The Federal Writers' Project

The Federal Writers' Project

A Study in Government Patronage of the Arts

Monty Noam Penkower

UNIVERSITY OF ILLINOIS PRESS   Urbana Chicago London

Publication of this work was supported in part by a grant
from the Andrew W. Mellon Foundation

Library of Congress Cataloging in Publication Data

Penkower, Monty Noam, 1942-
   The Federal Writers' Project.

   Bibliography: p.
   Includes index.
   1. Federal Writers' Project.   2. American literature
—20th century—History and criticism.
PS228.F43P4   810'.9'0052   77-2801
ISBN 0-252-00610-0

To My Mother and Father

Preface

HISTORIANS HAVE LONG DEBATED the innovative, revolutionary nature of the New Deal and the merits of its relief program, the Works Progress Administration. In discussing the more prominent aspects of both, they have given insufficient attention to the federal government's patronage of the arts during the Depression years. This study aims to correct that balance, as well as to shed additional light on the New Deal itself, by focusing on one of WPA's most significant achievements, the Federal Writers' Project.

The necessary understanding would come, I first thought, from a social history of the project and its relationship to the cultural spirit of the 1930s. This would establish the FWP's relationship to such thirties trends as regional effort, a growing interest in minority groups and socioethnic studies, and a reaffirmation of national values (as expressed in the wide popularity of history and folklore). Elucidation of the impact of the Depression on writers and a chronicling of their work on the FWP were the obvious objectives. However, I soon discovered that the project, in spite of its name, supported a great variety of personnel, not simply writers. Indeed, unlike the other Federal Arts Projects of the WPA, its program was not specifically geared to professional talent. This fact may have been responsible for its relatively high turnover of workers (who had to be trained in the first place). It also necessitated—for the production of the project's raison d'être, the American Guide Series—long-distance editing and intensive research in many unexplored fields. Yet the project overcame such difficulties to fulfill its primary objective, to be an agency of conservation and rehabilitation of skills and professional pride. Moreover, the combined effort of its 4,500–5,200 creative writers, researchers, clerical workers, and gifted administrators—an effort the like of which had never been seen before, anywhere—brought successes which seem almost incredible.

No less remarkable were the administrative hurdles which had to be met—relief laws, bureaucratic procedures, federal-state rivalry for control of the project, censorship, sponsorship arrangements, publication contracts, and a host of others. Congressional attacks on the project, whether as a part of WPA or as a front for Communist party activity and propaganda, provided an even greater challenge. The assaults finally achieved their objective, the end of the FWP, but not until June, 1939.

What was it that gave the project its strength to withstand these challenges until then and to survive in a revised form even thereafter? The answer to this question directs our attention to and provides an understanding of the FWP's enduring achievement.

This manuscript profited from the help of many individuals; unfortunately, the limitations of space permit me to mention but a few of them. Robert Kvasnicka of the National Archives proved very valuable in guiding me through the WPA and FWP records under his supervision. The executive board of the Authors' League allowed me to examine its files. Many wonderful hours were spent with people whose vivid memories illuminated my understanding of the project and the 1930s; I am especially grateful to Katherine Kellock and the late Florence Kerr. The first ten chapters of this book are based upon a Columbia University doctoral dissertation; Chapter 11 has been added to the earlier study. As the sponsor of the dissertation, John A. Garraty helped in countless ways. William E. Leuchtenburg proposed the topic and later gave the second draft a searching review which improved the work considerably. I am greatly indebted to them for their many suggestions and evaluations. Robert M. Friedberg's editorial skills were indispensable, as were those of David A. Rosen for Chapters 2 and 10. The final, exacting review given the manuscript by Chrystal Stillings Smith of the University of Illinois Press certainly added to its merit. I wish to extend special appreciation to Richard L. Wentworth, Associate Director and Editor of the University of Illinois Press, and to Burl Noggle of Louisiana State University for their confidence in my work. A word of loving thanks is due my wife, Yael, who has aided me immeasurably during the years of our marriage by her patience and especially her optimism that the manuscript would see print and thus be read by our Avram Yair, Talya Chana, Yonina Rivka, and Ayelet Sara. I finally want to pay tribute to my dear parents, Rabbi Murry S. and Mrs. Lillian S. Penkower, for their unfailing encouragement and interest. My father, in particular, gave me the benefit of his keen mind and gifted style from beginning to end. The dedication is a modest token of profound gratitude.

Contents

Prologue: The Writer in Crisis

February 25, 1935

THE PICKET LINE PASSED BACK and forth in front of the entrance to New York's Port Authority Building. It was an orderly demonstration; the police would have no trouble. Marching in twos, the twenty-odd men (joined by three or four women) appeared presentable, even well dressed, on the brisk February afternoon. Some smiled and chatted with lookers-on, while others gazed sternly into photographers' lenses. Normally, the press would not have bothered to cover the episode. Such lines were thrown up every day. But it sensed a news item which made this protest different: at the head of the procession, a man had tied a placard around his neck which read: "CHILDREN NEED BOOKS. WRITERS NEED A BREAK. WE DEMAND PROJECTS."[1]

Writers in search of jobs had never dramatized their needs in such fashion in this country, but those who marched that day were desperate. The public did not recognize the fledgling writer Earl Conrad or the poet Leon Srabian Herald, but it spotted the legendary Greenwich Village bohemian Maxwell Bodenheim in the front ranks. His risqué novels had been the toast of literary circles in the 1920s, but Bodenheim had publicly repudiated this earlier work a short time ago in favor of a fervent allegiance to Communist doctrine. Further back in the line strode Samuel Putnam, the noted literary critic and translator of Pirandello and Rabelais, who had recently returned from seven years of expatriation in Paris. Upon his arrival he had become a member of the Communist party because he wanted his young son's later respect. Both men, along with most of their unknown colleagues, now found themselves in such straits that federal relief rolls were their one source of security. Dissatisfied with a dole, they wanted the government to give them work befitting their talents. Perhaps some publicity will help, the picketers thought, as they quietly broke formation after an hour or so.

---

[1] *New York Daily Mirror*, Feb. 26, 1935.

But the *New York Daily Mirror*, with little sympathy for their demands and cultural concerns, chose to photograph the event for posterity with the caption "our future Walt Whitmans." Latest reports, the morning paper declared, were "that the only work in sight was for the writing of more placards." Other city newspapers neglected the incident entirely, focusing on leads such as "Fervor for Nazis Waning in Munich," "Babe Ruth Claims He Is Good for Several More Years," and "Jimmy Walker Broke, Wife Foots Bills." The feeble protest, it appeared, had accomplished nothing.[2]

This unusual scene could not be considered surprising in early 1935, another year in the Great Depression. This decade, as no other in the history of the United States, saw the nation threatened with special economic and psychological devastation. At the same time that it reached into every home or "Hooverville," the Depression challenged the very mythology that had buttressed what Jefferson had termed "the great experiment." The sense of America's uniqueness, of a land where hopes became realities and paupers self-made men, seemed to vanish, as breadlines and "bindle stiffs" captured the public imagination. All could agree with Marc Connelly's Angel Gabriel that "everything nailed down is comin' loose," as the sum of industrial wages and farm incomes plummeted from $81 to $41 billion. The only rising figures were market losses, which increased from $30 to $75 billion, and unemployment, which more than tripled to pass 12 million in 1932.[3]

At the beginning of the Depression, people still maintained great confidence in the titans of industry and finance. President Herbert Hoover himself regularly pointed out, every few months, that the worst had passed. The Democrats adopted "Happy Days Are Here Again" as their song for the 1932 campaign, but "Brother Can You Spare a Dime?," written the same year, caught the true mood. One historian has suggested that the new *Zeitgeist* was reflected even in the popularity of Donald Duck, symbol of "strident panic," which was growing at the expense of that of Mickey Mouse and his "crassy individualism."

[2] *Ibid.*; Jerre Mangione, *The Dream and the Deal*, p. 37; *New York Times* and *New York Herald Tribune*, Feb. 26, 1935. For the birth of the march's sponsor (the Writers' Union), see pp. 12, 15 below.

[3] Richard Morris, ed., *Encyclopedia of American History* (1965), p. 338; Dixon Wecter, *The Age of the Great Depression*, p. 17; Marc Connelly, *The Green Pastures* (New York, 1930).

Critics sneered at the President's philosophy as "ragged" (rather than "rugged") individualism; the Twenty-third Psalm underwent some alteration to read "Hoover is my shepherd; I shall do nothing but want."[4] Businessmen began to speak of economic "maturity" rather than "prosperity," while panaceas galore were offered by Democrats, Republicans, Communists, Trotskyites, Socialists, Farm-Laborites, Huey Long, Fathers Divine and Coughlin, Dr. Townsend, and a host of others.

In addition to challenging the national mythology, the economic shock raised the question of whether the diseased patient could recover at all. The emergency suggested the steady decline of the West which had been pessimistically forecast by Spengler in 1918. The closing of the country's Western frontier had, moreover, long since ruled out the traditional possibility of turning in that direction for hope.[5] America was no longer certain of its providential future. "B.C." and "A.C." might take on additional meaning as "before the Crash" and "after the Crash" and, whatever the final economic effect of this challenge, the nation and its citizenry would never be the same.

The convulsions of what Edmund Wilson called "the American Earthquake" were graphically registered by writers in the turbulent thirties. These "seismographs of social shock" reacted in different ways; yet for the overwhelming majority certain underlying responses could be discerned. Having denounced the shallowness of the bourgeois mentality in the 1920s, retired to Proustian introspection and "l'art pour l'art," or boarded the first ship for Paris, many writers now felt vindicated by the collapse of the market and of the businessman's prestige. The Great Depression did not seem altogether depressing to writers who, having pointed out the follies of the system, found a new sense of freedom and power with "the sudden, unexpected collapse of that stupid fraud."[6]

In their exhilaration, many became *engagé* in the fundamental, revolutionary sense. "Gone the bohemianism and cynicism, the con-

---

[4] Arthur M. Schlesinger, Jr., *The Age of Roosevelt*, vol. 1, *The Crisis of the Old Order*, pp. 162-73; Wecter, *Great Depression*, pp. 13, 19; Rita Simon, ed., *As We Saw the Thirties: Essays on Social and Political Movements of a Decade*, p. 110.

[5] William E. Leuchtenburg, *Franklin D. Roosevelt and the New Deal, 1932-1940*, p. 29; Daniel Boorstin, *America and the Image of Europe* (New York, 1960), pp. 31-32 and chap. 1.

[6] Edmund Wilson, *The American Earthquake*; Walter Rideout, *The Radical Novel in the United States, 1900-1954: Some Inter-Relations of Literature and Society*, p. 133; Theodore Dreiser, *Tragic America*; Edmund Wilson, *The Shores of Light*, p. 498.

cern with sex and aesthetics that I remembered,'' noted the poet Orrick Johns in recalling the excitement which pervaded literary circles. ''A madly hopeful time,'' wrote Malcolm Cowley of this period, and he concluded *Exile's Return* in 1934 with a plea (struck from a second edition) that art and propaganda merge ''to take the worker's side.'' One of his disciples later reminisced about Cowley's belief that ''salvation would come by the word, the long-awaited and fatefully exact word that only the true writer would speak.''[7]

Such feelings separated many writers from the majority of Americans, but the Great Depression forced them into a common position with their neighbors. Even while the spirit of the writer stirred in revolt, his physical wants had to be satisfied. The Depression caught the writer especially unprepared to win food and shelter with his talents. Wherever he turned for work in his trade, only very limited opportunities presented themselves.[8]

The economic crisis rocked the publishing world with considerable violence. Firms which in 1929 had taken in an estimated $42 million from the sale of trade (non-textbook) publications found four years later that their proceeds had dwindled to half that amount. Unable to afford to buy books, readers increased their borrowing: the American Library Association estimated that between 4 and 5 million new borrowers registered with public libraries in this time, and the total circulation of public library books in the United States increased by nearly 40 per cent. But this provided little comfort to publishers and authors, who only had to scan the monthly production statistics to realize the extent of their catastrophe: 9,035 new books and editions were printed in 1931-32, a decrease of 1,272 from the preceding year. The first five months of 1933 yielded 460 fewer new printings than the corresponding period a year earlier; by December there were 950 fewer new printings. Faced with such figures, *Publishers Weekly* could only advise pub-

[7] Orrick Johns, *Time of Our Lives*, p. 399; Malcolm Cowley, *Exile's Return: A Literary Odyssey of the 1920's*; Alfred Kazin, *Starting Out in the Thirties*, p. 5. In this period of fundamental dislocation, writers drifted steadily leftward toward the Communist party. For the political and emotional aspects of this affiliation, see Daniel Aaron, *Writers on the Left* and Malcolm Cowley *et al.*, ''Memories of the First American Writers' Congress,'' *American Scholar* 35 (Summer, 1966): 495-516. This relationship affected the future writers' project as well. See chap. 9 below.

[8] This point is overlooked by Leslie Fiedler, who argues that the division between writers and the American public created ''two memories'' of the Depression. See Fiedler, in David Madden, ed., *Proletarian Writers of the Thirties*, pp. 3-25.

lishers with filled warehouses to grind up all unbound sheets or else be prepared to sell their books cheaply.[9]

Not even recognized professionals could be assured of economic security. Writing for a living was a terribly hazardous affair, even if talents were compromised for the pulp czars or Hollywood. For example, after twenty-five years of writing and almost the same number of books, Sherwood Anderson admitted he found himself "always in need of money, always just two steps ahead of the sheriff." Only fifteen authors could claim that their books sold 50,000 or more copies in the United States in 1934. Royalties of truly established writers whose books customarily sold over 10,000 copies had dropped 50 per cent below the 1929 level by 1935.[10]

How much greater, then, were the needs of unestablished authors. Rates fell from one-fifth to one-third in quality and slick magazines and had plummeted from two cents to one cent per word in the pulps. Uncertainty marked all free-lance outlets, with editors buying very little for the future. As magazine advertising linage fell over 20 per cent from the 1930 figures (30 per cent from 1929) from January, 1931, to January, 1932, there was good cause to wonder about the very continuation of the magazines. Advice to maintain courage in the face of adversity had little meaning when the editor of *Atlantic Monthly* noted that only one out of over 400 manuscripts submitted each month saw print.[11]

Even those writers who found jobs as newspaper reporters and editors did not escape the catastrophe. Many newspapers folded, and others had to resort to sharp retrenchment or consolidation as scores of advertising accounts were cancelled. In twenty-three leading cities, the total of newspaper agate lines for 1933 hit the lowest figure since 1918 (over 40 per cent below the 1928 peak). Petitions of bankruptcy, suggestions of lower rates to save classified advertising, and the cancellation of daily editions were regularly recorded in issues of *Editor and Publisher* during the first half of the decade. The net rate of mortality in

[9] Edward Weeks, "Hard Times and the Author," *Atlantic Monthly* 155 (May, 1935): 551-62; *Publishers Weekly* 123 (Jan. 21, 1933):191; 124 (Dec. 21, 1935):1955; and 122 (Dec. 3, 1932):2102.

[10] Sherwood Anderson, *Memoirs*, p. 433; Weeks, "Hard Times." The writers' pose of the previous decade—the lonely individual against the Philistines—or self-exile to the banks of the Seine could not present easy solutions after cuts in advances and the fall of the gold standard in 1933. Isidor Schneider interview, May 30, 1968.

[11] *Editor and Publisher* 64 (Jan. 23, 1932):5; *Author and Journalist* 19 (June, 1934):2.

the field reached 48 per cent, and by the end of the Depression only about 120 cities had more than a single newspaper publisher. In the same week that the *New York Times* closed its Brooklyn plant for all but Sunday editions, a leading columnist estimated that in New York alone 1,500 craftsmen were out of work. In May, 1934, replies from hundreds of New York newspapermen to a questionnaire showed that the majority could not live on their present savings for more than six months; many could not do so for more than six weeks. A comparison of editorial salaries on thirty-one dailies by the Bureau of Labor Statistics in the fall of that year revealed that almost 17 per cent earned less than $20 a week, 28 per cent earned between $50 and $100, and only 3.4 per cent received $100 or more weekly.[12]

Competition from radio and the motion picture industry also added to the woes of the authors. While, for example, magazine advertising linage dropped 22.5 per cent in 1931, broadcasting advertising continued to climb, with that of the National and Columbia radio systems increasing 33 per cent during the same twelve months. The end of 1933 saw a gain of 23 per cent over totals reached by December, 1932, in this field. As for seeking refuge in Hollywood, almost any published novelist had the opportunity to work for twelve weeks at good wages, but conditions were so unstable that the majority often found themselves out of a job and without prospects at the end of this period.[13]

All these facts, however, did not change overnight the popular image of the writer's lot. An aspiring poet just out of Vassar in the depths of the crisis had been brought up with the idea that "writers weren't living people." "The public saw them as trash," in Muriel Rukeyser's opinion. "Living meant going to the office. Writing for magazines was jeered at, unless it was for the *Saturday Evening Post*. That meant acceptance, money and the proper capitalist virtues." Privation and suffering were the writer's proper lot, argued a syndicated columnist: "No writer is worth shucks until he can and has taken punishment. . . .

---

[12] *Editor and Publisher* 64 (June 11, 1932):7, 38, 52, and 66 (Jan. 27, 1934):110-11; Wecter, *Great Depression*, p. 245; *Guild Reporter* 1 (May, 1934):12; *Monthly Labor Review* 40 (May, 1935):1137-48. By contrast, in April, 1930, these figures had been 13, 41, and 5.7 per cent, respectively.

[13] *Editor and Publisher* 64 (Jan. 23, 1932):5, and 66 (Jan. 27, 1934):6; Robert Spiller *et al.*, eds., *Literary History of the United States* (1948), 2:1265-66. Even the highly successful F. Scott Fitzgerald became disillusioned with Hollywood's mediocre and depersonalized corruption of the American dream of success, as he made clear in the *Last Tycoon* before his fatal heart attack. Spiller et al., *Literary History*.

He's supposed to go hungry and ragged and cold, to drudge at chores he loathes, to suffer endless humiliation and rejection doing the thing he loves in infrequent, stolen moments or baking beans. It MAKES a writer, and weeds out the POSEURS, the people with a smattering of talent but no salt or spunk, lacking which no writer is worth a hoot.'' Ensconced in the editorship of the *Saturday Review of Literature*, H. S. Canby pontificated that authors should not go on salary, since "profits in themselves don't stimulate good literature.'' Regrettably, the editor did not disclose any basis for his concluding claim that "no good (and celebrated) story-teller or playwright, even in 1932, can fail of a decent reward.'' Such views, moreover, took no account of the observation of Dr. Johnson, "This truth is ev'ry where confess'd / Slow rises worth by poverty depress'd.'' Instead, the *New York Times* concluded its criticism of "lazy'' American writers by asking: "Can it be that they waste too much time attending literary teas?''[14]

Most writers had to forego such pleasures to attend to the job hunt. But the Depression caught them particularly ill equipped, since they had little or no training and experience for anything except their métier. Anxious interviewees often discovered, as a short story of Saroyan well related, that their one stock of possible value was the ability to use a typewriter. Greenwich Village's intellectual colony could therefore consider itself most fortunate in getting free lunches and suppers for a quarter at the privately organized Artists' and Writers' Dinner Club. Others borrowed small sums from the Authors' League fund or, swallowing their pride, applied for the $2-a-week food check at Home Relief bureaus and became euphemistically known as "clients of the government.'' In March, 1935, about 1,400 writers who had been sacked from various journalism posts were listed on the relief rolls. However, many of their colleagues refused to submit to the often excruciating experience of application, including the humiliating procedure of attaining relief certification and of proving that one met the arbitrary eligibility standards set up by relief agencies. Some tried their hand at odd jobs, which were few and far between. Harry Roskolenko became a ditchdigger in the Eighth Avenue subway. Harvey Breit delivered telephone books, and Studs Terkel counted bonds for the

[14] Muriel Rukeyser interview, Mar. 12, 1968; *St. Louis Dispatch* (Elsie Robinson), Mar. 25, 1938; Henry Seidel Canby, "Should Writers Go on a Salary?'' *Saturday Review of Literature* 9 (Nov. 26, 1932):270; Samuel Johnson, *London* (1738); *New York Times*, Apr. 19, 1931, III, p. 1.

Treasury Department. With "the world falling around me," Josef Berger left New York for Provincetown, where he lived largely on free fish from native fishermen.[15]

Outside sources could not be depended on for adequate help. Private organizations attempting to establish a specific program for white-collar workers quickly discovered that the lack of funds vitiated the best intentions. Thus, the Philadelphia Committee on Unemployment Relief and the New York Emergency Work Bureau, both begun toward the end of 1930, soon had to cancel their efforts. Municipal and state governments lacked sufficient funds and taxing power to offer adequate relief. Those state programs that did exist generally provided work of the lowest manual type. The New York state legislature took a significant step in September, 1931, by passing the Wicks Act. Creating the Temporary Emergency Relief Administration, it ruled that the state had to refund 40 per cent of all municipal expenditures for home and work relief. In time, Governor Franklin D. Roosevelt and TERA's head, Harry Hopkins, gave the nation its first comprehensive relief program. But it only represented a start and did not offer anything definite for writers and others in the creative arts.[16]

Offering a luxury item on the public market, most writers in the Depression years could only await an arbitrary return on their stock in trade. They did not care for the prescriptions of the *New York Times* for literary inspiration, such as Victor Hugo's diet of orange peel scraps and the claws of crayfish, or George Eliot's—red pickled cabbage, onions, and coffee.[17] But many, unprepared to work in other fields, did not have money even for meals such as those. Picket lines, at the same time, led nowhere. Unless new champions were found to help them meet their economic needs, the future seemed bleak, even hopeless.

[15] William Saroyan, *The Daring Young Man on the Flying Trapeze and Other Stories* (New York, 1932), p. 22; Harry Roskolenko interview, Nov. 21, 1967; Harvey Breit interview, Nov. 16, 1967; Studs Terkel interview, Mar. 29, 1968; Josef Berger interview, Nov. 13, 1967.

[16] William McDonald, "Federal Relief Administration and the Arts" (Library of Congress, 1949) (Music Division, Reel MUS 64), chap. 3; Harry Hopkins, *Spending to Save*, chap. 2.

[17] *New York Times*, Sept. 10, 1930; Maristan Chapman, "The Trouble with Authors," *Bookman* 74 (Dec., 1931):368-70: "The baiting of authors has become a recognized sport . . . [they are] bandied about like inanimate objects."

1   The Birth of a Federal Project

WITH ROOSEVELT AT THE HELM in Washington after the 1932 election, American writers had reason to hope that their condition would improve. FDR began experimenting to save the country from despair and decay. Outright relief grants worth $500 million (as opposed to grants-in-aid totaling $300 million under Hoover's Reconstruction Finance Corporation) became available to the states with the passage, in May, 1933, of the Federal Emergency Relief Act (FERA). Most important, Roosevelt picked Harry Hopkins to head the new relief program.[1]

Hopkins, the former head of the Temporary Emergency Relief Administration, brought to his task a radically new concept of relief. An extensive background in social work had provided him with a particularly sympathetic perspective on the needs of the destitute and a contempt for red tape. His varied experiences with settlement houses, the Association for the Improvement of the Conditions of the Poor, the Red Cross, and TERA had convinced him of the need for jobs that would fit human wants and skills. And so, under his supervision, FERA would attempt to substitute work relief for direct relief and to use the special abilities of those on relief.[2]

Hopkins also developed a specifically white-collar relief program. Immediately after his appointment, he ordered a survey of the occupational characteristics of families on relief; covering 180,000 families, the survey indicated that the particular skills of white-collar workers, including writers, were not being used. FERA, as the person who directed this survey later put it, had "scratched its head and come up with dandruff." A second study determined the number of unemployed in the cities and revealed the predicament of creative artists. A third

---

[1] Arthur M. Schlesinger, Jr., *The Age of Roosevelt*, vol. 2, *The Coming of the New Deal*, pp. 263-65.

[2] *Ibid.*, pp. 265-66; McDonald, "Federal Relief," p. 71.

Hopkins request led to an analysis of state-administered relief. Through these studies Hopkins obtained a grasp of the special problem of the white-collar unemployed; he then sought to provide programs for them. He was to prove particularly receptive to ideas to benefit writers and other creative people.[3]

If Hopkins was the perfect man at the top, Jacob Baker represented the ideal choice for organizing a white-collar relief program. When he was called by Hopkins to be his assistant as director of Work Relief and Special Projects in the summer of 1933, "Jake" Baker had had a varied background in management. He had been an engineer in California and Chicago and had helped organize and then manage the Vanguard Press in New York. His job, as well as a philosophy based on Kropotkin's "mutualism" and on "Wobbly" doctrine, had led to close ties with writers and artists in Greenwich Village, and he would think of their welfare when contemplating relief programs.[4]

The initial FERA experience helped professional writers very little. Since FERA relief rules required that states initiate work programs, the first effort made was to get state and local authorities to accept professional projects. Because their conventional view of work as primarily manual labor usually caused these authorities to refuse, a program with authority to operate the work projects directly from Washington seemed the only alternative.[5]

Cultural projects first became part of a comprehensive white-collar program in December, when the Public Works of Art Project was established under the Emergency Civil Works Administration (CWA).[6] The director of the Museum of Modern Art had first suggested that relief be provided for indigent artists. FDR, who simply styled himself "a Christian and a Democrat," seconded the proposal on the ground that artists, as human beings, also had to live. Using ideas from artists George Biddle and Edward Bruce, the PWAP, which functioned under the Treasury Department, proceeded to decorate

[3] Sol Ozer interview, Aug. 13, 1968; Robert Asher interview, Aug. 26, 1968.

[4] Isaac Don Levine interview, July 31, 1968; Blair Bolles, "The Federal Writers' Project," *Saturday Review of Literature* 18 (July 9, 1938): 3-4.

[5] McDonald, "Federal Relief," pp. 80-89.

[6] The CWA was set up in November to carry millions of jobless workers through the winter of 1933. This distinctly federal program provided minimum wages for over 4 million unemployed in its half-year existence. Schlesinger, *Coming of the New Deal*, pp. 269-71.

public buildings. It also encouraged professional organizations, unions, and guilds to seek the creation of relief projects in the other arts.[7]

The Special Projects Division had little precedent to consult in formulating a relief program for creative artists. Rulers had often subsidized artists on an individual basis. Augustus and many of the popes were their benefactors. Henry VIII aided Holbein, Francis I supported da Vinci, Maximilian favored Dürer. Shakespeare received support from James I, and Ben Jonson from Charles I. Richelieu established the French Academy, and Philip IV organized a similar institution for Spain. In the twentieth century, a number of governments expanded their aid, and the agency devoted to the arts became either a section or a subsidiary of the department of education. However, no precedent existed anywhere for large-scale government aid to creative people who were jobless.[8] In addition, the Special Projects Division soon realized that a plan for writers presented unique difficulties. At no time could the number of "unemployed writers" in need of relief be obtained, since that term could cover just about anyone who lifted pen to paper. Equally important, even if Washington could define the term, it would have great difficulty evaluating creative work.[9]

In the absence of precedent, the division at least offered a few tentative suggestions for employing writers. One, for "projects for the improvement or the preservation of public records and documents," was adopted in New Mexico with considerable success: the CWA unit there began to translate the state's Spanish archives. The Connecticut Planning Board initiated a survey of places of scenic and historic interest as a follow-up to all the material accumulated for the state's tercentenary. At least 1,000 writers received employment on various CWA state research projects and at universities. Seventy-five unemployed newspapermen found themselves writing the news of more than

[7] Jo Ann Wahl, "Art Under the New Deal" (M.A. thesis, Columbia University, 1966), pp. 7-9; Richard D. McKinzie, *The New Deal for Artists*, chaps. 2-3; Frances Perkins, *The Roosevelt I Knew*, pp. 75-76. Roosevelt's sentiments, coupled with his knowledge of geography and wide reading in American history and travel, later made it easy for him to support a writers' relief project which would produce U.S. guidebooks and other offerings. Perkins, *Roosevelt I Knew*, chap. 7 and p. 33.

[8] Grace Overmyer, *Government and the Arts*, chaps. 1-4. For the limitations of the Weimar Republic's efforts in this regard, see Alfred Fried, "Intellectual Starvation in Germany and Austria," *Nation* 110 (Mar. 20, 1920):367-68.

[9] Jacob Baker interview, June 27, 1967.

1,000 social service bodies, and a few did historical research on civil relief agencies in Cleveland. Such work did not provide creative satisfaction, however, and thus compared adversely with that of the artists on the Public Works of Art Project, who operated in their own métier.[10]

Since over 2,000 unemployed writers could be found in New York City, it is not surprising that the first attempts to obtain federal aid specifically for writers' projects took place there. A meeting at Irving Plaza in January, 1934, to discuss their economic situation attracted twenty-five writers. The provisional executive committee included the authors Samuel Putnam, Edward Dahlberg, and Robert Whitcomb. Soon there were 500 members, and the mailing list reached 1,200. The writers took the name Unemployed Writers' Association, elected Whitcomb their head, and asked a committee led by Margery Mansfield of the Poetry Society of America to iron out provisions. Demanding for each writer a minimum of $30 a week, the association asked that Congress appropriate the necessary funds a year in advance and establish a "national plan for all writers." Its proposals included the translation of foreign newspapers covering the U.S. artistic scene. The idea met with the approval of such literary figures as Theodore Dreiser, Floyd Dell, Ida Tarbell, Sherwood Anderson, and Maxwell Bodenheim.[11]

Another organization, one formed before the Depression to represent most of the country's established authors on issues of copyright and contract, also attempted to better the writers' economic condition. The Authors' League, with headquarters in New York and a membership of about 2,000, joined with the Unemployed Writers' Association to send a delegation to petition officials in Washington. Despite its report that the league's private sources of relief would be rapidly exhausted, the delegation was asked to request the league to continue such support

---

[10] Cassidy to Alsberg, Jan. 21, 1936, Box 110, Federal Writers' Project files, Works Projects Administration records, Record Group 69, National Archives, Washington, D.C. (hereafter FWPN); Eleanor Little to author, Oct. 11, 1967; *New York Times*, Feb. 16, 1934; *Editor and Publisher* 66 (Feb. 3, 1934):44,12.

[11] *Bulletin of the Writers' Union*. The *Nation* 138 (Feb. 14, 1934):171, seconded these demands but insisted that if "unemployed literature" were published at government expense, "the depression will become a holocaust." For the official CWA response, see Box 113, Civil Works Administration files, Works Projects Administration records, Record Group 69, National Archives, Washington, D.C. (hereafter CWAN).

while the government planned for future employment. The Authors' League council considered this a pledge of action to come and continued to assess league members. In the next two years it raised and spent over $100,000 for this purpose.[12]

On February 19, 1934, the Authors' League, fearing delay, suggested to CWA officials in Washington a project that would be of "social usefulness" to the government as well as to readers and writers. The plan, "a survey of varying aspects of everyday life as it is lived in all parts of the United States," was the first of many that would later be adopted as the American Guide Series proposal of the Federal Writers' Project. According to the league's plan, which was designed for trained writers, each writer would receive an assignment to supply an hour-by-hour account of one day in the life of a person in his community. Historians would consider the purely historical aspects of the community, and other writers would comment on its ethnological aspects. If all went well, the project could employ 500 writers for ten weeks.[13]

Individual professionals who were contacted about the feasibility of a permanent "division of fine arts" to include writers preferred more creative programs. Conrad Aiken, Babette Deutsch, and Theodore Dreiser suggested regional and national journals; others advocated large-scale translation projects. Marianne Moore and Ridgely Torrence, offering no detailed plans, proposed the preparation of guidebooks and state histories. All, however, wondered with Booth Tarkington and Sinclair Lewis whether the federal government could identify creative talents, and they expressed doubts about the necessary Washington controls and possible regimentation. Still, those questioned agreed with William Carlos Williams's parting observation: "Wonders might come from such a move as you propose, for letters are the wave's edge in all cultural advance, which, God knows, we in America ain't got much of."[14]

---

[12] Reel no. 144, Authors' League of America papers, Authors' League of America, New York, N.Y.

[13] *Ibid.*, Feb. 18, 1934, proposal. When a year had passed with no concrete federal program, the league decided to sponsor its own guidebook to the free leisure facilities available in the city. Only congressional approval of a similar project for the entire country put an end to this plan. July-Sept., 1935, Authors' League papers.

[14] Cited in Kathleen O'Connor McKinzie, "Writers on Relief: 1935-1942" (Ph.D. diss., Indiana University, 1970), pp. 9-12.

Though government supporters of white-collar projects were unable to accede to such private requests immediately, Jake Baker, who had been in charge of the FERA Emergency Works Program since April, set up a section for Professional and Non-Manual Projects under the supervision of his assistant, Arthur "Tex" Goldschmidt. Baker insisted that the establishment of working procedures, which had started under the CWA program, be continued.[15]

As the new acting director of Professional Projects, Goldschmidt made his office a clearinghouse for the exchange of information between the state ERA administrators. Soon after his appointment, he chose two administrative assistants to help formulate proposals. Nina Collier (daughter-in-law of the federal Indian commissioner), who had prepared a survey of Indian arts and crafts for the PWAP, concentrated on art, music, and theatre, and Clair Laning specialized in his field of publishing and literature. The efforts of this inner circle, with its extremely informal relationships, would finally succeed in persuading state executives and politicians that a relief program for needy creative people could be both economical and worthwhile.[16]

The FERA experience confirmed Baker's initial worry about a writers' project in particular. As the result of various surveys, he continued to uncover many white-collar workers who presented special problems of classification of employment. By 1933, some 200,000 certified teachers found themselves out of work. Cuts in appropriations severely hurt college faculty. Librarians received dismissal notices with increasing regularity, and thousands of ministers were out of pulpits. The country had an overabundance of lawyers. These and thousands of other white-collar professionals possessed one skill in common—their writing ability. Presumably, therefore, such professionals, although not creative artists, might be classed as "unemployed writers." How would socially useful employment, Washington's prime concern, be provided all these people? And how could Washington deal with the fact that even if the Professional Projects Division drew up worthwhile

[15] McDonald, "Federal Relief," chap. 5. After winter ended, and in response to cries from Southern Democrats and the director of the budget, FDR decided to terminate the expensive CWA program and have FERA again take over the full burden of relief in April, 1934. Schlesinger, *Coming of the New Deal*, p. 277.

[16] Arthur Goldschmidt interview, Jan. 31, 1968; Nina Collier to author, Aug. 27, 1968; Laning, in Holger Cahill Memoir, Columbia University Oral History Collection, New York, N.Y. (hereafter COHC), p. 441.

plans, local relief offices had the power to assign such workers independently to other jobs?[17]

In spite of such problems, several states put FERA working procedures and other individual ideas into effect between July and October, 1934, thereby aiding professionals with some writing skills. Former CWA operations, like the New Mexico archival translations and Connecticut's survey of interesting places to visit, continued. In Utah, writers collected histories and social data of Washington County. The Minnesota Historical Society, under the guidance of Theodore Blegen, began a local archives survey. A local history project in Port Jervis, New York, indexed local newspapers for ready reference in high school classes. Four newspapermen on the relief rolls in Oregon received an assignment to write a history of Salem.[18]

The Unemployed Writers' Association, dissatisfied with these programs, adopted a more aggressive stance which reflected the pervasive influence of the Communist party. Some of the association's members, frustrated by unsuccessful attempts to get federal help for writing projects per se, voted in April, 1934, to become the Writers' Union. A member of the party's district headquarters soon was instructed to organize a faction within the new union to use as a recruiting medium. He accomplished his task so well that a number of party representatives gained spots on the union's executive committee and he became its first president.[19] The union subsequently became a local of the City Project Council (an affiliate of the Workers' Alliance), another party front.[20]

Robert Whitcomb's renewed enthusiasm after the union's formation

[17] Baker interview; Wecter, *Great Depression*, pp. 189-91; *Nation* 137 (Aug. 23, 1933):213-14 and (Jan. 17, 1934):66-67. The final FERA *Occupational Classified Index* simply listed "authors" and "special writers" as undefined categories. McDonald, "Federal Relief," pp. 143-44.

[18] Howe to Alsberg, Nov. 11, 1935, Box 45, FWPN; Blegen to Alsberg, Jan. 17, 1936, Box 20, FWPN; Baker interview.

[19] Ralph De Sola to author, Dec. 26, 1967; *New York Herald Tribune*, Nov. 2, 1936. Ivan Black, like most organizational leaders, was convinced that the union had brought about practically every idea adopted by the writers' project (Black interview, Feb. 15, 1968). As this chapter relates, a number of groups and individuals played at least as substantial a part in the project's formation. Moreover, the union's tactics, especially in New York, brought great harm to the project in general. See chap. 9 below.

[20] *Bulletin of the Writers' Union*. Most members of the union could not be classed as party members. They joined the union because it seemed to be doing something to halt the "feeling of waste," including holding a public meeting on behalf of a writers' project with Ford Madox Ford and Edward Dahlberg. Rukeyser interview and Edward Dahlberg interview, Apr. 11, 1968.

had little effect on Washington circles. He drew up a project for twenty-five writers to do research on unemployment and the writing profession and even succeeded in interesting the local relief administration in the plan. After obtaining the support of both Al Smith, the former governor of New York, and Hopkins, whose office sent the plan to Goldschmidt, Whitcomb was "confident something would be done in the near future." By October, however, it became clear that, as in the past, all projects still had to be initiated locally and approved by the state administrator.[21]

Fortunately, one state ERA administrator did grant approval for a project which came closer to meeting the needs of unemployed writers. With the aid of local California organizations, Hugh Harlan, a former classmate of Hopkins's at Grinnell College who was now in the SERA Los Angeles reports department, drew up a series of projects for unemployed newspapermen and writers. In August, 1934, the state administrator approved a plan known as the Newspaper Writers' Project for Los Angeles County, and Harlan became its supervisor and managing editor.[22]

This successful project was an important model for Goldschmidt in drawing up plans for a federal program. By February, 1935, fifty-one men and five women had been placed on the project at a cost of $16,000. Their work included reports on subsistence homesteads, histories of the Los Angeles police department and school system, and studies of racial groups in southern California. Joseph Gaer, the adapter of folk legends and author of *How the Great Religions Began*, served as chief editor for the program. Professional writers submitted a drama based on the state's early history and prepared extensive bibliographies of California authors. At the close of the project, a formidable amount of research had been done and forty-four of eighty-three workers had gone on to full-time jobs.[23]

Armed with examples of successful state ERA units and suggestions from professional organizations, unions, and individuals, Baker and

[21] The correspondence can be found in Box 57, Federal Emergency Relief Administration files, Works Projects Administration records, Record Group 69, National Archives, Washington, D.C. There is no evidence that Whitcomb's project was ever begun, although this assertion has been made in McDonald, "Federal Relief," p. 730.

[22] McDonald, "Federal Relief," pp. 727-28.

[23] Newspaper Writers' Project files, Box 337, Works Projects Administration records, Record Group 69, National Archives, Washington, D.C.; McDonald, "Federal Relief," p. 720.

his group were able to draw up some general FERA procedures for writers' projects by the end of 1934. The first and second of these reflected the influence of the Writers' Union and the Authors' League: for creative writers, individual projects, and for general writers, specific commissions under the sponsorship of public institutions. The two vaguely worded procedures, or proposals, reflected the difficulty of providing appropriate employment for members of this dichotomous "profession." They also presented the possibility of competition with private publishers, which was clearly at variance with the aims of federal relief. For these reasons, the idea of the government as "an unfailing patron . . . fathering and producing the masterpieces a crude world had scorned" was quickly shelved.[24]

Another FERA proposal, a project to interview ex-slaves in the Ohio River valley, was suggested by Lawrence D. Reddick of the history faculty of Kentucky State College. The plan, he wrote Hopkins, which would initially provide jobs for twelve black college graduates for one year, represented the last chance to collect this historically priceless testimony. The project received approval and, by July, 1935, had conducted about 250 interviews. The venture also suggested to Negro leaders that black personnel should be employed on any of the writers' projects dealing with their race. It would only be a small step to considering the collecting of black folkways and folklore.[25]

A fourth proposal, under the rubric of general folklore, contained an additional emphasis on preserving as much as possible of the country's rapidly fading folk heritage, Joseph Gaer, of California's newspaper project, even suggested that the entire federal operation be called the American Folklore Project. This proposal and the one for interviewing ex-slaves, presented problems, however, because such work required

[24] FERA Procedural Publications, VII, Oct. 12, 1934, Works Projects Administration records, Record Group 69, National Archives, Washington, D.C.; Katherine Kellock, "The WPA Writers: Portraitists of the United States," *American Scholar* 9 (Oct., 1940):473-82. As with all the major proposals for the FWP, other individuals also suggested this idea. See p. 13 above. Also, Cater to Sillcox, Jan. 26, 1935, Authors' League papers, and Colby to Billington, June 9, 1936, Box 99, FWPN.

[25] FERA Procedural Publications, VII, Oct. 19, 1934; Norman Yetman, "The Background of the Slave Collection," *American Quarterly* 19 (Fall, 1967):535-53; Charles S. Johnson, "A Proposal for a Regional (or National) Project under the FWP," n.d., Federal Writers' Project file, Schomburg Collection, New York Public Library. While not included in the preliminary plans of the Federal Writers' Project in July, 1935, Reddick's suggestion was taken up independently by other states and eventually became a separate unit of the project. See chap. 7 below.

expertise and the Professional Projects Division could not cope with thousands of "writers" unprepared for such tasks.[26]

A final proposal suggested work which might solve this problem. It stemmed from an idea imparted to Baker by a successful journalist, Robert M. Buck, which called for the production of an "iconography"—as Baker would later define it in the FERA procedure, "a compilation of pictures, broad-sides, hand-bills, and all the other original source material that describes the events, attitudes, and customs of a given place, region or group."[27] Though the iconography proposal found advocates in some state programs, it did not satisfy Goldschmidt: while all writers out of work could do this "collating job," the task would not fulfill his division's purpose of preserving and improving writers' skills while providing relief. "That had always been the trouble," he thought: "What should writers do as *writers*?"[28] As yet, Baker and the inner circle had not found a satisfactory answer.

II

One man thought he had the solution. Born in 1881 in a home in New York's prosperous East Seventies, Henry Garfield Alsberg received a strict upbringing from his German-Jewish father. A great procrastinator, when only twelve he remarked: "Never do what you can't do tomorrow, because maybe you will never have to do it." His father's will prevailed, however, and he was sent to the Sachs Collegiate Institute, a remarkable private school which prepared him to enter Columbia College at fifteen. Limiting his circle to classmates John Erskine, Melville Cane, Simeon Strunsky, and Harold Kellock, he refused to be photographed for the senior yearbook of 1900 with what he would later call "the average American middle-class citizen." After graduating from Columbia Law School, he practiced in the office of the attorney for New York's Port Authority for three years, but turned down a junior partnership, contending that law was a "dirty business." After a year in Harvard's graduate English department, he decided that

---

[26] FERA Procedural Publications, VII, Nov. 24, 1934.

[27] *Ibid.*, Oct. 12, 1934. Robert M. Buck covered the District Building in Washington, D.C., was also the *Daily News*'s chief editorial writer on municipal affairs, and became a "pioneer performer" in the events leading up to the formation of the American Newspaper Guild. Richard Hollander to author, June 3, 1969.

[28] McDonald, "Federal Relief," p. 731; Goldschmidt interview.

the discipline of academia did not suit him. He finally secured a spot on the editorial board of the *New York Post*.[29]

At heart a free, creative soul, Alsberg wanted to be a writer and see the world. He got his first chance in 1917 when his legal connections secured him the post of secretary to the U.S. ambassador to Turkey. Awkward in hat and tails, he was more comfortable as a foreign correspondent for the *Nation*, the *London Daily Herald*, and the *New York World* from 1919 to 1922. He served the American Joint Distribution Committee by bringing funds to starving Jewish refugees in the Ukraine; met Prince Kropotkin, whose philosophical anarchism resembled his own; and formed strong friendships with Alexander Berkman and Emma Goldman, who later remembered the tall, witty correspondent for his "sincerity and easy joviality, directness and *camaraderie.*" His first book, an edited collection of letters by Russian dissidents, done in conjunction with Isaac Don Levine, revealed prodigious work, required considerable editing, and gave his co-worker the impression that it had been "put together in a back alley in Greenwich Village." The effort of a highly creative mind, it showed his small concern for detail and a weakness in administrative precision and organization. These elements reflected Alsberg's character. Tolerance for the opinions of others, coupled with an easygoing nature, endeared Alsberg to all who knew him. At the same time, his combined traits often led to permissiveness—a quality unsuitable for executive duty.[30]

Alsberg's temperament fitted the Bohemian, intellectual world of the Village, in which he moved for the next few years. While working for Roger Baldwin's International Committee for Political Prisoners, he became associated for a short time with the Provincetown Players through his ties with Emma Goldman and Berkman. As a producer and member of its advisory board, he finally achieved the literary recognition to which he had always aspired by translating, adapting, and producing S. Ansky's *The Dybbuk* in this country; its debut in 1926 was a literary event. Bored and bogged down with detail, Alsberg gave up on a history of the Joint Distribution Committee that subsequently was assigned to his past collaborator, Isaac Don Levine. A bachelor with no

---

[29] Julius Alsberg interview, Aug. 5, 1968, and Katherine Kellock interview, June 23, 1968; *Columbia University Twenty-Fifth Anniversary Alumni* (New York, 1926), p. 22.

[30] J. Alsberg interview; Levine interview; Emma Goldman, *Living My Life*, pp. 794-95; *Letters from Russian Prisons*; see chap. 2 below.

responsibilities or fixed occupation, the lumbering six-footer seemed most at ease in the company of a few intimate friends with whom he shared apartments in New York and Washington. He cared little about his image as an unkempt, shaggy-maned, absent-minded professor.[31]

This "lovable St. Bernard" and "fountain of knowledge" received a call from Jake Baker in mid-1934 to come to Washington to work with the national relief program. Baker wanted people to know about the work of the CWA and thought that his friend from the Village, whose philosophical and creative temperament resembled his own, could use and do the job. The result, *America Fights the Depression*, revealed hack work and hasty arrangement. Yet the volume accomplished its purpose, and Baker succeeded in getting Alsberg appointed as supervisor of the reports and records issued by FERA, where he served primarily in an editorial capacity.[32]

Realizing his friend's weakness in administration, Baker chose Reed Harris to become Alsberg's assistant. A few years earlier, as the editor of the undergraduate *Columbia University Spectator*, Harris had come to the public's attention by being expelled for reprinting a report against the excessive prices, poor quality of food, and mistreatment of waiters in Columbia's dining halls. Sixteen Columbia College faculty members, the National Students' Union, and the American Civil Liberties Union had come to his defense, raising the issue of free speech. After three weeks of agitation and national headlines, Harris was reinstated; he immediately withdrew in protest. He next tried his hand as newspaperman, production manager for an advertising agency, ghost writer of *A Guide to Czechoslovakia*, and editor of a pulp fiction magazine. With the publication by Vanguard Press of his harsh attacks against the professional racketeering aspects of college football, he came to Baker's attention.[33]

Harris's appointment had tangible effects on Alsberg's success in the federal organization. Some of Alsberg's directives had to be reviewed after he told Harris, "Hell, I don't keep carbons!" (Washington circles still talk of "the Henry Alsberg filing system: if he were interested, it

[31] J. Alsberg and Levine interviews. Alsberg listed "saving the world from reactionaries" as his work. *Columbia University . . . Alumni*, p. 200.

[32] J. Alsberg, Baker, and Walter Frese (Sept. 13, 1967) interviews; Russell Lord, "Books," *New York Herald Tribune*, Oct. 7, 1934, p. 4.

[33] Reed Harris interview, July 17, 1968; *Columbia Spectator*, Apr. 1-21, 1932; Reed Harris, *King Football* (New York, 1932).

went into his desk; if not, into his wastebasket.'') With the FERA supervisor of records concentrating on the editing of material and Harris focusing on administration, reports like a history of unemployment relief in Louisiana and a survey of Key West were finished. These studies served to supplement material which various Washington officials were gathering for future relief plans, and, at the same time, the surveys gave Alsberg and Harris a chance to develop ties with the state ERA administrators and to provide jobs for unemployed newspapermen.[34]

Concerned with the plight of his New York literary circle, Alsberg kept in close touch with Goldschmidt's Professional Projects Division and subsequently developed his own idea for a writer's project. His contacts with the inner circle of planners made him aware of the various suggestions it had received. In Alsberg's mind, the proposal for a series of guidebooks became transformed into the broader concept of a diverse collection of essays which could ''attract attention to the whole of American civilization and its development.'' The new concept effectively encompassed FERA's iconography and folklore ''procedures'' and held the promise that creative writers could find fulfillment in its employ. Armed with imagination and a creative vision, Alsberg was largely responsible for the eventual acceptance of production of a guidebook as the major purpose of a writers' project. He himself told his brother, ''the guide series was Hopkins's idea,'' but Julius Alsberg never found the assertion totally convincing: ''I always suspected Henry suggested it to Hopkins, because he was so heart and soul in it.''[35]

Throughout 1934, suggestions for state and national guidebooks had been received by Goldschmidt's division from the Authors' League and various individuals. In submitting one such idea, one person expressed his confidence that a federal project would ''build the foundations of patriotism'' and even stimulate foreign travel to the United States

[34] Harris and J. Alsberg interviews. This experience would prove to be very useful when the two men became assistant and executive directors of the Division of Reports, Statistics, and Records for WPA. The FERA reports themselves suggested the first federal project for writers, the WPA Narrative Reports, which served as a ''transition,'' with respect to both personnel and organization, to the FWP and its main concern, the American Guide Series. McDonald, ''Federal Relief,'' p. 737.

[35] Bolles, ''Federal Writers' Project,'' p. 3; Alsberg to Gruening, Apr. 23, 1936, Box 133, FWPN; J. Alsberg interview.

—reasons that would be used by the division to advance the need for the project. What finally convinced Goldschmidt was a chance meeting at a cocktail party. As he recalled it: "Baker left me stuck in the corner with a garrulous gal who kept asking 'What will you do for writers?' I couldn't easily escape and, besides, I decided to listen. You never knew where a good idea would come from. Her proposal was guidebooks. The next morning I said to Jake: 'Iconography is for the birds. I've got the answer.' " The suggestion particularly impressed the head of the Professional Projects Division because he thought that "writing guidebooks was making history," while iconography represented "just the writing of it," and he henceforth steered his staff to focus on this one proposal.[36]

To Katherine Kellock, "the garrulous gal," history and guidebooks went together. While aiding the Quakers in their relief work against famine in southern and central Europe after World War I, Kellock had realized the value of the world-famous Baedeker guides. Returning to New York, she did nursing work for Lillian Wald's Henry Street Settlement and attended Columbia, where she majored in history. Her talents went into the research and condensation of the authorized biography of Houdini written by her husband, Harold Kellock, and into forty articles for the *Dictionary of American Biography*. Dissatisfied with the 1909 Baedeker for this country, she decided to champion a national guidebook for the United States. Letters to publishing firms brought the same reply: "when we get three-dollar wheat again we will consider it." Undaunted, she pushed her project at Washington cocktail parties, finally snaring Goldschmidt. Guidebooks, she argued, would also provide almost unlimited work for white-collar workers and get tremendous community support—vital considerations for Baker's program.[37]

Katherine Kellock later broached the subject to Alsberg, her husband's close friend from Columbia days. He mentioned that a guide to Connecticut had just been done and, with the ease with which the New Deal was run in those days, suggested: "Why don't you take it to Nina? She's interested." Collier gave her visitor specifics about budgeting and planning for programs, especially that of the Connecticut guide. While writing up a proposal then and there, Kellock, who had figured on a $400-$500 thousand budget for a nationwide project,

---

[36] McDonald, "Federal Relief," p. 741; Goldschmidt interview.
[37] Kellock interview, June 23, 1968.

was "shocked beyond words" at Nina Collier's $2 million estimate. Her interest in the guidebooks remained so strong that, when she was later offered a post in the Resettlement Administration, she agreed only on the condition that she be released to the writers' project if and when it materialized. In the interim, she did "little chores" for Alsberg and proved instrumental in the formulation of the American Guide program.[38]

The publication of the Connecticut Guide in May, 1935, persuaded Jake Baker that a guidebook series was feasible. This "survey of places of scenic and historic interest," initiated in the winter of 1934 under CWA and completed with FERA funds, was published by the Hartford Emergency Relief Commission. Compiled with the aid of a few relief workers and about 1,000 volunteers, the pioneering effort had a brief introductory history and architecture essay, offered a list of hotels and a short bibliography for tourists, and covered all 169 of the state's towns. At last, as Baker put it years later, the FERA had "found something that literate people could do." The volume had several shortcomings, including stress on the past and dull prose. But William Lyon Phelps of Yale's English faculty called the FERA Guide a "veritable Baedeker" and hoped that every state would produce its own. The book sold more than 10,000 copies in two months, returning all costs to the state ERA administrator.[39]

While only Connecticut succeeded in publishing a guide at this time, other states, businesses, and individuals sought to put out such volumes. The Michigan and Kentucky state organizations worked on various local histories. The editors of the Americana Corporation became convinced of the necessity for a "gazetteer of the U.S. along Baedeker lines"; they had been contemplating issuing such a volume, but the Depression made this private effort impracticable. A student at the University of Chicago had begun work in early 1935 on an auto tourist's guide to the immediate vicinities of the highways between the larger cities of the country. Later, hearing about the federal program, he would cry "plagiarism!"[40]

A "geographical encyclopedia" for the nation had also been sug-

[38] *Ibid.*; Collier to author, Aug. 27, 1968.

[39] *The Connecticut Guide, What to See and Where to Find It* (Hartford, 1935), pp. xvii, 234; Baker interview.

[40] McDonald, "Federal Relief," p. 731; McDaniel to Hopkins, July 1, 1935, Box 460, Works Progress Administration state file series, Works Projects Administration records, Record Group 69, National Archives, Washington, D.C.; Nathan Morris interview, Mar. 30, 1968.

gested to Baker by an old friend, George Cronyn. Author of *The Fool of Venus* and *Fortune and Men's Eyes*, English instructor, stonemason, stage manager, cowboy, movie scenarist, and plumber, Cronyn had as rich a past as Alsberg and Katherine Kellock. His more imposing duties had included editorial positions with the *New Standard Encyclopedia* and the *Columbia Encyclopedia*, which had led to his appreciation of certain fields never before approached by guidebooks, including "the social, scientific, economic, and folkways backgrounds of the entire country, and of every section of it." His ideas had had an effect on Baker, who soon called him to Washington to help start the program.[41]

The country had a number of guidebooks. Baedeker's 1909 volume had warned foreign visitors about the lack of public lavatories and noted that pistols could be left at home (since the Indians had been subdued). Chamber of commerce pamphlets offered superlatives and some facts. A few more informative guidebooks were outdated, such as King's *Handbook of the U.S.* (1891) and Rider's guides to New York (1924) and the capital. The U.S. Geological Survey put out a *Guidebook of the Western States* (1922) in five pamphlets, and the National Park Service offered handouts to its visitors. To meet the demands of the automobile age, which necessitated drastic revision of Baedeker *et al.*, the Continental Oil Co. put out "touraids" and the A.A.A. published its three-volume guide—"the nearest thing to a comprehensive guidebook," in Alsberg's opinion. There were also such recent works as the studies of Louisiana by Lyle Saxon and Percy Viosca, Cornelius Weygandt's volumes about Pennsylvania, and the more comprehensive *Vacation Travel-charts and Travel Chats* and *Double-Crossing America by Motor*.[42]

None of the nationwide travel guides adequately covered the country, however; all suffered in comparison with Europe's Murrays, Guides Bleus, and Baedekers. Even the better books were generally descriptive travel books rather than guidebooks. They also concen-

---

[41] Harris interview; Cronyn to Cronin, Oct. 26, 1936, Box 461, Works Progress Administration general file series, Works Projects Administration records, Record Group 69, National Archives, Washington, D.C. (hereafter WPA).

[42] Karl Baedeker, *The United States*; Alsberg to Stokes, Nov. 1935, Box 2446, WPA; Lyle Saxon, *Old Louisiana* (New York, 1929); Percy Viosca, *Out of Doors* (New Orleans, 1933); Cornelius Weygandt, *The Wissahickon Hills* (Philadelphia, 1930); Frederick Collins, *Vacation Travel-charts and Travel Chats* (Indianapolis, 1930); Edward Dunn, *Double-Crossing America by Motor* (New York, 1933).

trated on a few principal cities, partly because of the influence of the master, Baedeker.[43]

The vast extent and rapidly changing conditions of the United States made the production of a satisfactory guidebook difficult. Indeed, Baedeker found the effort to produce one so arduous that he gave up after several attempts. The country's vastness led the author of Mussolini's official biography to declare that she managed to "do" America in less than four months in 1934 only by flying from major city to major city.[44]

The dearth of worthy guidebook examples immediately became evident to the Washington officials interested in the guide series proposal. Researching the files of the National Geographic Society, Reed Harris found that "practically nothing good" could be found for the United States. Without decent guidebooks, Americans sped through towns and past scenery on the best highways in the world, unaware of the rich variety of their history and folklore.[45]

The various ideas for a series of guides as the *raison d' être* of a writers' project proved most satisfactory to Baker and Goldschmidt's division for a number of other reasons. While mapping an uncharted America, the volumes also would benefit a depression-ridden economy. The series would stimulate business as people began to "See America First." (Alsberg later argued that had Americans spent at home the billions they poured into travel abroad in the twenties, the total would have surpassed the Roosevelt deficit.) The guides, at the same time, would answer the needs of many Americans who had abandoned annual visits to Europe because their funds were low or because of political unrest on the Continent. In 1935 alone, 35 million vacationers took to the nation's highways. The guides would serve the rapidly growing number of visitors to national parks, as well as the newly emerging youth hostel movement, the American Camping Association, and the Scouts. They could also help in the rediscovery of historic landmarks and scenic wonders.[46]

Most important, the guide series would be the perfect answer to the gnawing dilemma of how to provide employment both for white-collar

[43] Kellock interview, June 23, 1968.

[44] Baedeker, *United States*, preface; *Chicago Herald and Examiner*, Oct. 14, 1934.

[45] Harris interview.

[46] Henry Alsberg quoted in *New York Herald Tribune* (clipping), Box 201, FWPN; Wecter, *Great Depression*, pp. 233-35.

workers having some writing ability and for true literary craftsmen. It could solve Baker's primary problem of finding meaningful jobs for professionals, most of whom could hardly be considered creative artists. The Connecticut FERA Guide, for example, had made use of the writing ability of many jobless preachers, and this impressed Baker greatly. As for actual writers, Goldschmidt's principal concern, they could focus on Alsberg's interest in essays for the guides.[47] These disparate groups would not be engaged in a useless operation. If the avowed aim of WPA was "to help men keep their chins up and their hands in," working on a national guide could give such professionals a sense of dignity and value.[48]

Although convinced of the value of a guide series for needy writers and miscellaneous professionals, Baker and the Professional Projects Division had to wait patiently while their superiors in Washington deliberated and fought over control of a new relief organization. Roosevelt, hoping to substitute work for relief, had suggested an emergency works program to remove 3½ million employables from relief rolls and put them in steady jobs at a "security wage." At first, the new works proposal, presented to Congress in January, 1935, was viewed as almost exclusively supporting construction operations. Hopkins himself only mentioned the white-collar aspect twice during hearings in February, and he made no reference to arts projects at all. The passage in March of the Emergency Relief Appropriation Act of 1935 led to a struggle between Hopkins and the Public Works Administration's Harold Ickes for control of the President's discretionary use of almost $5 million. Hopkins wanted the funds used for immediate work relief, whereas Ickes hoped to "prime the pump" to national recovery with large public works projects. In May, an executive order established the new Works Progress Administration; Hopkins received authority over WPA soon thereafter.[49]

Since the battle for control of the ERA's $5 billion allotment had not clarified whether WPA (the federal government) or the states were

[47] Baker and Goldschmidt interviews.

[48] Wecter, *Great Depression*, pp. 189-91.

[49] William E. Leuchtenburg, *Franklin D. Roosevelt and the New Deal, 1932-1940*, pp. 124-25; McDonald, "Federal Relief," pp. 168-92. Roosevelt specifically wanted WPA, according to the executive order, to "recommend and carry on small useful projects designed to assume a maximum of employment in all localities." Quoted in Ronnie W. Clayton, "A History of the Federal Writers' Project in Louisiana" (Ph.D. diss., Louisiana State University, 1974), p. 11.

entitled to the ERA funds for white-collar programs, the fate of the cultural projects remained to be settled. Anticipating some favorable decision at the end of May, the head of WPA began appointing state administrators. Reflecting his concern for white-collar professionals, he chose his former FERA secretary, Bruce McClure, to head the new WPA Professional and Service Projects Division (covering all white-collar units), with Tex Goldschmidt as associate director. By mid-June, there still had been no sign that the arts projects would be operated under WPA sponsorship. Finally, as a result of the Comptroller-General's response in early July, the $300 million earmarked in the ERA act for "assistance for educational, professional, and clerical persons" passed into WPA hands. A rushed effort to promote white-collar projects tentatively included thirteen federal units; six were eventually established. Federal Project, No. 1, to cover four fields in the arts, became the first of these.[50]

The Federal Writers' Project (part of Federal #1) stemmed directly from the formal proposal submitted on June 25, 1935, by the WPA Professional and Service Projects Division before the Comptroller-General's breakthrough decision. The proposal called for the preparation of a guidebook of the United States, reports of WPA progress, an encyclopedia of government functions, and a limited number of special studies by qualified individual writers. The draft suggested that the major work be issued in five regional volumes and be hence-forth called the American Guide. The division's report estimated that the project would last for one year and cover 6,742 relief workers at a cost per man-year of $912.54. With other local and regional costs, the total budget reached $6,285,222.72. These precise figures (short of the final budget by less than $3,000!) represented part of the outline budget and general plan for the arts program drawn up by two members of the inner circle of planners; that outline, with final approval, subsequently became the "Bible" for all units of Federal #1.[51]

[50] McDonald, "Federal Relief," pp. 192-98; Goldschmidt interview. This $300 million appropriation had spurred PWAP's Edward Bruce to ask Eleanor Roosevelt to support cultural projects which would "enrich the lives of all our people by making things of the spirit, the creation of beauty, part of their daily lives." Mrs. Roosevelt gave this memo to FDR in early May. Bruce memo, n.d., Series 70, Box 643, Eleanor Roosevelt papers (hereafter ER papers), Franklin D. Roosevelt Library, Hyde Park, N.Y. (hereafter FDRL); Eleanor Roosevelt to Bruce, May 8, 1935, Series 100, Box 1330, ER papers, FDRL.

[51] "Project Submitted," June 25, 1935, Box 461, WPA; Nina Collier to author, Aug. 27, 1968.

Baker next had to choose a national director for Hopkins's consideration. Years later he recalled that moment: "Alsberg was sitting around,
listening. Tex said, 'Give it to Alsberg or he'll be disappointed.'"
Another federal director later disagreed with this decision: "Henry
Alsberg . . . was a very odd duck. I don't know why in the devil he was
the Director of the Writers' Project anyway, because he isn't a writer."
Alsberg got the post because Jake felt he was "the right man, of some
stature in the publishing and writing field." Then, too, he had played a
vital role in the formation of the project, and his creative ideas closely
resembled Baker's interests.[52]

In Baker's fertile mind, Federal #1 suggested more than the regener-
ation of professionals in need. It also offered a rare opportunity, under
the proper supervision, to revitalize the arts to an extent heretofore
unknown in America. Seizing this chance, he largely chose national
arts directors who, like himself, were liberal nonacademicians and to
whom "the arts were alive and experiment was still possible." With
money he received from the *New York Times* for a magazine article
on relief and skilled workers, Baker gave a dinner at Alsberg's apartment for Hopkins to meet the newly selected executives and discuss
their ideas.[53]

Exalted plans ran through excited conversation that evening. The
various project administrators, with ideas for guides, the Index of
American Design, and community art centers, theatrical productions,
and concerts across the country, all shared the brilliant vision of a
renascence and democratization of the arts for the nation as a whole.
Hopkins served as a catalyst. With his uncanny perceptiveness, the new
head of WPA suggested procedures by throwing out questions as if he
were leading cards to be picked up by those in the audience. Though
he sensed that Federal #1 would represent the "touchy" aspects of
WPA's relief program ("that's where we'll get hell," he told Florence
Kerr as he was about to receive an honorary degree from Grinnell), his
determination never wavered.[54]

Along with his fellow directors on Federal #1—Hallie Flanagan for

[52] Baker interview; Cahill Memoir, p. 352; Harris interview.

[53] Baker interview; "Unemployed Arts," *Fortune*, 15 (May, 1937):108-17.

[54] Cahill Memoir, pp. 424-37; Florence Kerr interview, July 7, 1968. Later, reviewing the
initial contribution of Federal #1 to the "renascence of the arts" in the country, Hopkins wrote
that this "certainly betokens a deep spiritual change and re-estimate of what is valuable in
American life." Hopkins, *Spending to Save*, p. 174.

theatre, Holger Cahill for art, and Nicolai Sokoloff for music—Henry Alsberg received his official appointment on July 25, 1935: his title was National Director of the Federal Writers' Project. Of the nearly $5 billion appropriated to WPA, a little over $27 million was granted to the arts by presidential order at the end of August. Because of the change to WPA sponsorship of federal projects, additional rules and procedures had to be drawn up, and only on September 12 did the arts program receive final executive approval. At long last, with a six-month allotment of $6,288,000 for some 6,500 persons, Alsberg and his staff had their chance to serve as guidemakers to America.[55]

[55] *New York Times*, July 27 and Aug. 7, 1935; McDonald, "Federal Relief," p. 201.

2   Administration

AS SOON AS THE FEDERAL WRITERS' PROJECT received approval in July, 1935, Alsberg plunged into his new role with a zealot's conviction. The proposal submitted by the WPA Professional and Service Projects Division a month previously—for a five-volume American Guide to cover the Northeast, Southeast, North Central, South Central, and Pacific Coast areas—served as his basic plan. Information would be received from the states, and a professional staff of writers in Washington would then turn out the final manuscript. Twelve regional offices would be set up as administrative centers.[1]

The regional emphasis had several drawbacks. George Cronyn, the newly designated associate director of the project, objected that beyond New England and the South no one could agree on the boundaries of a region. He also believed that this arrangement would be unfair to the states, which would be obligated to send all their material to Washington. The contemplated organization, in addition, could not administer state units for WPA as its planners had originally intended. Furthermore, quick results were needed to mollify skeptics at both the congressional and local levels, and regional guides would take too long. Finally, Katherine Kellock argued that regional guides could not be expected to gain state and local support, not a small matter in the minds of legislators on the Hill.[2]

Cronyn proposed guides on a state-by-state basis. To avoid the delay that any rewriting of the project might involve, the state guides could be completed and then used to produce the regional volumes. The amended plan received final authorization in October, 1935.[3] The plan

---

[1] *New York Times*, July 27 and Oct. 11, 1935; Cronyn to von Auw, Jan. 4, 1936, Authors' League papers.

[2] Cronyn telephone conversation, June 30, 1968; Kellock telephone conversation, Aug. 25, 1968.

[3] Cronyn telephone conversation; Harris to Morris, May 12, 1937, Box 52, FWPN; *New York Times*, Oct. 11, 1935.

required further modification, however. Alsberg's assurances to one irate member of the Westchester County Realty Board that the project's administrators did not contemplate the publication of any local or county guides, which might compete with realtors' publications, proved worthless. Project officials soon discovered that state workers would first focus on city guides, because they were most familiar with the locale and had some source material from which to copy. The slow progress of the state guides[4] quickly convinced the Washington office that the five-volume regional guide—the American Guide—would be elusive and probably unattainable. Cronyn's proposal for state guides thus prevailed, and in October, 1935, Alsberg and his staff began work.[5]

The central office now had to consider what form the state guides should take. Alsberg posed this problem at the first official meeting of the central staff, attended by Alsberg, Harris, Joseph Gaer (formerly of the Los Angeles newspaper project), Katherine Kellock, and Lawrence Morris.[6] Alsberg and Cronyn favored a small encyclopedia for each state, which would contain essays on its history, education, agriculture, industry, and topography. Kellock preferred a volume concentrating on tourist routes with a brief background of the state. Alsberg's view assumed that the staff would write primarily for *readers*; Kellock's, that their audience was *tourists*. The compromise was a guide beginning with a variety of essays followed by comprehensive tour descriptions.[7]

To avoid confusion, Alsberg and Cronyn had American Guide manuals prepared for the various states. While some state executives praised the first manual issued, other reviewers called for fundamental revisions. Confusing instructions from Washington to the states reflected the central staff's uncertainty about the makeup of the guidebooks. Alsberg's preference for essays contrasted with Cronyn's encyclopedic approach to town and city coverage. Thus, the second

[4] For the reasons for this, see chaps. 3 and 4 below.

[5] Alsberg to Nuttall, Dec. 12, 1935, Box 36, FWPN; Kellock telephone conversation; *New York Sun*, June 26, 1935. When an attempt was finally made, in mid-1938, to begin a New England regional guide, it collapsed. Manuel to New England directors, July 14, 1938, Box 19, FWPN.

[6] Morris, past coeditor of *New Democracy* (the Social Credit movement's journal), had turned down Bruce Bliven's offer to become literary editor of the *New Republic* on the ground that he wanted to write a novel. Discovering that part-time freelancing could not carry him through the Depression, he quickly accepted an editorial position on the FWP from Alsberg. Morris interview.

[7] Morris interview; Kellock interview, June 23, 1968.

manual, devoted to state guides, set up a uniform system for city and district material. The requirement of uniformity immediately elicited cries of despair from the states, notably from the South. The manual required indexing of specialized subjects; this was practical in Charleston or Jacksonville, but not in areas of the country with limited research and travel facilities. Alphabetizing, moreover, required the tourist to "tie up fragments" by thumbing through maps, making lists of places, and referring back and forth to cities on his planned route.[8]

Kellock endorsed many of these complaints—she thought the manuals unworkable. The first manuals also lacked clear directions on the use of source materials and established questionable schedules of production. Kellock suggested, therefore, that workers be encouraged to refer to works such as the Beards' *Rise of American Civilization* as an example of writing which fulfilled the Guide's purpose: "to educate Americans to an evaluation of their own civilization." As for production, the quota of an average of 1,500 words a week represented "an invitation to dawdling and padding." The page allotments in the second manual also appeared much too rigid and gave more room to essays than to tours or points of interest.[9] It did not help to assure confused state directors that they could change these divisions at their discretion, for most blindly accepted instructions out of lack of experience and a veneration for "Washington" and central authority.

Alsberg had to admit that, almost a year after the project began, there still existed doubt in a number of states about the nature of a guidebook. Was it a gazetteer? A state encyclopedia? A device for attracting settlers?[10] In this preliminary disorder, instructions from Washington underwent frequent revision. Changes quickly made earlier manuals outdated, causing one state administrator to declare that his staff had to redo practically all of three months' furious efforts when they received new orders in January, 1936.[11] Indeed, after the original plans had been approved, a year passed before the central staff drew up definite outlines for the state guides. Though this delay might seem excusable in a pioneering effort, the many changes in regulations often led to

[8] Harlan to Alsberg, Nov. 27, 1935, Box 3, FWPN; Kellock to Alsberg, Feb. 18, 1936, Box 58, FWPN. There were sixteen manuals in all. See Box 69, FWPN.

[9] Kellock to Alsberg, Feb. 18, 1936, Box 58, FWPN; Manual #2, Box 69, FWPN.

[10] Alsberg to Gruening, Apr. 23, 1936, Box 35, FWPN.

[11] Ulrich R. Bell, quoted in *Louisville Courier-Journal*, Nov. 27, 1938; Kellock interview, June 23, 1968.

frustration. One exasperated state editor penned these lines:

> I think that I have never tried
> A job as painful as the Guide,
> A guide which changes every day
> Because our betters feel that way,
> A guide whose deadlines come so fast
> Yet no one lives to see the last,
> A guide to which we give our best
> To hear: "This stinks like all the rest!"
> There's no way out but suicide
> For only God can end the Guide.[12]

Chaos, subsided, though, after the central staff adopted new procedures in mid-1936 to enhance the final product. Within about a year, supplementary instructions eliminated the overlapping, and the required new arrangement of material brought about smooth narrative in state copy.

Alsberg had to reassure Hopkins before the FWP was approved that the work could be completed in a half-year's time. In fact, Cronyn wrote Baker and McClure that the six-months' allotment given the guide project by Congress would hardly suffice. But WPA's chief needed the reassurance that the FWP's task could be completed by July, 1936, when Congress's annual fiscal appropriation came to an end. Knowing that only in this way could he get the necessary funds to proceed, Alsberg told Hopkins what he needed to hear. The national director sensed a lengthening Depression and reasoned that Congress would have to extend his appropriation.[13]

Uncertain of the talents of their future charges, aware of the dearth of solid guidebook models, with little time to produce results, the easiest course for the central staff would have been to turn out dry, uncontroversial "booster" books. Some observers, expecting no more, dismissed the new project with a sneer. Wrote Robert Littell:

> It is Baedeker's business to steer his readers to flawless churches and flealess hotels. I'm afraid the U.S. Guidebook, compiled with funds derived from taxes paid by its eventual readers, will not say very much about flaws and fleas. If the Squeedunks and Linoleumvilles of the

[12] Supplementary instructions 11B, Box 69, FWPN; Stella Hanau papers, private collection, New York, N.Y.

[13] Morris interview; Cronyn to McClure, Sept. 18, 1935, Box 461, WPA.

United States are omitted from the Guidebook, or truthfully described as being of small interest, they will raise hell enough to ripple all the way to Washington. . . . I shall want a guidebook that can stifle its passion for statistics and arrowheads long enough to leave some room to write about American people. But I'm afraid I'll be disappointed, and that guidebooks will continue to treat people as they always have—as ethnological wax groups frozen behind the glass exhibit-cases of a natural-history museum.[14]

For Alsberg, however, a man deeply committed to the production of an enduring literary monument, both the flealess and the fleabitten aspects of the American scene would be woven through the Guide.

II

Alsberg's faith alone could accomplish nothing without a skilled administrative organization. Second in command was Associate Director George Cronyn, picked by Baker to add "exactness" to Alsberg's work. At the start he exercised both administrative and editorial authority, but although his sense of precision in both areas was invaluable, his approach to administrative matters made a clash with Alsberg inevitable. More practical than his chief, Cronyn fully sensed the pitfalls into which the Guide might stumble as an officially sponsored government publication. As a result, he was cautious in approving guide copy and quickly objected to the "higher-ups" when other editorial supervisors and Alsberg ignored his opposition to questionable passages and phrases.[15]

A few months after the project began, Cronyn's precision proved to be excessive: sent to straighten out a muddled situation in the newly organized California project, he held public hearings to the delight of the opposition press and drew conclusions which, ironically, a second investigation proved to be in error. In Baker's words, he was "too damned exact," and at the end of January, 1936, Baker was forced to ask Cronyn to relinquish his administrative authority and to focus solely on editorial matters.[16]

As the managing coordinating editor, Cronyn proved highly compe-

[14] Robert Littell, "Putting America on Paper," *Today* 5 (Nov. 30, 1935): 6-9.
[15] Baker interview.
[16] *Ibid.*; see pp. 43-44 below.

tent, and, with his extensive knowledge of the country (matched only
by that of the tours editor), he was able to suggest points of departure to
floundering state editors and directors.

Cronyn's administrative duties passed into the hands of Reed Harris,
assistant director of the project, who until then had been serving as
executive editor and acting chief of the Section of Special Reports and
Photos of WPS's Division of Research, Statistics, and Records.[17] As
the FWP's principal administrator, Harris promised to run a smooth
organization, thereby satisfying the WPA Finance Division that its
funds would not be squandered. In fact, Hopkins and his administrators
doubted the capacity of the four federal arts projects to handle money.
For this reason, Sol Ozer, formerly director of social work for the
Dallas County Board of Welfare, was asked by the Finance Division to
become the financial officer and establish fiscal controls for Federal
#1. Robert Asher, Ozer's co-worker, characterized Harris as having
"more the contact with reality" than the others, and he consulted with
Harris directly on most financial matters.[18]

The central office concentrated its efforts on editorial duties, exercis-
ing authority on all aspects of writing, research, and publication. By
March, 1936, Harris and Cronyn's efficient organization had sixty-two
employees, with nine in executive positions, five in the field, and
practically no duplication of functions.[19]

Alsberg had good reason to take pride in his Washington staff.
Besides Katherine Kellock, Lawrence Morris, and Joseph Gaer, its first
members included old friends of Alsberg's like Philip Coan, Roderick
Seidenberg, and Research Editor Lawrence Abbott, the former editor
of *Literary Digest*. Lewis Barrington, the associate research editor, had
been an assistant librarian at the Library of Congress for five years.
Edward Barrows, author and managing editor of the *National Municipal Review*, held chief editorial authority. Waldo Browne, past literary
editor of the *Nation* and editor of the *Dial*, served as research editor and
later literary editor. Floyd Dell, the noted author and critic, worked for

[17] That section, which Alsberg had headed as assistant director, passed, in January, 1936, into
the control of the Division of Information, leaving both men free to concentrate on the FWP.

[18] Ozer and Asher interviews. Their successor, Julius Davidson, continued to serve as "a
bridge between the tough boys in the Treasury and the screwballs at WPA." Davidson interview,
June 30, 1968.

[19] Harris to Stein, Mar. 26, 1936, Box 55, FWPN.

a time as advisory editor.[20] Different topics were assigned to separate editors throughout the project's existence. Architect and writer Roderick Seidenberg handled architecture and art; Darcy McNickle, author and member of the *Encyclopaedia Britannica* editorial staff, and then Edward Kennard, specialist on the Hopi and Sioux, handled Indians and archaeology; Edwin M. Williams, historian of New York State, Washington, D.C., and Delaware and history editor of the *Americana Encyclopaedia*, covered history; and Katherine Kellock, of course, had charge of tours.[21]

Members of the national coordinating staff often had to serve in the field as well, for the FWP lacked regional directors until 1938. At the outset, the executive staff divided the country into five areas and sent representatives to help organize the state units and choose their respective directors. Morris, promoted to chief field supervisor, stayed with the project one year, after which Jake Baker asked him to direct the WPA New England regional headquarters. Gaer then became chief field supervisor for the project, and he focused his attention on the publication of various books from the New England states. Occasionally, Gaer and other field people would act independently, causing more than one state director to react in consternation over conflicting directives. These difficulties were met by having state directors visit neighboring projects as field representatives to share similar problems and offer advice.[22]

Alsberg's demand for literary quality, along with Cronyn's vigilance on questions of policy, led to a decision to require every part of the work, both in copy and final form, to have editorial approval from Washington. To insure efficient copy flow, every manuscript arriving in the central office was passed to Alsberg and Cronyn (or Harris in their absence) for a brief inspection and then went, successively, to the state editor, a particular subject editor, and at last to the field editor. It next received the approval of one of the three project directors and, after

---

[20] Dell wrote progress reports for a year and inspired audiences with the achievements of the various white-collar projects until transferred to another federal agency. Miles to Alsberg, June 12, 1936, Box 1, FWPN.

[21] For other authorities on the D.C. staff, see chap. 7 below.

[22] Morris later became executive assistant of Federal #1. Morris interview. Harris to Alsberg, Apr. 19, 1937, Box 55, FWPN. Among other field supervisors was Clair Laning, who had previously worked in the inner circle of Federal #1 planners and later became assistant to the director.

making its way to the checker, who in turn sent it to the proper person for signature, finally arrived at state headquarters.[23]

Inundated by copy as the guides progressed, the central staff became increasingly overworked. Constant cuts in the project rolls slowed down the editorial machinery when fast results were called for. Waldo Browne tried to comfort the essays editor: " . . . remember that Atlas had to hold up the entire world, while you have only the weight of the United States on your shoulders."[24]

The problem of offices also plagued the central staff. The Washington headquarters of all the arts projects had first been assigned to a former theatre now known as the Old Auditorium. Files occupied elegant boxes and office cubicles hastily appeared where patrons of the arts had once taken orchestra seats. This setting seemed incongruous, especially with the huge organ pipes hovering above, and the airless gray hall offered little physical comfort. A rare respite occurred when a limousine, sent by the First Lady, abruptly whisked a few FWP planners to the White House. The perspiring administrators pleased Mrs. Roosevelt with reports of their initial effort to combine relief and the advancement of American culture, and they left Pennsylvania Avenue greatly encouraged.[25]

Just as Alsberg became accustomed to his office in a dressing room behind the stage, an order to move arrived, and Alsberg, his staff, and the other projects were squeezed into the Evalyn Walsh McLean mansion at 1500 I Street. The former residence of the owner of the Hope Diamond soon yielded an unexpected but fitting bonus, a case of champagne which, located in the basement one Saturday afternoon, was disposed of by Monday morning. But the gaudy edifice, with its ornate chandeliers, silken walls, and Greek statues, was ill equipped to house Federal #1. The ballroom, which housed the writers' project, lacked office space and was unventilated. The staff's cigars, Harris complained, smelled "like burned rubber in a badly ventilated zoo on a hot summer afternoon."[26]

[23] Harris to editors, May 4, 1936, Box 55, FWPN.

[24] Browne to Barrett, Dec. 5, 1938, Box 85, FWPN.

[25] McKinzie, "Writers on Relief," p. 19.

[26] Asher interview; Harris to staff, Oct. 15, 1937, Box 56, FWPN. At least in this respect, the office resembled WPA headquarters; the absence of air-conditioning in the summertime earned for the WPA the distinguished sobriquet "wet pants administration." Anne Cronin interview, Sept. 18, 1967.

Yet mere physical discomforts could not dampen the exhilaration and strong sense of fellowship of this gifted band for most of the project's existence. Blizzards of paperwork and recurring financial crises could not suppress absent-minded Alsberg jokes or halt jealous quarrels over the attentions of female staff members. One editor placed bets with his bookie at exactly the same hour each afternoon; another refused to allow his work to interfere with his drinking. An integrated project party enraged Mississippi's Senator Bilbo, especially when a lady from his own state (Alsberg's superior) stayed to enjoy the martini punches served, but he decided to overlook this revelry and drop his comments from the *Congressional Record*.[27]

The three executive directors sought to avoid rigid office rules, but soon found that the pressures of work called for closer cooperation and coordination. Attendance sheets became a necessary nuisance. And entry into Alsberg's or Harris's office after 11 A.M. had to be forbidden so these executives could concentrate on their own duties.[28] Gradually, the central staff became an efficient, closely knit unit, wedding discipline to devotion.

III

Having established the central office in Washington, the national director had to fill forty-eight state directorships (plus another for New York City and an additional one for California in 1937, when WPA split the state into separate northern and southern units). At the outset, Alsberg faced the project's major dilemma: whether its technical or administrative aspects should predominate. The matter of directorships involved the choice between editorial people—free-lancers, newspapermen, college faculty—and executives. The Guide was a literary endeavor, but its execution also called for administrative finesse, to organize workers and to placate local critics.[29]

There was no dearth of applicants. Telegrams and letters flooded the Washington office, with suggestions from state officials, universities, and writers' organizations. Since the directors received their appoint-

[27] Mangione, *Dream and Deal*, pp. 224-29.

[28] Harris to staff, Apr. 14, 1936, Box 55, FWPN.

[29] The pay of the state directors in April, 1938, averaged $207 a month. It ranged from $100 to $266 according to the quota of relief workers carried in the state. Cunningham to Pratt, Apr. 7, 1938, Box 41, FWPN.

ments from state WPA administrators upon Alsberg's nomination, politicking at all levels was inevitable. This was especially true for the WPA heads, many of whom had been contractors or road builders and were chosen to organize public works projects for thousands out of work. Caring little about a writers' project for a few people not prepared to haul wheelbarrows or dig ditches, they were prepared to tolerate this sideshow only if control rested in their hands. The question of federal-state rivalry would plague the FWP during its entire existence, and various attempts were made to turn control of the project over to the states. These efforts were not successful until 1939, but the administrative structure resulted in many ineffectual appointments.[30]

Such political interference became especially marked in the first months of the project. The incompetence of Tennessee's director, a county historian whose senilities kept two stenographers busy, was tolerated for almost a year, after which the assistant director replaced him. A division of responsibility between the associate director and the director of the Professional and Service projects kept the West Virginia unit from total collapse until La Vega W. Burns, a Mason, Rotarian, and member of the State Education Association (the strongest political group in the state), finally resigned for another state position a year later. It took only a little less time before an energetic and gifted administrator replaced the Nebraska director, who had obtained the post through the good offices of the editor of the *Lincoln Star* (the only New Deal paper in the state) and Senator George Norris. And Missouri's first project director, "a promoter and a politician" named Geraldine Parker, refused to delegate authority to a highly capable editorial staff, eventually causing them to strike.[31]

Political considerations also figured in the selections of replacements. Pennsylvania's directorship soon shifted from an associate of the public relations department of a railroad corporation to the Philadelphia supervisor (Paul French), who was vice-president of the American Newspaper Guild but, more important, a cousin of the state governor. After Geraldine Parker was dismissed from the Missouri directorship, the post went to an associate of the Daughters of the

[30] Morris interview. For more on these attempts, see pp. 47-50 below.

[31] Coppedge to Woodward, Dec. 22, 1936, Box 44, FWPN; Daryl McConkey file, Box 62, FWPN; Morris to Alsberg, Jan. 30, 1936, Box 60, FWPN; Morris to Alsberg, May 28, 1936, Box 60, FWPN; chap. 8 below.

Confederacy who, like her predecessor, buried creativity and individual opinion in the desire to publish nothing but "safe" material.[32]

Fortunately, the selection and replacement of state directors did not always depend upon political considerations, and the dangers such appointments presented to the quality of the guides were reduced after the central office secured the talents of writers like Vardis Fisher, Lyle Saxon, Ross Santee, John Davis, and John T. Frederick.

Vardis Fisher, no doubt the most outspoken and individualistic of these, had already achieved fame with the Testament of Man series and would soon be awarded the Pulitzer Prize for his *Children of God*. In a semiautobiographical novel, he later wrote that the offer from Cronyn (who had supported his candidacy) had three distinct advantages: he would be able to provide for his wife and two children; he would get to know his state (Idaho); and he could discover, by studying the "inner workings" of government, whether any form of socialism could succeed. The fellow director who had recommended him sent the following telegram: "Congratulations on your new position. Don't take it seriously. It is not intended that we should achieve anything but only that we should put the jobless to work so they will vote for Roosevelt. Take it philosophically and if they send you a telegram from Washington 150 words long, send them one 300 words long or call them long distance collect." Ignoring this advice, Fisher worked twelve- to fourteen-hour days, seven days a week, logging all the roads of Idaho in a new 1936 Nash (at $5 a day and four to five cents a mile), and wrote nearly all the copy for the state guide. He was sustained by his consuming desire to bring out the first state guide, or "break his neck" in the attempt.[33]

Fisher's creative colleagues also stamped their guides with verve and literary style. Saxon, whose authoritative and lively books on the land of the bayous had earned him the title of "Mr. Louisiana," wisely decided to relegate all administrative matters to an associate. Another

[32] For the story of the end of French's involvement with the FWP, see chap. 6 below. Harris to Cordell, Jan. 6, 1937, Box 55, FWPN. A strong endorsement from Senator Pat Harrison got Eri Douglass a directorship, although her only qualification was some experience in organizing private tours and a post in the music department of the Mississippi State College for Women. Cronyn to Alliston, Oct. 12, 1935, Box 22, FWPN.

[33] Vardis Fisher, *Orphans in Gethsemane: A Novel of the Past in the Present*, p. 733; Mangione, *Dream and Deal*, p. 78; Ronald W. Taber, "The Federal Writers' Project in the Pacific Northwest: A Case Study," (Ph.D. diss., Washington State University, 1969), p. 131; Fisher to author, May 19, 1968.

local colorist, the artist-turned-cowboy Ross Santee, became the director for Arizona after its first appointee had wasted three months writing "folksy" letters to ingratiate himself with the local powers. Wrote Santee to Alsberg, "Anyone who can wet-nurse a hundred and fifty saddle horses, know where they run, know all the quirks of each particular horse, ought to be able to wrangle a bunch of writers." Two other gifted local colorists served as project directors. John Davis, newspaperman and author of nearly 200 short stories and magazine articles, headed the Texas unit, and John T. Frederick, the first publisher of William March and James T. Farrell as the founder of *Midland* (1915), directed the Illinois project.[34]

Several diligent women also served as directors of the writers' project, although most did not have the prior reputations or attainments of their male colleagues. One of the few local historians in Florida, Carita Corse, held that state's directorship for more than six years. Especially impressive was the long service of Eudora Richardson, who took over the Virginia project after it had floundered a year and a half. A writer and member of the State Board of Public Welfare, she brought it up to a par with the best of the state projects in a relatively short time.[35] The rate of survival in the directorships was far higher among women than among men. However, there were far fewer women in such posts and they were often the beneficiaries of highly skilled associates and state editors, who regularly bore the burden of administrative or literary duties.[36]

The central office also searched the university English and history departments for able directors, and in communities centered around universities these appointments proved particularly valuable. Harold Merriam, editor of *Frontier and Midland* and chairman of the English faculty at the University of Montana, housed the main project office on his campus free of charge while serving part-time. Harlan Hatcher, a

[34] Saxon to Alsberg, Apr. 21, 1936, Box 15, FWPN; E. Current-Garcia, "Writers in the Sticks," *Prairie Schooner* 12 (1938):294-309.

[35] Carita Corse interview, Oct. 15, 1967; Ralston to Woodward, Sept. 21, 1937, Box 2694, WPA. Also noteworthy in this respect were South Carolina's Mabel Montgomery, New Jersey's Irene Fuhlbruegge, and Delaware's Jeanette Eckman. At the same time, another female director threw away letters from Washington ("those silly things") and ignored work on the guide in favor of having a staff of seventeen produce reams of poetry—her favorite form of literature. Mangione, *Dream and Deal*, p. 80.

[36] Kellock interview, June 23, 1968. For information on state editors and administrative associates, see chap. 4 below.

prolific author and professor of English at Ohio State University, revived Ohio's project after assuming the directorship in 1937. Leo Lyons, an English instructor at the University of Wisconsin, introduced order to that state's project following partisan quarrels between its Madison and Milwaukee branches. (The associate director, as a result of ministerial training, had apparently spent much of his time saving the souls of his charges.) Ethel Schlesinger, recommended at the age of twenty-three by the University of North Dakota English department, provided a pleasant surprise in her handling of North Dakota, a state of nearly 80,000 square miles, despite a dismal shortage of qualified personnel and the central office's preoccupation with the more-traveled states.[37]

Historians, apparently allergic to deadlines, fared poorest as state directors. Their insistence on superthoroughness was out of step with the guides' purposes. In Massachusetts, where the director, Clifford Shipton, exhibited an aggravating condescension toward his workers, a field worker charged that his "pernickety fidelity" to instructions stifled originality. Finally, two associates took over the administrative machinery and handled it until Shipton obtained a more suitable post with the State and Historical Records Project. His successor, Ray Allen Billington, proved a better choice; he and Jarvis Morse, who "jazzed down the hill" from his history classes at Brown University to work part-time in the Connecticut project's main office, resisted efforts to make "mountains out of some local historical molehills," and thus preserved the historical value of the guides.[38]

Other colleagues specializing in different fields preferred to follow their own interests, often with dubious results. An authority on Nevada mining camps, the septuagenarian T. D. Van Devort, assumed that his state had no points of contemporary interest for the tourist, and he sought to transform its guide into a history of Nevada's mining industry. He remained on the project as a history editor with the help of his old friend, Sen. Key Pittman. Ross Lockridge, an authority on Indiana's folklore, spent most of his time drumming up publicity for the

[37] Crane to Alsberg, Apr. 6, 1938, Box 23, FWPN; Gaer to Alsberg, Aug. 19, 1936, Box 62, FWPN.

[38] Seidenberg to Alsberg, Mar. 12, 1936, Box 59, FWPN. After examining letters written by his protégé, Samuel Eliot Morrison concurred with the central office's visiting representative and quickly dismissed the issue: "He's old enough to know better. Where would you like to go for lunch?" Roderick Seidenberg interview, Apr. 18, 1969; Jarvis Morse interview, July 24, 1968.

project by presenting performances (at $100 apiece) composed in part of dramatic recitations and folk songs. Although the central office ordered Lockridge to concentrate on the guide, he failed to assume this minimal responsibility and eventually "resigned."[39]

Bisodol, prescribed by Alsberg's doctor for his nervous stomach, came in handy when directors could not handle their own problems. A Midwest executive used project funds to pay visits to the females in his scattered harem. "If we made it a rule not to hire writers given to drink, we would probably not have a Writers' Project," said Alsberg to Eleanor Roosevelt on one occasion. His desire for girls and liquor helped the one-legged poet Orrick Johns lose the New York directorship. Arriving in his apartment one night, a bottle of brandy tucked under his arm, to continue an affair with an employee, Johns was beaten into unconsciousness by a redheaded seaman. The jealous boyfriend, who had also been refused a job by Johns, next set the director's wooden leg afire with the aid of the brandy. When Johns finally recovered and left the hospital, Alsberg asked for his resignation.[40]

In one instance, a conflict of professional interest almost destroyed an entire state unit before it had begun work in earnest on the Guide. California's director, the noted author and anthropologist Paul Radin, instead of focusing on the guidebook, pursued his specialty, racial minorities, as well as the uncompleted studies of the former Los Angeles Newspaper Project (which had been supervised by Hugh Harlan). Radin's intransigence and the fact that $1,200 a month was being lost by the guide project caused Cronyn to speed to California, where he reported "incompetence, grave irregularities, political maneuvering and sabotage of the American Guide." The associate director soon suspended Harlan from his post. Harlan immediately wrote Hopkins (his old Grinnell classmate) of the matter, pointing out that he had acted under Radin's orders and that continuing SERA research represented not "subterfuge" but true value for the guide project. In the meantime, George Creel, a member of the advisory staff of Federal #1, had allegedly told an angry group of talented San Francisco project writers

[39] Alsberg to McClure, Nov. 19, 1936, Box 2362, WPA; DuVon to Alsberg, Jan. 30, 1936, Box 59, FWPN. For information on Oregon's director, see Howe to Harris, Oct. 19, 1937, Box 40, FWPN.

[40] Mangione, *Dream and Deal*, pp. 68, 80-83. For more on Johns's incompetence, see chap. 9 below. Kansas's director set a dubious record when heavy drinking on the job led to his dismissal after eleven days.

that responsibility for Cronyn's order rested with "an s.o.b. in Washington named Jake Baker." Fortunately for the success of the project, a second investigation, conducted by Utah's director, recommended that Harlan be reinstated and Radin be demoted to a research editorship.[41]

The outcome drew mixed reactions. One newspaper complained that the new focus on an unnecessary "sublimated Baedeker" would at least be safe from attack by super-patriots, who formerly might have seen "a red behind every tree" whenever SERA labor or creative studies were involved. Another writer viewed the praise of chambers of commerce for the guide venture as the old story of the "American Guyed," with "the interests" out to destroy independent effort on the part of the intellectuals. But with Harlan's reinstatement and the choice of James Hopper, a short-story writer acceptable to Creel, the state WPA, and the Authors' League as the new director, the turmoil subsided. Project workers no longer had to worry about dismissal on political or personal grounds, and the guide project could finally begin in California.[42]

IV

Nationwide, the project had to contend with the normal dose of red tape. Obtaining typewriters presented a special problem; in a number of states, the guide manuscripts had to be written in longhand for months. Forms had to be filled out perfectly lest they be returned weeks later for the slightest error. In addition, directors were deluged with daily telegrams, letters, and wordy mimeographed bulletins from Washington. One state executive soon learned to pass them on to her secretary for a digest and instructed her: "If they have changed anything today, tell me."[43]

While Harris and his colleagues learned to live with red tape, they were less successful in preventing editorial delays in Washington. For two years the central office not only proofread everything but did

[41] Radin file, Box 5, FWPN; Cronyn to Baker, Dec. 26, 1935, Box 58, FWPN; Harlan to Hopkins, Dec. 17, 1935, Box 58, FWPN.

[42] Clippings from *Pacific Weekly*, Jan. 6, 1936, and *San Francisco News*, Dec. 13, 1935, Box 937, WPA.

[43] Lawrence Morris to editors, n.d., Box 52, FWPN; Mabel Ulrich, "Salvaging Culture for the WPA," *Harper's* 177 (May, 1939):653-54.

complete rewrites of doubtful passages. Alsberg finally proposed a decentralized system—one with regional directors—to clear the logjam. Alsberg had in fact contemplated using these regional appointees to edit local guides and special publications, but the sluggish performance of many states required that the regional people concentrate on the state guidebooks in order to complete them before the project closed.[44]

The central office selected four proved administrators as regional directors. Like John Frederick and Lyle Saxon (who received the Midwest region and the five states near Louisiana, respectively), William T. Couch of the Southeast region came from an executive post on the project and had a previous background in regional literature. He had been associate director of the North Carolina unit, had managed the University of North Carolina Press for over ten years, and had made it one of the outstanding university presses in the country. The editor of *Culture in the South*, a work aptly designated "a pathfinder" by Constance Rourke, Couch concentrated his skills on broadening the writers' project to include "life histories" of contemporary laborers in that region.[45]

Frank Manuel came to the project from Harvard's history faculty to serve as New England regional director and work on the New England regional guide. The complacency of the workers of that region after the last of its state guidebooks had been finished was rudely disturbed when Manuel began his task. He was intolerant of those unable to match his standards, and his curt manner and inclination to "hop all around" (secretaries called him a "jitterbug") alienated staff members and depressed morale on the project. Not a state or associate director, he occupied an undefined position vis-à-vis the Massachusetts director, with whom he shared headquarters. At the same time, he formulated and worked on proposals dealing with regional folklore and socioethnic studies, thereby earning the gratitude of the Washington specialists working in these fields.[46]

[44] Alsberg report to Morris, Nov. 4, 1938, Box 1, FWPN.

[45] Box 1, Library of Congress Federal Writers' Project files, Works Projects Administration records, Record Group 69, National Archives, Washington, D.C. (hereafter LC FWP). For Couch's work on "life histories," see chap. 7 below.

[46] Coxe to Branion, Dec. 17, 1938, Box 1, LC FWP; Morris to Alsberg, Mar. 20, 1939, Box 1529, WPA; McDonald, "Federal Relief," p. 783. For Manuel's work on regional volumes, see chap. 7 below.

While the central staff sought primarily to facilitate the production of the state guidebooks through these appointments, Alsberg also tried, unsuccessfully, to see his original hope for regional guides fulfilled. But publishers favored an emphasis on recreational regions (to the neglect of Alsberg's novel concept of interpretive essays) to attract the tourist book trade. In considering the publication of a regional guide, Houghton Mifflin drew upon the sentiments of Bernard De Voto: "For God's sake, make the New England volume a guide. I never yet saw a tourist who wanted to be preached at or even lectured to. He wants to know where the old mill used to be, how far it is to East Twinflower and where is the comfort station." Manuel agreed, hoping to forestall any criticism that the project had put out the book by "stringing together" sections of the separate guides. Alsberg's dream was never realized. Gaer's plans for a New England volume, which he formulated as early as August, 1937, had to be shelved, as did the idea of a one-volume guide to the United States, intended for the foreign tourist, in the 1939 prospectus.[47]

Of the various ideas for regional studies, only a few were brought to print. Frederick's suggestions for histories of the Great Lakes and the northern rivers and a census of newspaper files were endorsed at various regional conferences. He cherished the idea of collecting newspaper material by important frontier humorists, but ultimately was forced to abandon the idea. On the other hand, a combination of state efforts led to the success not only of Couch's "life histories" but of Manuel's *New England Hurricane*, an immediate attempt to follow the eye of that 1938 disaster.[48]

The project's regional organization, once established, served well. The regional directors read state copy voraciously and turned out presentable material. Couch, as the director of a major university press, invited the project to mount a display at the Southern Conference for Human Welfare, and Frederick occasionally reviewed FWP volumes over his award-winning CBS "Book Review" program. More important, Couch saved the Tennessee project—which had been "bogged down in mediocrity and misdirection"—by finding a capable replacement for its incompetent chief executive. Frederick recruited new state

---

[47] Linscott to Manuel and Manuel to Alsberg, May 18, 1938, Box 19, FWPN; p. 30 above; Howe to Mangione, Dec. 16, 1937, Box 462, WPA.

[48] Chicago and Boston regional conference files, Box 1, FWPN.

administrators for the disorganized projects of Ohio, Michigan, Indiana, Missouri, and Minnesota. By mid-1939, Alsberg had added Maurice Howe as another regional supervisor and Vardis Fisher as technical consulting editor. With such able assistants, he would have been able to proceed with his regional emphasis if events in Congress had not altered his plans.[49] The regional directors were, in any event, the most successful of his appointments.

V

While administrative inexperience, early confusion about long-range objectives, and a heavy dose of political appointments created a constant air of crisis, perhaps the greatest threat to the FWP emerged from the jealousy and contempt the project aroused among WPA state administrators. For most of them, the Federal Writers' Project represented a "stepchild" engendering constant suspicion. Jealous of their power and reluctant to exempt creative "prima donnas" from local jurisdiction, these executives immediately sought control of the FWP. Lawrence Morris understood, for example, that in the Midwest relief officials did not regard the FWP as a separate entity with a national existence but as a state project "lumped in" with the other segments of Federal #1. In their opinion, the entire arts program cost too much for the small number of unimportant people it employed.[50]

While state WPA representatives could not assume absolute domination over project salaries and cuts, they sought to exercise power in other ways. Reports Project and guide workers were ensnarled in red tape and used solely for publicity purposes. (The Reports Project ceased operations, with Alsberg's ready consent, in July, 1936.) More important, WPA officials quickly exercised their authority to approve project directors. Cursing "the whole God Damn White Collar Projects," Pennsylvania's administrator warned Cronyn that he would not tolerate any "people butting in" from Washington. Iowa's representative delayed organization of the FWP project in that state on the assumption that WPA would fare better by starting with visible work, such as the public construction programs, before turning to what he

[49] Perry to Hopkins, Aug. 20, 1938, Box 2576, WPA; John T. Frederick to author, Apr. 6, 1968.

[50] Kerr interview, July 7, 1968; Morris interview.

called the "tap dancing" units. The New Jersey WPA dismissed useful workers for union activity; Arkansas's chief editor suffered a similar fate.[51]

Some state executives tried to turn the FWP to local political use. One project director informed Alsberg in September, 1935, that the *Davenport Democrat's* first article on the local unit resembled "almost a help wanted ad directed to Democratic office seekers" in Iowa. A field supervisor found that the Paterson, New Jersey, project consisted of thirty-five gangsters, and he commented that "this wasn't boon-doggling, this was defiance." Kansas City rolls were swollen with Pendergast appointees who came to pick up paychecks; Vardis Fisher's workers were asked to wear buttons supporting Senator James Pope's bid for reelection.[52]

As the FWP approached the end of its first fiscal year and came up for a second congressional appropriation, WPA's Professional and Service Projects Division (to which Federal #1 belonged) posed the greatest threat to its security. Jake Baker, head of the division, keenly sensed the resentment harbored by state relief officials against the arts projects' national jurisdiction. To avoid further squabbles over divided control, he proposed that control of Federal #1 be given to WPA state administrations. Although Baker envisioned a setup whereby it would be "somewhat" under his authority, Hallie Flanagan and Holger Cahill of the theatre and art projects emphasized in an April, 1936, report that the projects could build up professional quality only if controlled by professional staffs in Washington. When Baker tried to delay showing the "boss" their memo—written in conjunction with Alsberg and Nicolai Sokoloff of the music project—until June (the close of the fiscal year), Cahill decided to take the matter directly to the White House. At the time, that also meant Eleanor Roosevelt, who had displayed particular interest in Federal #1. She immediately telephoned Hopkins and, upon hearing that his complaints about Federal #1 and its "very abrupt" and "imperious" directors mainly stemmed from his subordinate's reports, asked: "Have you ever thought that the difficulty might be with Mr.

[51] Cronyn to Jones (telephone conversation), Oct. 12, 1935, Box 52, FWPN; Rotch to Baker, Dec. 11, 1935, Box 17, FWPN; DuVon to Alsberg, Oct. 26, 1935, Box 13, FWPN.

[52] DuVon to Alsberg, Sept. 18, 1935, Box 31, FWPN; Seidenberg interview; Fisher to author, May 11, 1968. On the other hand, a project employee (the former head of the state Democratic party in Kansas) attacked Alf Landon in the pamphlet "Can a Leopard Change His Spots?" Bender and McConkey files (Kan.), Box 59, FWPN.

Baker?'' A short time later, Ellen Woodward of the Women's Projects Division replaced Baker, and the immediate crisis passed.[53]

Behind Hopkins's decision lay both a strong personality clash with Baker and the exigencies of politics. Baker, always an individualist, wore a black shirt to an affair in the White House to emphasize his belief that the New Deal had not gone enough to the left. His plain vocabulary had offended the First Lady. He proposed a system of cooperatives (in line with his belief in Kropotkin's mutual aid philosophy) in which mountain folk would produce handicrafts and sell them on the open market. His installation of such a unit in WPA's Professional and Service Projects Division seemed excessively enthusiastic and radical to some, including Hopkins, who lacked confidence in the scheme and feared it might endanger the entire WPA program, which was coming under increasing fire in Congress. By contrast, Ellen Woodward of the Women's Projects Division was a respectable Southerner with close political ties to her mentor in the Senate, the highly influential Pat Harrison, and could assuage legislators worried about radicals and ''artists.'' The P. and S. Division shifted to Woodward's jurisdiction under a new name, Women's and Professional Projects Division, in July, 1936, and Federal #1 temporarily became ''more respectable.''[54]

WPA state officials who had been lobbying in support of Baker's plan for Federal #1 did not intend to let this major defeat end the issue. Montana's administrator tried to keep the central staff's office within his jurisdiction in Butte or Helena (rather than Missoula), and protested the appointment of its first director because he had hoped to squeeze his publicity director into the post. A new WPA administrator decreed that all letters from the Oklahoma project to Alsberg's office had to be prepared for his signature. Assuming that the writing of guidebooks was a shorter and less exacting job than the construction of suspension bridges or high schools, administrators in Tennessee and some Midwestern states spoke of shutting down their projects when no guides had appeared.[55]

New York City's WPA administrator proved particularly bothersome to the local unit in its final years. Colonel Brehon Somervell, an

[53] Baker interview; Cahill Memoir, pp. 379-86.

[54] Kerr interview, July 21, 1968; Ozer interview.

[55] Cahill Memoir, p. 387; Polk to Hopkins, Feb. 25, 1938, Box 41, FWPN; Kerr interview, July 21, 1968.

army engineer, continued to bear down on what he considered "the most controversial elements in the WPA program." Reliefers received contemptuous treatment by having to take a specially colored elevator to reach his headquarters. A translation of King Solomon's *Song of Songs* from Hebrew into Yiddish by Nathan Ausubel brought an objection because of Somervell's assumption that they were the same language.[56]

Though some administrative officials outside the FWP proved helpful, it is extremely doubtful whether much could have been accomplished if the project had been turned over to the state relief administrators. WPA's administrator in Tennessee, according to regional director Florence Kerr, "wouldn't have spent a nickel— he was crazy about little airports." South Dakota's Democrats were "few and far between"; few of the state's citizens had much interest or faith in the project's value. Nebraska's administrator only wanted to placate the local politicos who had secured posts for him and an inefficient project director. Some of their colleagues in other states would have closed the local units if the choice had been theirs to make.[57]

The fact that FWP state units remained under national jurisdiction meant that salaries, cuts, and the writing and publication of guide copy ultimately could not be tampered with for personal ends. As Florence Kerr concluded years later: "Federalization saved the arts projects."[58] Jake Baker, WPA administrators, and various state politicians could not bring the writers' project under absolute state control or close it entirely. The FWP therefore succeeded in maintaining literary standards and in developing editorial cooperation between its member units which led, finally, to the production of works of lasting value.

VI

Miraculously surviving the political imbroglios and administrative chaos which threatened to tear the project apart, Henry Alsberg

[56] *New York Times*, Nov. 26, 1936; Kerr interview, July 7, 1968; Carl Malmberg interview, Nov. 22, 1967. Somervell later assigned word production quotas, before he finally left WPA to assume duties more suited to his talents as chief of the Construction Division of the Quartermaster General and to build the Pentagon.

[57] Kerr interview, July 7, 1968.

[58] Kerr interview, July 21, 1968.

emerged as its central, creative force. By nature relaxed, friendly, and carefree, he drove himself mercilessly to improve the content and style of its publications. Together with an overworked but dedicated staff which drew inspiration from his eager absorption of fresh ideas and his perceptive editorial skill, Alsberg attacked the wave of manuscripts inundating his headquarters. To the casual visitor, the cigarette ashes and food spilling over Alsberg's clothes, his fumbling with a maze of telephone cords, and his penchant for delivering suffocating monologues might have suggested a befuddled patriarch misplaced in time. But Alsberg's outward appearance was belied by his relentless devotion to high literary standards. Hardly pausing to eat and sleep, he stuffed his briefcase with evening work to be done in his rambling house on Wisconsin Avenue. Seeking precision in every word, perfection in every phrase, he could never call a job finished.[59]

Unhappily, Alsberg's literary skills and friendly personality were combined with the habits of an absent-minded professor, which ill suited him to serve as an administrator. He found it difficult to fire incompetent workers and naïvely assumed that people did not need direction—"if they're good, they'll produce." A philosophical anarchist, he had no comprehension of fundamental administrative procedure. Creative innovation suited his character, not methodical or firm executive control. Offhanded promises of salaries ("how about $75 a month?") and putting people down on sick leave with no standards were frequent occurrences. When his fellow directors met with Hopkins one day to complain about rigid WPA regulations, he remarked: "I don't have any gripe, Harry. I haven't had as much fun since I had the measles."[60]

The national director's very personal identification with his work also resulted in illogical decisions. These included the granting of posts to writers who, as Harris later put it, "looked good on paper or knew

[59] Gorham Munson interview, Feb. 11, 1968. Alsberg went through eleven FERA secretaries in one year because of his habits before a Radcliffe graduate decided to take the job, owing to his "great respect for words" and his command of German (which she spoke fluently). She stayed on, devoted to him, for the next four years. Dora Thea Hettwer interview, July 11, 1967.

[60] Harris interview; Mangione, *Dream and Deal*, p. 193. "A colossus of chaos," concluded a former member of the D.C. staff. *New York Times*, May 18, 1969, VII, p. 2. The same individual was cured of his fear of flying when Alsberg, forgetting that South Dakota's director had written him more than a month earlier of local arrangements to print the guide, dispatched Mangione on a "wild goose chase" through thunder, snow, and sandstorms to try to get the book issued by a national publisher. Mangione, *Dream and Deal*, pp. 235-37.

him years ago.''[61] Alsberg's administrative shortcomings would prove especially harmful to the FWP when it came to his relations with the state directors. He asked Maryland's original director to reconsider a proposed resignation, despite that individual's unsuitability for the post. Form letters went out to WPA administrators telling them of the successful work being done by actually incompetent directors in West Virginia, New York State, and Indiana, leading these officials to assume that Alsberg was satisfied with the quality of the local projects. The continuing presence of Missouri's Geraldine Parker reflected poorly on Alsberg, since his reluctance to go through with the disagreeable job of firing her led to indecision and delay until a strike by her editorial staff brought this matter to a head. The best way to dispose of incompetents, in his opinion, was "to promote or transfer them to better jobs." Rather than create a "blowup" with Nebraska's Elizabeth Sheehan, he kept her on the project for two more years. Paul French should not have been allowed to continue as Pennsylvania's director for four years, nor should Bernice Babcock (who had already made a bad impression on Baker and on her project colleagues at an early regional conference) have been retained as Arkansas's for three. Similar difficulties occurred with James Egan in the state of Washington. The deterioration of the New York City unit was largely a result of Alsberg's administrative inadequacy.[62]

Alsberg's slipshod administration affected the writers' project in another way. A Princeton instructor named Luther Evans, in answer to Hopkins's suggestion (during the formation of Federal #1) that a national project to be set up to take care of old records in the capital, had proposed an inventory of federal archives located in the states; at the suggestion of the National Archives' Philip Hamer the plan was extended to include local and state records. The eventual Survey of State and Local Archives, more commonly known as the Historical Records

[61] Harris and Morris interviews. It also led to a deep suspicion of Ellen Woodward, whose conservatism, political temperament, and Southern emphasis on tribal loyalty differed radically from his cosmopolitan, left-wing, intellectual disposition, in spite of her sincere efforts to fight for Hopkins and the arts projects against Congress and the Dies Committee. See chap. 9 below.

[62] Alsberg to Singlewald, July 7, 1936, Box 52, FWPN; Kerr interview; Alsberg to Gaer, May 10, 1936, Box 60, FWPN; Miller to Alsberg, Mar. 11, 1936, Box 59, FWPN; Morris to Harris, Mar. 4, 1936, Box 67, FWPN; see chap. 9 below for New York. Alsberg should also have appointed regional directors before or soon after the project began—as did his colleagues on Federal #1—and not waited until 1938.

Survey, was authorized in November, 1935, and began work under Alsberg's supervision.[63]

Difficulties arose immediately. Alsberg wanted to supervise the HRS to demonstrate the FWP's varied activities to Congress and the public. He juggled HRS state funds and gave second priority to its employment quota needs. Evans, who sought the management of his own project, resented such treatment and the administrative snarls in which Alsberg's laxness had entangled him. An efficient executive, Evans called for regular summation reports, "had his finger on everything," and never hesitated to fire incompetents. The clash of personalities and interests finally ended with the complete severance of the HRS from FWP control; the survey became a full member of Federal #1 in November, 1936.[64]

While Alsberg's intense personal involvement in the project amplified the adverse effects of his administrative incompetence, his gifts as editor, innovator, and inspirer left a permanent mark on the project's publications. With a central staff no more than one-third the size it should have been, he brought to print accurate, well-written guidebooks and a number of other significant works. Although the writers' project faced inevitable turmoil, it managed to run, perhaps in spite of Alsberg. The central staff arrived at decisions regarding the format and style of the Guide, sent style manuals to the states, and developed reasonably ordered operational procedures. Reed Harris, who "by default" directed supply and other routine procedures, was particularly efficient; and the District of Columbia unit and the field supervisors proved very valuable in the formative months of the project. Here and there, excellent, hard-working state and regional directors appeared. Even where political considerations threatened to choke a local office with posturing incompetents, the national office was often able to salvage considerable research and writing worthy of publication.[65]

Political pressures and errors of judgment notwithstanding, the overall organizational picture was stable. Practical ability marked the executive echelons of the project. This, together with a gifted central staff in Washington and administrators like Couch, Hatcher, Fisher, Saxon,

[63] Perry Morrison, "Everyman's Archive," *The Call* 18, no. 2 (Spring, 1957): 4-9; Luther Evans interview, June 19, 1967.

[64] B1000-26-10A file, Authors' League papers; Kerr interview, July 21, 1968.

[65] Harris interview.

and Frederick in the field, gave the FWP a good chance of employing to the fullest the unknown talents of workers at the lower levels and, in the process, of converting Henry Alsberg's rhetoric into reality.

TOSSED ABOUT IN THE DEPRESSION, most writers were desperate. One Miami resident wrote Alsberg: "How would you like a steady diet of black-eyed peas (no seasoning) such as my family had been enjoying (?) for several days?" A Maine editor's hopes for an old-age pension vanished when the state legislature allocated its last $50,000 for the beleaguered Aroostook potato farmers. Younger writers had recourse to public construction projects, but shovel-stiffened fingers and weariness from unaccustomed physical labor made continuing at their true craft very difficult, as did the attendant damage to morale.[1]

Word of the Federal Writers' Project came as a miracle to stricken white-collar workers, many of whom thought it provided for subsidies to stimulate literary efforts and get the results published. From the first news of the project, applications poured into the Washington office for funds to publish such things as a translation of the *Memoires* of Le Cler Milfort (an Alabama frontiersman), sonnets, biographies, and a manuscript on the Creole patois. Even after the Guide Series had achieved widespread recognition, requests for subventions continued: for books on American customs jurisprudence, Bulgarian fairy tales, and an autobiography centering on military life in India. Some writers, pursuing contemporary themes, offered inspirational poems "in tribute to our beloved President" or novels whose heroes extolled the virtues of WPA. Still others provided solutions to the daily crisis with works on monetary theory, religious bigotry, and the creation of the Samaritan Order for world peace.[2]

Other requests for financial aid revealed the varied possibilities that writers saw in the project. One applicant proposed the indexing and

---

[1] Hawkins to Alsberg, Oct. 13, 1935, Box 23, FWPN; Elder to Hopkins, Sept. 30, 1935, Box 16, FWPN.

[2] Galbraith to Alsberg, Oct. 19, 1936, Box 6, FWPN; Aycock to Kerr, Mar. 12, 1939, Box 1585, WPA.

cataloging of the world's largest collection of Lincoln titles. Others sought the creation of writing courses for beginners. And when attacks on the FWP and the New Deal mounted, an applicant suggested that writers be hired to reply to this "untrue vociferous vituperation."[3]

Most writers demanded not special favors but a job. One wrote to Alsberg: "Kind of work: will accept any position. Salary: Enough to make a living on. At present: Broke." Another offered to exchange geological equipment and services for an opportunity to do research on upper cretaceous fossils in eastern Colorado. Hundreds of penny postcards reached Washington with the pathetic message: "The wolf is at my door." Some applicants seemed almost resigned to failure, but a note of defiance also came through the swell of despair: "I'm not a Ph.D. or a G-man, but I don't see why I haven't as much right to the work as they have."[4] Knowing that upward of 4,500 jobs were available on the FWP, thousands rushed to get them.

Official regulations formed the first barrier to these eager applicants. Roosevelt's earliest executive order stipulated that at least 90 per cent of all workers on the project (as part of WPA) had to be selected from the public relief rolls. It had been on the assumption that they would be so chosen, WPA's Aubrey Williams pointed out, that Congress had voted appropriations for the relief program. But in order to get on the rolls, individuals had to undergo a "means test" to show need for relief. One applicant wrote Hopkins that in addition to suffering the immediate degradation of getting a relief job, a candidate who was successful would experience great difficulty later in securing a private editorial post if the fact became known. As a result, he added, "your broke writer is most apt to get a new typewriter ribbon on the cuff, bum the money for stamps, roll in a clean sheet, and start 'Sylvia swooned in the muscular arms of Herman etc.'" Critics constantly assailed the humiliating means test. Even before WPA began, Governor Herbert Lehman of New York had attempted to convince Harry Hopkins that workers should be drawn from the U.S. Employment Service offices

[3] Rogers to Harris, Feb. 11, 1936, Box 3, FWPN. A WPA writing course in Anacortes, Washington, resulted in *The Tramp*, a poetry quarterly which lasted to the outbreak of the war. G. W. Sherman to author, May 30, 1968.

[4] Sherry to Alsberg, Nov. 8, 1935, Box 17, FWPN; McKenzie to Harris, June 1, 1938, Box 19, FWPN.

instead of from the relief rolls, but the needs requirement harassed applicants throughout WPA's existence.[5]

For the overwhelming majority, those who were willing to swallow their pride and apply for relief certification, other obstacles presented themselves. The sincere wish of WPA administrators to employ those destitute longest gave rise to the initial project rule that the 90 per cent on relief had to have been on the rolls before November 1, 1935. However, many for whom such aid was designed had not gone on relief because no special project had existed to provide for them. It seemed that people who had done their best to stay off the rolls now were receiving a penalty instead of a job from the very taxpayers who had benefited from their sacrifice. All state directors with whom Alsberg spoke recognized this injustice. Furthermore, relief officials in all states disqualified applicants for failing to meet the two- to three-year local residence rule, even though the writers' project had national scope. Those who were fortunate enough to get certified often became enmeshed in red tape that was not disentangled for weeks, even months.[6]

Having achieved certification, a motley crew applied for posts on the FWP. It took Reed Harris some time to discover that a "20-pound poet" had that amount of poetry waiting for a publisher. Because a social worker who checked his case had called him "a man of letters," an unemployed mail carrier insisted that he deserved a position in New York. A bricklayer's claim to a project job was defended by a Haverford College professor of English on the grounds that Ben Jonson had practiced this noble trade.[7]

Relief regulations hampered Alsberg from getting his first choice of personnel on the FWP. Because he wanted to concentrate on the writing of the guides, the national director gave preference to free-lancers, editors, and journalists. The census of 1930 had reported that of the

[5] Donald Howard, *WPA and Federal Relief Policy*, chap. 14; Wheeler to Hopkins, Nov. 18, 1935, Box 19, FWPN; Florence Kerr interview, Oct. 18, 1963, American Archives of Art, Detroit, Mich.

[6] Alsberg to Baker, Nov. 15, 1935, Box 52, FWPN. A woman could also get a post by befriending the relief investigator on occasion, which led one man to complain in mock bitterness, "Why can't a man sleep his way into a job like those luscious babes?" "Brother," retorted a female employee, "bitching from bed to bed is specialized work." Anzia Yezierska, *Red Ribbon on a White Horse*, p. 168.

[7] Harris to Peason, Nov. 1, 1935, Box 462, WPA; *New York Times*, Jan. 10, 1937, II, p. 9.

10,499 people who listed "writing" as their gainful occupation, most were located in California, Illinois, Massachusetts, and the Middle Atlantic states. It is thus not surprising that probably half of the project's actual writers would come from New York City, Chicago, Boston, Philadelphia, and Los Angeles. But, when such individuals were located, they often had a difficult time getting on the FWP because of the 90 per cent relief regulation. Alsberg himself understood their plight under the existing relief laws. Relying on letters received from his state directors, Alsberg wrote Baker in mid-November, 1935, that changes in the relief laws had to occur if the project were to succeed. His chief may have been able to assure one correspondent, perhaps for the sake of public relations, that "pretty capable writers" already on the relief rolls were staffing the project "on the whole," but he failed to satisfy more knowledgeable professional organizations.[8]

Outside the densely populated states, with their clusters of needy writers, directors found it very difficult to locate professionals. The relief rolls of thirteen North Carolina cities contained the names of 518 schoolteachers, three librarians, and no writers. It took "a great deal of scratching among the cornfields of Iowa" for Lawrence Morris to come across three people with writing experience. Vardis Fisher discovered no other writer besides himself in Idaho. The spinster schoolteachers who dominated the Kansas project "possessed an idea of writing which centered around the split infinitive."[9]

Thus the FWP was forced to consider personnel other than writers for its state units. The compilation of the American Guide, according to the Professional and Service Projects Division's proposal of June, 1935, called for: "writers, editors, historians, research workers, art critics, architects, archeologists, map draftsmen, geologists, and other professionals . . . although a major part of the personnel will be made up of writers exclusively." Presidential letter no. 321, which sanctioned the project two months later, included similar guidelines. But, as Alsberg immediately realized, the term "writers" would require great latitude of interpretation. Reed Harris satisfied the Georgia WPA administrator that the project for "writers" would be feasible in her state by expanding the term to include "almost any other occupation that involved an

[8] Folder B 1000-5, Authors' League papers; Alsberg to Baker, Nov. 15, 1935, Box 52, FWPN; Baker to Hoey, Dec. 2, 1935, Box 57, FWPN.

[9] Morris to Alsberg, Apr. 2, 1936, Box 59, FWPN; Fisher to Alsberg, Mar. 22, 1937, Box 11, FWPN; McConkey report, Oct. 25, 1935, Box 59, FWPN; Dickinson to Alsberg, July 21, 1937, Box 23, FWPN.

understanding of the English language and some training and observations in the preparation of records."[10]

Those who ended up on the project's rolls in this manner included some unusual people. The Pennsylvania and New York City units claimed two former American consuls on their payrolls. Cornish and Balkan miners were employed to tell their stories for the Arizona Guide. The explorer of Labrador got appointed to the Dutchess County, New York, unit. A descendant of Pontiac became the personal file clerk of Michigan's first director. The daughter of a woman who had endured the siege of Vicksburg for half a year in a cave got hired for one month to record her mother's story. Joe Gould, whose oral history of his life from his graduation from Harvard in 1911 to mid-1937 would total 8.8 million words, obtained a post to write a biographical dictionary of early New York settlers.[11]

However, colorful personnel could not counter the existence of government regulations which put the project's literary worth in doubt from the very beginning. At the end of 1935, Harold Merriam of Montana warned that unless the 10 per cent nonrelief quota could be raised, professionals from Chicago or New York would have to be imported to produce his state guidebook. The central office faced the additional problem of classifying people because the U.S. Civil Service Commission gave architects, historians, and geologists "professional" ratings, while listing writers and editors as "clerical" personnel. Under these circumstances, all hopes for literary masterpieces seemed doomed; at best the guides would be objective, factual accounts. It would be difficult to edit indifference out of the final result unless more nonrelief professional writers could be assigned to the project. However, the fact that other skilled workers and supervisory personnel also had to fit within the 10 per cent noncertified allowance stymied this possibility at every turn. The FWP, seemingly anything but a writers' project, appeared doomed to futility.[12]

Certain writers' organizations soon made attempts to improve this

[10] "Project submitted," June 25, 1935, Box 461, WPA; letter quoted in William F. McDonald, *Federal Relief Administration and the Arts: The Origins and Administrative History of the Arts Projects of the Works Progress Administration*, p. 683; Harris to Sheeperson, Oct. 12, 1935, Box 1138, WPA.

[11] Chittenden to Alsberg, Jan. 9, 1936, Box 20, FWPN; Alsberg to Corse, Apr. 22, 1936, Box 52, FWPN; *New York Herald Tribune*, Apr. 10, 1937.

[12] Merriam to Alsberg, n.d., Box 23, FWPN; Kellock interview, June 23, 1968; Santee to Harris, Sept. 26, 1936, Box 2, FWPN: "Why work a good cuttin' horse to the wagon?"

situation. With the formal announcement of the FWP's creation, the executive board of the Newspaper Guild had approved a conference of writers' groups to work as a unit to secure and maintain posts for professionals in need. The established Authors' League, viewing this move with distrust and an air of superiority, did not attend the first organizational meeting, held in a Times Square hotel, which included the guild, the Writers' Union, and the League of American Writers. It also hesitated to permit Alsberg to insert its name on the project's letterhead as a cooperating agency. The league's conservatism may have been ruffled by the call of these left-wing organizations for ''a real united front.'' The Authors' League insisted that the militant Writers' Union, in particular, discontinue all activities (except to get work relief for unemployed writers) which duplicated its work and recognize its position as ''the basic union in the industry.'' These demands reflected the league's sense that a good number of the union's members could be termed anything but professionals. Some token pledge must have been given to secure its allegiance, for the league joined these groups and two Yiddish writers' organizations to picket for additional jobs in front of WPA headquarters on Eighth Avenue and Fifteenth Street. It also used its influence to get members like John Morosso, Edwin Bjorkman, Edward Dahlberg, Rebecca Pitts, and John Davis into supervisory nonrelief positions in various states and and it recommended many others to the project's directors.[13]

The first attempts of these groups on behalf of recognized talents who were off relief failed to achieve their objective. The Authors' League was particularly concerned about the means test and the November 1 deadline, which nullified all its previous efforts to keep writers off the rolls. Though George Cronyn ordered the New York City project's rolls increased from 250 to 400 after a meeting with the newly formed Joint Committee of Authors' Organizations in early November, his superiors rescinded this action as soon as he returned to Washington. At the end of that month the Authors' League and the Newspaper Guild received Hopkins's promise that he would talk with Baker about increasing the quota of noncertified workers in New York and substituting another test for the present relief examination, but he failed to communicate further with these groups. The head of the league's fund, George Creel, had to

[13] Sillcox to Black, Oct. 30, 1935, and von Auw to Alsberg, Oct. 14, 1935, Authors' League papers; *New York Times*, Nov. 24, 1935, II, p. 1.

write his friend Hopkins that such silence was "mystifying," especially since WPA rules which called for a certain number of employees per state had failed to distinguish between areas that had many or few writers. He received no reply from Hopkins either.[14]

The Authors' League soon realized that the project had only succeeded in destroying its private relief resources, since the league's past contributors had received the false impression that WPA had taken over the entire economic burden. The league decided that it had no recourse but to appeal directly to President Roosevelt. In an attempt to obtain publicity while WPA was still "live news" in the New York papers, Henry Pringle drafted a letter dated December 27, 1935, which received the support of members like Marc Connelly, Sherwood Anderson, Oliver LaFarge, Matthew Josephson, and Ida Tarbell and of representatives of the other organizations. The letter discussed the virtual collapse of the project for needy professional writers and informed the chief executive that 800 writers had been "outrageously discriminated against" in their search for work on WPA. After discussing the league's past record in providing for such people, the remonstrance noted that organization's encounters with red tape: "Our representatives have been tossed from Chief of Division 22Q to Chief of Division 36R . . . and nothing has been done."[15]

The protest had its desired effect. Within twenty-four hours after the letter's receipt in the White House, an executive order authorized raising the nonrelief quota to 25 per cent. Hopkins assured the league's secretary that some 1,800 additional writers would be taken on through the State and Local Historical Records Survey, with an additional 200 in New York City alone. Nevertheless, the Authors' League and the other members of the Joint Committee regarded this ameliorative step as only a temporary measure. Most galling was the fact that the basis of eligibility remained receipt of relief through the hated means test.[16]

The Joint Committee also would have to guard against future cuts in the relief rolls, which were foreshadowed by a severe one at the end of December. It appeared likely that these reductions would cripple the project, especially in many Midwestern and Southern states which had

[14] Cronyn to von Auw, Jan. 4, 1936, Authors' League papers; Sillcox to Creel, Dec. 4, 1935, and Creel to Hopkins, Dec. 14, 1935, Authors' League papers.

[15] Correspondence re "Letter to the Press," Authors' League papers; *New York Times*, Dec. 30, 1935.

[16] Hopkins to Sillcox, Jan. 14, 1936, Box 460, WPA.

been forced to accept clerical workers in lieu of scarce professional writing talent.[17] Whether the highly diversified federal writers now under Alsberg's charge could overcome these difficulties remained to be seen.

II

The number of FWP employees varied according to the general trend of the WPA rolls. By the end of November, 1935, 4,016 had gotten on, and the figure rose to over 6,000 by the first of the new year. On the average, 4,500-5,200 people worked constantly on the FWP during its four-year existence. These infinitesimal figures compared with the average of 2,060,000 persons a month for the WPA in general.[18]

As with all other WPA units, the prevailing wage varied according to regional living costs, but it remained higher on FWP payrolls than in manual-labor relief projects. Urban centers, understandably, had higher relief payments than rural areas. The highest wage, from $93.50 to $103.50 a month, was paid in New York, to professional workers; their counterparts got $39 in Georgia and Mississippi. Relief funds had been assigned just "to keep body and soul together," but such funds actually did far better than that for workers on the writers' project. Precisely because the FWP served as a white-collar operation, the project's members were overwhelmingly placed in the skilled and professional-technical security wage classifications.[19]

The advantages enjoyed by the federal writer within the framework of the WPA system became manifest in other areas as well. Realizing that a large number of qualified writers were not on the relief rolls or refused to go on, the Finance Division permitted the project a larger nonrelief quota. Whereas most WPA projects eventually had to cut noncertified personnel from 10 to 5 per cent, the FWP received permis-

[17] *New York Times*, Dec. 21, 1935.

[18] "The American Guide," n.d., Box 50, FWPN; Howard, *WPA and Relief Policy*, p. 531.

[19] Howard, *WPA and Relief Policy*, pp. 182-87; Davidson interview. From February, 1937, to December, 1938, 75 to 85 per cent of the project's employees filled the two highest paid categories, whereas only 14 to 17 per cent were so registered in other WPA projects. Project supervisory personnel also fared better, with their non-security wage classification in these months averaging 13 per cent as compared with 3.7 per cent for those outside Federal #1. "A Brief History of the FWP," p. 11, Katherine Kellock papers, Federal Writers' Project file, Library of Congress, Washington, D.C. (hereafter KK papers, LC).

sion to raise that limit to 25 per cent two months after it began.[20] This allowance, as the division's two officers overseeing Federal #1 later admitted, signified a contradiction of the major purpose of WPA—to provide jobs for those certified as "needing relief." The division justified these high quotas of professional people not on relief as being the only means of creating jobs for the vast majority of research and clerical workers who were on relief; the latter would never have been able to produce the guides on their own. Personnel who had to transfer from one state to another for health or other pressing reasons received similar leeway. In this fashion, Kenneth Patchen and Ross Santee left the New York and Delaware projects for those of New Mexico and Arizona.[21]

Such preferential treatment rarely drew positive acknowledgment because of the pervading anxiety over staff reductions, which occurred every few months. These cuts were part of and paralleled those being carried out in other WPA projects, as Hopkins and his subordinates tried to explain, but statistics and reports proved small comfort to the many thrown back on pitiful resources. The time of signing in, once the social hour of the day, became "the silent meeting of the condemned waiting for the ax of the executioner." The dreaded pink slip dismissal, commonly referred to as being "403'd," often appeared the result of blind chance, and assurances that dismissed writers would be absorbed by private industry were not very persuasive in a period when newspapers and magazines were folding regularly.[22]

The first cuts after the December, 1935, reductions drew the particular concern of professional organizations. With a drive under way in early March, 1936, to drop 700,000 from the WPA rolls by July (the time of the next congressional appropriation), the secretary of the Authors' League anxiously sought information about the upcoming congressional committee hearings. To insure that all would be well "after the political whip begins to snap," the league and the Newspaper Guild wrote to Carter Glass, chairman of the Senate Appropriations Committee, urging that funds be made available for the continuation

---

[20] Although the figure dropped to 7 per cent at the close of 1937, it climbed to over 11 per cent in March, 1939. "Brief History," KK papers, LC; Howard, *WPA and Relief Policy*, p. 356*n*.

[21] Ozer interview.

[22] Yezierska, *Red Ribbon on a White Horse*, p. 198; Roskolenko interview.

and expansion of the project. But the new law lowered the nonrelief quota for the FWP to the original 10 per cent, and further reductions were made in the project's rolls. The situation appeared so disastrous that Fannie Hurst, a friend of Hopkins's, wired him on behalf of a special means test. Countee Cullen, Stuart Davis, and others wired against the "UNFULFILLMENT OF ADMINISTRATION PROMISES TO THIS GROUP OF NEEDY AMERICAN CITIZENS." The league council itself went on record against the WPA shortly thereafter for never having given ''adequate or intelligent consideration to the problems involved in trying to rehabilitate needy writers.''[23]

Though the project's membership reached its peak in the months that followed, the danger of reduction in its rolls again plagued the FWP when the third congressional WPA appropriation fell due. Drastic slashes of 25 per cent in all the federal arts projects by July 15, 1937, and the accompanying drop of about 40 per cent in nonrelief certification a year later, added to the daily uncertainties facing the project's administrators in Washington. At one point, only a dramatic appeal by Hopkins convinced Roosevelt not to cut Federal #1 entirely. But the President, worried about the danger of inflation, continued to cut WPA rolls. As a result, the few state units in New England which had completed their guidebooks all but closed on Alsberg's order, while most others faced considerable delays in meeting production deadlines. Maine's director, who joined the FWP after she had been fired from a $12-a-week newspaper job for smoking, replied to two Washington telegrams calling simultaneously for more production and cuts in staff: ''No workers, no copy.'' Alsberg tried to substitute reductions in selected areas having incompetent writers for the prevailing across-the-board cuts, but did not succeed.[24]

Project employees, seeing the inability of professional groups to aid them, decided to protest by following the trend of the thirties and

[23] "Correspondence re Letter to Sen. Carter Glass," Apr. 29, 1936, Authors' League papers; Harris to Morris, Nov. 21, 1936, Box 55, FWPN; Dec., 1936, file, Authors' League papers. Since just before the 1936 election FDR had promised "useful work for the needy unemployed," Edna St. Vincent Millay had cause to criticize his neglect of those who had provided the President "so many nourishing votes." Quoted in McKinzie, *New Deal for Artists*, pp. 97-98.

[24] *New York Times*, June 13, 1937, II, p. 1; "Brief History," p. 11, KK papers, LC; McDonald, *Federal Relief Administration and the Arts*, pp. 223-29; Leuchtenburg, *Roosevelt and New Deal*, p. 244; Mangione, *Dream and Deal*, p. 91; Alsberg to Gaer, July 8, 1937, Box 59, FWPN.

picketing or engaging in sit-down strikes. The federal writers' newly felt "craft consciousness" exhibited itself in a number of states. As might be expected, the first demonstration took place in New York City; it was organized by Greenwich Village artists and writers against the *Daily Mirror*'s attacks on Federal #1. There was mass picketing, and ten were found guilty of disorderly conduct. Threats of sit-downs or actual sit-downs occurred in Philadelphia, Boston, Newark, Portland, San Francisco, and Oakland in protest against the 10 per cent nonrelief quota and general cuts in the rolls.[25]

Sit-down strikes occurred most frequently during congressional deliberations about relief appropriations. The most noted of these was staged in June, 1937, after Congress, agreeing with Hopkins's assistant that "WPA as an emergency program is over," ordered a 25 per cent slash in the WPA relief allocations for 1938. New York City workers, realizing that about 150 FWP personnel would be affected, brought mattresses and food into their director's office and remained there for four days; at one point it took four people to restrain one girl who was about to be fired from jumping through an open window. The project strikers also joined 600 of their counterparts on Federal #1 in virtually imprisoning Harold Stein, the special overseer of all the projects, in his office for twenty-four hours. Warned by an engineer that the floors would give way if there was any commotion, Stein refused an offer from WPA guards of safe conduct out of the old building and spent all night talking on the telephone with his Washington superiors. Hopkins's assistants could not agree to rescind the dismissals or set up a special review board in New York City; the bleary-eyed strikers agreed at 4 A.M. to finally let their hostage go when he promised to meet their demands to the limits of his authority.[26]

While these demonstrations had little effect on the policies of WPA and its Finance Division, administrators in Washington discouraged all attempts at strikebreaking and lent a sympathetic ear to labor complaints. The assistant administrator of the Women's and Professional Projects Division recalled many long days spent in the offices of Federal #1, often until 2 A.M., listening to the petitions of labor

[25] *New York Times*, Sept. 13, 1935.

[26] Anne Cronin interview, Mar. 30, 1965, Archives of American Art, Detroit, Mich.; *New York Times*, May 25, 29, and June 26, 1937; McKinzie, "Writers on Relief," pp. 184-90.

representatives. As a result, project workers received the sense (shared by all WPA workers) that at least their demands would receive careful, if not always productive, consideration.[27]

The principles which motivated Hopkins and his staff to give a fair hearing to all employees led to the formulation of WPA's ideal of equal opportunity in getting these jobs and assured the good intentions of the project's principal administrators toward the Negro. Members of Harold Ickes's so-called "Black Cabinet," including John Davis, Robert Weaver, and William Hastie, insisted that blacks be represented on the federal projects. Alsberg and Cronyn wanted to fulfill this request and, at Howard University, met with James Weldon Johnson and Alain Locke to draw up a section, "Negro Culture in America," for the American Guide. Davis, NAACP's Ralph Bunche, and Alfred E. Smith (Hopkins's chief assistant for Negro matters in WPA) then persuaded the Negro author Sterling Brown to accept an appointment on the Washington project as editor of Negro affairs, and Alsberg began to push for Negro employment.[28]

These efforts went slowly. Davis, executive secretary of the Joint Committee on National Recovery, complained that his office had received nearly 300 white-collar applications, only to be told by Aubrey Williams and others that such job seekers could not investigate discrimination against blacks or receive appointments in the South. Alsberg admitted this to Williams, but noted that there existed "very little cause for complaint in the North," as these applicants usually lacked the necessary qualifications. The issue of qualifications was also raised by project executives in Kentucky and the Carolinas and echoed the observation of New Mexico's director that nearly all of the "colored people" in her state were cooks and chauffeurs. Many of her colleagues argued that the few blacks who possessed a higher education at the time could usually step immediately into private jobs.[29]

The greatest number of blacks worked in the New York City, Illinois, and Louisiana projects, where they had been assigned to prepare histories of their race in these states. "For the first time since the Harlem period of the '20's," reminisced Arna Bontemps of the

[27] Harris to Harlan, Feb. 4, 1936, Box 3, FWPN; Cronin interview. For a study of these unions, see chap. 9 below.

[28] Sterling Brown interview, June 11, 1968; McKinzie, "Writers on Relief," p. 136.

[29] Davis to Williams, Dec. 12, 1935, and Alsberg to Williams, Dec. 16, 1935, Box 15, FWPN; "Letters to Negroes Employed" file, Box 200, FWPN.

Chicago unit, "Negro writers had a chance." New York boasted professionals like Roi Ottley, Claude McKay, Helen Boardman, Ted Poston, Charles Cumberbatch, Henry Lee Moon, and the young Ralph Ellison; Chicago claimed Richard Wright, Willard Motley, Margaret Walker, Bontemps, Frank Yerby, and Katherine Dunham. Other projects had less fortune. Directors located one qualified Negro in Indiana, Rhode Island, and Nevada, and two in Iowa, but none in Oregon or Connecticut.[30]

In the South, clear cases of discrimination emerged, and even qualified Negroes could not get into various state units. An employee in Tennessee was made so uncomfortable by co-workers that she asked to be transferred to another project. Although a black became an assistant editor on the Texas unit, his attempts to give a proper version of Negro life for the state guide were called "insolence." The director of the Atlanta School of Social Work located a number of qualified jobless Negro writers, but they were not employed. Years later, the Georgia director admitted: "Looking at the matter from the viewpoint of 1968, I wonder why we did not have Negro representation on our State staff, but in the 1930's it didn't seem so urgent, *if indeed we ever thought of it*" (italics mine).[31]

A report in February, 1937, disclosed that only 106 blacks—of some 4,500 workers—had been employed on the project. Even in the New York unit, with many talented Negro writers, there was only one black in a supervisory post. Moreover, with WPA their only real chance for employment, Negroes were especially hurt by cuts. In sum, discrimination and the lack of qualifications (often accounted for by poverty) explain the small number of blacks on the FWP.[32]

Other minorities suffered less discrimination. In New York City, a Jewish unit had been set up for the guide's Racial Group Section to help Yiddish writers, who had been especially hurt by closing markets for Yiddish literature and by the absorption of the *Tageblatt* by the *Jewish Morning Journal* in 1938. Lamed Shapiro, Baruch Weinreb (B. Rivkin), Isaac Rontch, and Halper Litvick wrote on facets of Jewish life and literature in America. Other writers like Philip Rahv, Nathan

[30] Arna Bontemps interview, Mar. 31, 1968.

[31] Harmon to Alsberg, June 4, 1937, Box 53, FWPN; Washington to Alsberg, Dec. 31, 1935, Box 10, FWPN; Carolyn Dillard to author, Apr. 28, 1968.

[32] Feb., 1937, report, Box 200, FWPN. For the one letter in all of Alsberg's correspondence which was from a Negro praising the FWP, see Alsberg to Hopkins, July 2, 1936, Box 22, FWPN.

Ausubel, and Nathan Asch translated these articles from Yiddish or delved into other Jewish themes. Charges of discrimination were leveled at this project as well as at units in New Jersey and New Hampshire, but such claims usually arose when the inevitable cuts in the rolls occurred. When members of both the Yiddish Writers' Union and the *Freiheit* (Socialist) group received discharges in these reductions, it became clear that political motives had played no part in the matter.[33]

The one clear instance of discrimination against Jews occurred in Massachusetts, where because of his religion Bert Loewenberg, assistant director of the project, did not get the directorship after Clifford Shipton's resignation. Subsequently, he became responsible for the appointment of a ''proper gentile,'' his friend Ray Allen Billington, to the post. The episode, Billington later wrote, indicated that Washington officials feared Loewenberg's appointment would fan the flames of anti-Semitism, already directed against the ''Jew Deal,'' and have some influence on the 1936 election. No inclination toward religious discrimination existed within the project itself—Alsberg and Gaer were both Jews—but ''they acted with votes rather than efficiency in mind.''[34]

With respect to other minorities, the project had a mixed record. Necessary cuts, not prejudice, explain the reductions in German- and Dutch-American personnel on the New York project. Still, aliens whose citizenship papers met bureaucratic delays and who therefore either could not qualify for relief or were cut at the earliest opportunity did truly suffer. While the 1937 Emergency Relief Appropriation Act gave understandable preference to U.S. citizens, it was unfortunate that many who seemed ''no more fitted for it than for piloting an airplane across the Atlantic'' got on, instead of some gifted writers bedeviled by regulations. The conclusion must be drawn that although the WPA projects certainly ''played an important if often forgotten role in the battle of discrimination,''[35] the battle had yet to be won.

III

The forlorn individuals who came on the project underwent a rapid transformation. Hopelessness gave way to enthusiasm. A freshly

[33] Donald Thompson interview, Nov. 28, 1967.

[34] Bert Loewenberg interview, Apr. 30, 1968; Ray A. Billington, ''Government and the Arts: The W.P.A. Experience,'' *American Quarterly* 13 (Winter, 1961):466-79.

[35] Woodward to Hoffman, July 26, 1937, Box 34, FWPN; Weiss to Hopkins, May 11, 1938, Box 801, WPA; Billington, ''Government and the Arts.''

pressed suit and shined shoes served as signs of moral and physical rehabilitation. ''Men who hadn't had a job for years fondled five-and ten-dollar bills with the tenderness of farmers rejoicing over a new crop of grain,'' Anzia Yezierska recalled. New employees lavishly praised FDR and Hopkins, whose ''humane and living sympathies'' dispelled the popular notion of impersonal government. Workers developed loyalty as they achieved a sense of security from the knowledge that weekly bills could be paid for the first time in many months.[36]

Many white-collar professionals genuinely believed in the Guide as a social obligation which could, at the same time, free them from inactivity. A Mississippi worker thought that the state guide would do much to dissipate sectional jealousies; another worker said it had made him more charitable and tolerant toward the many new ''isms'' of the 1930s and liberal organizations generally.[37]

Although the project failed to develop an adequate reemployment service, it provided employees with assurance in their craft. Workers returned to former jobs as pulp, publicity, radio, and script writers, teachers, salesmen, and ministers. The co-author of a project history of Cincinnati received an appointment as a University Fellow in history at the University of Chicago. The departure of these good writers hurt the project but accomplished its major purpose. Sixty-one writers in six states won permanent positions in the first half of 1936.[38]

In most instances, however, state directors did not need long to realize that art and relief were uncomfortable bedfellows. Unlike the other federal arts projects, the FWP's program was not specifically geared to professional talent. The white-collar workers only remotely connected with writing were for the most part a willing crew, but the need for true writers became ever more pressing. Planners of the FWP had originally hoped that project workers would possess imagination and the ability to select pertinent facts for the guides, but many who fancied themselves writers turned out to have more ambition than talent. The majority, especially in rural states, could not even handle spelling and syntax. In addition, since criteria remained subjective, even the meeting of vague requirements did not insure future perfor-

[36] Ulrich, ''Salvaging Culture,'' pp. 653-54; Koch to Hopkins, Nov. 27, 1935, Box 9, FWPN; Yezierska, *Red Ribbon on a White Horse*, p. 161.

[37] Miscellaneous file, Box 101, FWPN.

[38] Crosby to Fuhlbruegge, May 23, 1938, Box 26, FWPN; May 22, 1936, report, Box 74, FWPN.

mance. Higher nonrelief quotas for actual writers hardly met the demands of frustrated directors. Relief workers complicated matters by giving reporters with almost no experience "professional" ratings, while placing in the lower classification employees with degrees in English from Columbia. Within a few months after the project had begun, rumors started spreading that it conveniently served as a dump for everyone but writers, a convenient retreat for duds and psychopaths.[39]

In addition to the matter of personnel, the FWP faced another distinct disadvantage when compared with the other arts projects. The fact that it could not perform immediately before the public led many to think that the project did nothing but waste its time and the taxpayers' money. "NATION DESCRIBED AT DOLLAR A WORD" typified headlines across the country after the conclusion had been drawn that the $2,689,000 allocated the project would produce a 2,689,000-word WPA guidebook. Cronyn noted in defense that the cost did not take into account the 15 million words which would go into local and state volumes, the benefits accruing from tourist travel, the advantages to future writers and students searching for source material, and the "incalculable cultural dividends" from the stimulation of local interest in historic and material resources. However, attacks continued throughout the FWP's history. Arch critics of the New Deal like the *Baltimore Sun* and the *New York Herald Tribune* opposed "made literature" as "made work."[40]

As part of WPA, the FWP received its share of heavy fire from New Deal opponents as a "boondoggling" operation. As soon as the project was announced, the *New York Herald Tribune* suggested that some writers work on a statistical guidebook to New Deal spending. The *Los Angeles Times* editorialized that the city's previous FERA Newspaper Writers' Project had done what the new project proposed to do. Such efforts appeared no better than the digging of ditches or the counting of tombstones, chickens, or electric light bulbs on other WPA projects. Even Alf Landon, in an address in Cleveland, saw fit to sneer at FDR's tourist guidebooks as comparable to another project concerned with "classifying fossils." Later critics charged that the FWP sought to

[39] See chap. 1 above; Morris to Alsberg, Jan. 27, 1936, Box 61, FWPN.

[40] *New York Times*, Jan. 27, 1936; *New York Herald Tribune*, Sept. 14, 1938; *Baltimore Evening Sun*, Feb. 24, 1939.

present its originating agency in the best possible light just before the 1938 congressional elections. Defenders of the FWP implored fellow editors to desist from snickers at the expense of unemployed colleagues in vain. The New York City project tried to retaliate with "the Boondoggle and the Fact Series" to show that charges against the WPA had their basis in political persuasions rather than pertinent truths.[41] But the press's image of WPA workers as leaners on shovels ("We Poke Along") became transformed into that of pen-chewing WPA writers.

The activity of various white-collar workers on the project gave weight to these charges. Many employees proved to be pedantic, careless with factual information, or sloppy in their writing. Rhode Island's director later recalled the day when, in response to his request that more precise information be added to "a big white house," one worker returned with a description of eight blocks of concrete and twelve pieces of glass in its door. Smooth passages became immediately suspect; they often turned out to be from studies such as those by John Fiske on Massachusetts or E. M. Coulter on Georgia. Alsberg's warning that plagiarism might be considered grounds for summary dismissal did not halt the practice.[42]

Some seriously handicapped the work by their lack of sincerity or conflicts of interest. The supervisor of Michigan's Benton Harbor district condescended to visit WPA offices in Kalamazoo for ten minutes, just enough time to catch a return bus for full-time work on a daily newspaper. Seeking additional income, a Kentucky lady got paid to include hotels and bordellos ("rooming houses") in that project's local guidebooks. Some directors found that habitual inebriates did not show up for days or weeks, while others, like Orrick Johns, faced threats and physical harm for refusing to hire personnel.[43]

The project's staff and its friends offered several responses to the boondoggling charge. A large group of Massachusetts writers received publicity when they replied that the project had given honest employment to millions, regardless of political affiliation, "who otherwise would have no recourse but to charity." Tennessee's research editor

[41] *New York Herald Tribune*, Sept. 23, 1935; Harlan to Alsberg, Dec. 11, 1935, Box 14, FWPN; *Washington Morning Herald*, July 13, 1936; chap. 10 below; Magraw to Harris, Jan. 6, 1936, Box 30, FWPN.

[42] Morse interview; SGS, May 5, 1937, report, Box 97, FWPN; Alsberg to state directors, Sept. 8, 1937, Box 56, FWPN.

[43] Isbell to Harris, Nov. 9, 1936, Box 20, FWPN; p. 43 above.

took the trouble to remind the editors of *Time* that a recent issue had four mistakes of fact in less than five lines, thereby suggesting that the magazine's experienced board had committed the crime of boondoggling itself. Investigations revealed that charges of waste and incompetence had been regularly leveled by persons who had themselves been fired from the project for incompetence. Vardis Fisher noted that his state had spent very little time bringing out Idaho's guide and other volumes. When publications began to appear, they went a long way toward refuting the boondoggling accusation.[44]

Attacks against the FWP also often failed to grasp the nature of the project's undertaking. Solemn edicts calling for fixed quotas did not recognize, as Josef Berger later put it, that "a novel is not like a pair of shoes." Aesthetic quality could not be judged by quantitative standards. The writers' project suffered from a relatively high turnover of personnel (which created a training problem), long-distance editing, and the necessity for intensive research on many themes never undertaken by earlier guidebooks. These factors made production a slow process. The project's volumes, unlike the 11 million words of the professionally written *Dictionary of American Biography*, for example, would come to some 20 million words—edited down from ten times that amount of copy. The associate director also noted that, unlike the *DAB*, the guides had to satisfy the reading public and, therefore, could not afford to be dull. Finally, the central office could not bestir "any accusing ghosts," especially since its volumes represented the printed word of the federal government.[45]

Boondoggling did exist on the Federal Writers' Project, but hardly to the extent pictured by vociferous critics. Because the project focused on providing relief, many workers were employed who never should have been. In most cases, though, relief employees realized their literary limitations and seemed to be trying earnestly to make up this shortcoming. In his travels, Lawrence Morris continually found people so afire with the idea of putting out a book about Nebraska, for example, that they spent weekends digging through libraries and historical archives at their own time and expense. Today, many seasoned bureaucrats who received their baptismal training in WPA claim present-day govern-

[44] *Boston Globe*, Oct. 15, 1936; Newman to editors of *Time*, July 3, 1936, Box 44, FWPN; Fisher to Hood, July 28, 1937, Box 11, FWPN; see chap. 6 below.

[45] Berger interview; Cronyn to Woodward, Dec. 31, 1936, Box 461, WPA. For "ghosts," see chap. 5 below.

ment operation does not compare favorably with the federal agencies of the Depression years, in which people became motivated to do their best.[46]

Since relief remained essential, project directors kept incompetents on as long as possible. This consideration led John T. Frederick to refrain from dropping a calligrapher on the Illinois unit, even though his only contribution was the printing of calling cards for fellow employees. When asked about boondoggling artists, Hopkins quietly replied: "We employ carpenters, plumbers, in our Works Program. They're hungry and we find work for them, put them to work. We do the same for artists because they're hungry, too." Any judgment, therefore, of the inadequacies of this emphasis on relief as against performance must take into account the circumstances which brought the project into being. In this light, too, must be seen attacks from an obviously partisan press.[47]

Indeed it seems surprising that so little boondoggling occurred. An amazing amount of production took place despite the project's severe handicaps, and this record of accomplishment could not have been realized without the dogged research of the project's regular employees. Their persistent efforts also resulted in the unearthing of vast quantities of resource material which would benefit contemporary readers and future scholars.

The FWP cannot, of course, be considered a writers' project per se. In response to a celebrated attack in which it was charged that few "professional writers of experience" could be found on the project's rolls, Alsberg gave the names of only twenty-nine acknowledged creative writers, nine established professionals as state directors and editors, and three Guggenheim winners who served on the project. The one detailed reply to a survey of personnel, which was conducted by the Washington office in mid-1938, revealed that 82 (of some 4,500 workers) could be designated as recognized writers, while 97 had held important editorial posts. The report also listed 238 as "having sold to newspapers and magazines" and 161 as being "beginning writers with promise"—vague criteria, to say the least. Some projects, especially those in New York, California, and Illinois, had an abundance of

---

[46] L. Morris interview; Mildred Portner interview, Aug. 21, 1968.

[47] John T. Frederick to author, Apr. 6, 1968; Florence Kerr interview, Oct. 18, 1963, American Archives of Art, Detroit, Mich.

creative writers. But, as will later be shown, this did not guarantee adequate production.[48]

Yet the project's very conglomerate nature enabled it to overcome its limitations. While rehabilitating people wrecked by the Depression, the FWP also contributed to the growing realization that "putting words together" involved a pooling of diverse accomplishments, the whole only possible through the sum of its parts.[49] This collective endeavor —the like of which had never been seen before, anywhere—resulted in final successes which mark the project as one of WPA's most worthy achievements.

[48] *New York Times*, July 22, 1937; Hower to Laning, Oct. 5, 1938, Box 48, FWPN. See chap. 8 below for an analysis of the creative writers on the FWP and chap. 9 for information on the New York project.

[49] *Raleigh News and Observer*, May 11, 1938.

THE WRITING OF GOOD GUIDEBOOKS proved to be a formidable task for the FWP, especially considering the country's affinity for boosterism. The United States had always been a nation of "upstarts," spokesmen for progress and future growth. The "frenetic search for community" in the nineteenth century, as one historian described it, had been marked by feverish competition for county seats, colleges, and political favors. Rivals tried to outdo one another in bestowing superlatives on fledgling, often evanescent towns, and a fresh vocabulary developed to describe a vast new country. Chamber of commerce brochures soon replaced promotional presses in asserting local superiority, and towns vied for the title of "Athens of America" or for recognition as possessor of the "longest main street West of the Mississippi."[1]

The project's central office wanted to avoid indulging this excessive local pride—which some might call provincialism. The Washington staff hoped, indeed, that a writing style new to America, one "restrained and dignified," would be introduced through its efforts, and eventually even replace chamber of commerce "ballyhoo." For that reason, the members of the central office decided early that certain words ("interesting," "unique," "unusual," "quaint," "odd," "amusing," "famous," "well-known," "shrine") should be used only in rare instances. To avoid the obvious, the facetious, and the banal, restrictions were placed on some specific booster cliches: "panorama," "kaleidoscope," "quest for pleasure," "amusement," "cornucopia," "beauty of the deep," "loves of the sea," "altogether colorful," "thousand and one services," "infectious spirit of play," and "innumerable quiet havens."[2]

The central staff soon learned that these taboos had little effect in combating the traditional booster approach. "Crossroads of the Na-

---

[1] Daniel Boorstin, *The Americans: The National Experience*, part 3.
[2] Cronyn to Gaer, June 28, 1937, Box 127, FWPN.

tion" had several claimants, which led the Kansas project's supervisor to comment that this rivalry prevented his state from appropriating its rightful title. Denver and Lead, South Dakota, each tried to usurp "Mile-High City" as its unique possession. Some projects artfully qualified their enthusiasm: for instance, Maine's copy emphasized that the state was "not surpassed by an equal area in the U.S." In editing the Nevada Guide, Vardis Fisher made short work of its "parks," explaining that in his barren state the designation was applied as soon as "two trees and a drop of water were found together."[3]

The most common danger proved to be the use of "first" and the suffix "est." The Washington office had ruled from the project's inception that all authoritative sources be listed in such cases. It suggested consulting the *World Almanac, Who's Who in America, Famous Trees, First Facts*, and various encyclopedias to confirm claims of primacy, but workers relying on their own authority gave Dearborn the title "largest industrial organization in the world" and claimed that Pittsburgh was the possessor of the "biggest array of earth-moving machinery" ever assembled in one locality.[4]

In submitting copy for the state guides, many project writers tried to resume past rivalries of various sorts. Washington vied with Oregon as the home of the discoverer of anesthesia, and Plymouth Rock with Provincetown for the landing of the Mayflower. Old feuds surfaced in the disparaging comments of Kansas City, Kansas, workers about their city's Missouri counterpart and in slurs by New Jersey personnel against the long domination of New York and Philadelphia. These historical differences also loomed in the competition for state guide copy between Madison and Milwaukee, St. Paul and Minneapolis, Birmingham and Mobile, San Antonio and Houston. When it became apparent that the Civil War was still being fought in some states, the Washington office decided that "War between the States" could be substituted for that term in Dixie guidebooks.[5]

The central office could put curbs on local patriotism in a number of ways. It often suggested that "perhaps" be affixed to any questionable statement. That the first instance of crushing cottonseed for oil on a commercial basis occurred in Columbia, South Carolina, was accepted

[3] *Wichita Eagle*, Dec. 27, 1936; Fisher to Alsberg, May 9, 1939, Box 106, FWPN.
[4] Alsberg to Corse, Sept. 1, 1938, Box 51, FWPN.
[5] Barrett to Alsberg, Jan. 13, 1938, Box 100, FWPN.

when the state project director submitted proof. However, the Southern regional director had to be reminded by Alsberg that the permission previously granted some New England guides to include several pages of "firsts" had since been revoked for other state volumes, because it invited both counterclaims and the charge that the government was "taking sides."[6]

In adopting a promotional attitude, zealous workers often made contributions of some note. Their enthusiasm usually represented a combination of naïveté, inexperience, and a desire to put their state on the map. Hearing a project employee alter his claim that a university in St. Louis was the "first American university" to the "first in Missouri," Lawrence Morris realized that the superlative remained a great temptation to the inexperienced writer. When the central staff, to remove such lures, stressed the need to let the facts speak for themselves, some workers went too far in the direction of fact finding. But most, by limiting themselves to local archives, soon found a vast quantity of material which disproved many local tales written on bronze memorial tablets. Many Indian "legends" were merely white men's inventions, every state having its "lovers' leap." Workers discovered that primary sources on colonial history were biased and that standard books on historical battlefields were faulty guides for the present-day sightseer.[7]

A wide variety of statements were scrutinized by the central office to insure accuracy and objectivity. Why did John Brown choose Harpers Ferry, and did his action signify a slave revolt? What were the "ground nut" cakes so popular in Charleston made of? Did Arizona's Bloody Tanks Massacre get its title from the color of the floodwater coming from the copper content in its hills? Washington did correct the dominant notion that what Indians did to whites was frightful, but the reverse noble: frontier cruelty was portrayed as commonplace on both sides.[8]

Errors of omission as well as commission were common. One guide manuscript failed to mention the largest single migration in the country's history, that of 16,000 Mormons on trails through Wyoming. No more than a summary account of Idaho history after 1860 could be located in the state's copy, and the Palo Alto write-up in California's

[6] Alsberg to Couch, Apr. 8, 1939, Box 113, FWPN.

[7] L. Morris interview; Harris to Fuhlbruegge, Mar. 13, 1936, Box 26, FWPN.

[8] Alsberg to Kresensky, Jan. 28, 1938, Box 90, FWPN.

manuscript omitted mention of that city's most widely known resident, former President Herbert Hoover.[9] Most omissions resulted from a strict adherence to the chamber of commerce tradition. Blacks and the massacre of Indians received little mention. Political machines in Kansas City and Memphis and the Socialist character of Milwaukee's government went unnoticed. Project employees covered up the sordid history of the Dutch government of New York as well as the bawdy saga of Dodge City, and the fleeting discussion of the casinos of Reno and Las Vegas caused one editor to deplore the many pages devoted to campus life compared with "only two nervous paragraphs to AFTER DARK." Climatic conditions in Puerto Rico and Florida were placed on the Guide's extended *index rerum prohibitarum*, in spite of the discovery of a cemetery headstone marking the grave of sixty-nine people killed in a West Palm Beach suburb during the 1928 hurricane.[10]

While crusading against boosterism, the Washington office had considerable difficulty revolutionizing the guidebook approach by focusing on the present. "Old fogies" in Connecticut gave the impression that the state's history ended with the eighteenth century. Workers placed too much emphasis on Virginia's aristocracy and paid little attention to the common man. Even in the relatively newer states, points of interest mentioned most were courthouses, city halls, jails, and churches, rather than industrial and recreational areas. When descriptions of present conditions could be found, they either strained the reader's credulity or lacked utility and interest for the tourist. Incredibly, a discussion of Hollywood contained no mention of how a movie is made or if the disintegrating stuffed figure of King Kong still littered a lot at RKO.[11]

Even fact-filled accounts often made no effort to engage the reader's attention through vivid prose. As a result, the facts seemed detached from their environment, as if lifted from an encyclopedia. In some cases the drab character of the area in question contributed to such detachment, but most cities were vital enough that Washington editors had no trouble enlivening guide copy. Knoxville's mailboxes on con-

[9] Alsberg to Christensen, Sept. 22, 1937, Box 132, FWPN; Alsberg to Fisher, Oct. 29, 1936, Box 11, FWPN.

[10] Fisher to Williamson, n.d., Box 106, FWPN. For a discussion of copy relating to blacks, see chap. 7 below.

[11] Morse interview; June 1, 1939, report, Box 1, LC FWP.

veyances, Poughkeepsie's Vassar girls on bicycles, Las Vegas's gambling houses going full blast, and Sarasota's circus headquarters added spice to final guide manuscripts.

To satisfy the tourist, the Technical Project pointed out the quaint, the unusual, or the picturesque. Thus it preferred a discussion on checking out books to one on the size and type of marble used in the New York Public Library. Mention of any of the great American industries called for descriptions of people at work: Oregon lumberjacks, Maine lobster fishermen, Pennsylvania steelworkers, and Georgia saltpeter miners. Finding references to only the dead in Lynchburg copy, Cronyn wrote the Virginia director: "Even mention of a single pedestrian would galvanize this museum piece. . . ."[12]

Alsberg's wish for a natural, vivid style seemed a particularly demanding one. The first copy for the American Guide Series had, indeed, come from a professional writer, Achmed H. Mundo, of Alabama. He had been managing editor of the *New Orleans Times-Picayune* and with Lyle Saxon had helped found the city's writers' and artists' colony. His confident style bore little resemblance, however, to that of most of the manuscripts which found their way to project offices. Many workers labored under a great feeling of inferiority—often valid—which could not easily be overcome. Stylistic flourishes substituted for exact words in forceful combination. When members of the central office had finally weeded out booster rhetoric and hyperbole, they found that the thinness of the remainder called for added research. It was 1938 before one field worker could rejoice in his successful drive to introduce vivid, factual language into Florida copy.[13]

Style remained a problem because the assembled bits of information did not produce a steady and logical progression. Besides choppy sentences, simple infelicities and errors crept into copy, like "rainfall fell," "shoo-flu" (for "shoo-fly"), "encounted" (for "encountered"). Some unusual dialect which sounded like Li'l Abner had been included for the Southern highlands. A chatty, discursive style made pleasant reading, but did not suit the needs of a guidebook: "to those in

---

[12] Cronyn to Richardson, Mar. 29, 1939, Box 51, FWPN.
[13] Publicity report, n.d., Box 74, FWPN; McConkey to Alsberg, Mar. 25, 1938, Box 58, FWPN.

the know,'' ''furry and feathered tribes,'' and ''many a swank hostelry'' were offered instead of forthright statements.[14]

In short, the federal writers lacked the ability to respond to the appeals of the Washington office for a combination of fact and vigorous language. These were amateur craftsmen who were also subject to local prejudices and loyalties and who lacked any great perspective on their individual states and the nation as a whole.

II

Unsure of a second congressional appropriation, the project's administrators in Washington had set a deadline of May 15, 1936, for all state copy for the original five-volume American Guide. They had assumed that the District of Columbia staff would then concentrate on this material and quickly put it into shape for publication. Their expectations were dashed, however, when the preliminary ''dummy'' manuscripts arrived. Many states did not even send their material until two months late, but this delay did not result in improved copy. Almost without exception, the dummies displayed poor organization and shoddy writing. The two general principles of a guidebook—that it should inform and do so entertainingly—had been neglected in most cases.

Workers gave little thought to proportion and balanced accounts. Chicago, Detroit, and Baltimore overshadowed the rest of their respective guides. Colorado's history essay devoted one paragraph out of twenty-two pages to post-1894 events. Minnesota's history section entirely omitted the struggle for railroads and timber, and its contemporary essay contained heavy editorializing about the ''neuroses of Swedes'' and the ''appalling number of seasonal workers.'' The reference to the ''remarkable growth of manufactures in Alabama'' ignored the $250 million drop in the value of the state's production between 1919 and 1935. Southern copy spoke throughout of the harmony of ''friendly and stimulating rivalry'' between Negro and white and

---

[14] One example of a local attempt to weave words: ''Her little homebuilt ship of state— buffeted by storms beyond her control, endangered by dissension and even mutiny among the crew, sometimes unwisely but always daringly manned—was safe in the harbor at last. Vermont has retained and maintained, in significant ways, her own inviolable identity; but her political, governmental and military history after 1791 is essentially that of the U.S.'' Quoted in Williams to Cronyn, Oct. 20, 1936, Box 105, FWPN.

praised mining companies. Montana's offering, its first director admitted later, represented "a god-awful draft." Although Mississippi, New Hampshire, Ohio, Wisconsin, and New York City had fuller, more thoroughly researched essays, they contained masses of obscure data. Only in the case of Louisiana, whose director Lyle Saxon presented a massive three-volume dummy, could Washington speak of success. Except for this "swell job" (to cite Hopkins's reaction), little copy was ready for final editing.[15]

Realizing that worthwhile results would not be quickly forthcoming, the Washington staff began focusing its attention on the most novel and exciting part of the Guide Series—the essays. These chapters, with their broad cultural approach, offered the tourist a valuable introduction to any state in a picturesque style that even the Baedekers lacked. It took almost two years for some state projects to realize that these diverse topics could not simply be lumped under such a general division as "Natural Setting" or that certain subjects, such as religion, could not be dismissed in one sentence. Massachusetts initially proposed to group a number of major topics under "History" within 10,000 words, while giving no less than 23,000 words to literature and the arts. Statistical tables in industrial and racial articles only slowly gave way to human interest stories and local color.[16] In time, new topics like flora and fauna, folkways, and Indians took on independent significance. Recognizing the special nature of certain states, the central staff permitted the insertion of additional essays—on Florida sports and recreation, Idaho tall tales, Arizona ranch life, Utah religious urban planning, and the like.

First priority went to the history essay. Fifteen pages out of twenty-three was too much to devote to prehistory, as South Dakota's project originally wanted to do. The writers of the Virginia and Massachusetts history essays possessed too much expertise in the field, which caused the Old Dominion and Boston to crowd the center of attention. One specialist overemphasized the part played by Kentucky's troops in the War of 1812 and asserted that the country got New Orleans because it was "Kentucky's seaport" and "Kentucky compelled expansion." In another example of "ballyhoo" copy, Vermont played up the Benning-

---

[15] Preliminary reports, Boxes 101, 78, 81, and 132, FWPN; Harold Merriam to author, Apr. 6, 1968; Alsberg to Saxon, June 22, 1936, Box 52, FWPN.
[16] Cronyn to Billington, Apr. 23, 1937, Box 97, FWPN.

ton victory during the American Revolution, but neglected to point out that the state had been neutral some two years before the war's end. Blatant errors cropped up in other states, like the Alabama claim that General Albert Sidney Johnston had planned the Battle of Shiloh in 1865 (three years after he was killed in it).[17]

The central office wished to call attention to important matters that had heretofore gone neglected because of their controversial nature and therefore accorded the labor and industry essay special attention. Information on contemporary events, such as the clash between CIO workers and Chicago police near the Republic Steel Corporation plant on Memorial Day, 1937, the strike at the Johnstown Bethlehem Steel plant, the La Follette Committee hearings, and tenant farming and its close connection with soil exhaustion in the South, had to be added by editors in Washington. In the dummy manuscripts, accounts of an earlier day usually reflected the conventional nineteenth-century view which opposed union interference with a laissez-faire economy. Labor troubles, it seemed, were confined to areas with a dominant foreign population. It was as if the Haymarket riot, Al Capone, the Socialist government of Reading, Pennsylvania, the Molly Maguires, and the Wobblies had never been. The District of Columbia staff rectified these and other gross omissions.[18]

The literature essay had particular importance, since editors believed that critics would immediately focus attention on this segment of the Guide. As a federally sponsored publication, no guidebook could commit itself on issues of literary and cultural preference. Mark Twain's art could not be labeled "a sick and sorry compromise," nor could Whitman be dismissed as "an old stick" who "sat and munched peanuts." Catalogs of mediocrities had to be avoided as well. Something appeared fundamentally wrong when Ohio's copy devoted one sentence to William Dean Howells and treated at length the writing of S. G. E. Heckewelder, Daniel Drake, Timothy Flint, and the Carey sisters. At first, Georgia and Iowa copy entirely omitted authors critical of these states, noticeably Erskine Caldwell and Josephine Herbst.[19] Fortunately, specialists like Lawrence Abbott, Waldo Browne, and George Cronyn in the Washington office were able to correct errors

[17] Alsberg to Miles, n.d., Box 78, FWPN.

[18] Apr. 20, 1937, report, Box 92, FWPN.

[19] Cronyn to Gaer, Mar. 26, 1937, Box 102, FWPN; Cronyn to French, May 5, 1937, Box 121, FWPN.

of fact and judgment and transform dry, encyclopedic accounts into sparkling copy.

Of all the essays, those on architecture and art, under the supervision of Roderick Seidenberg, appeared the most novel. Seidenberg had shared Alsberg's friendship through Columbia days, Seidenberg's stay at Leavenworth as a conscientious objector during World War I, and the Provincetown Playhouse years. He later achieved recognition as the architect of the New Yorker Hotel and as a writer on cultural themes. Disgusted with the ruling architectural norms, which took no account of the new functional concepts then flourishing in Europe, he saw in the guides a rare opportunity to help awaken the American public to an appreciation of its native and contemporary architecture. The manual Seidenberg drew up reflected his progressive convictions, with an emphasis on plan and inner structure rather than the traditional reliance on external style alone. Since the eye of the tourist always fell upon architecture, Seidenberg thought it essential that a measure of professional guidance be provided in this relatively unfamiliar field. To help bring out a serious, localized history of architecture and art in every state, he secured the services of Donald Kline of the George Washington University department of art (later succeeded by Harold Rosenberg of the New York City project).[20]

Most project workers came particularly unequipped by education or experience to deal with architecture. Often they failed to recognize the treasures their states possessed, such as the Nebraska state capitol, the first of its kind to have a tower instead of a dome. Notable contemporary works, such as grain elevators, town forms, factory and farm buildings, tenements, bridges, campuses, tourist camps, and gas stations, also had to be pointed out by Seidenberg and his associates as proper subjects for study.[21]

Some directors objected to this emphasis. Vardis Fisher asserted that sagebrush had more significance than architecture for Idaho tourists. The assistant director of South Carolina's project best expressed the reaction of even professional writers to Seidenberg's requests:

> It makes me chortle
> To think that the portal
> Rests upon brackets reversed in detail;

[20] J. Alsberg interview; Donald Kline interview, Aug. 25, 1968; Seidenberg to Mumford, July 14, 1936, Box 36, FWPN.

[21] Seidenberg, North Carolina report, Oct. 13, 1937, Box 51, FWPN.

Shall I doubt whether
'Twill stand the weather
With its acanthine octagonal rail?

. . . .

If I were able
I would forget all this wordage and vault—
Vault to the tree tops
Quick as the tree hops,
Gothic and Roman and Classic forgot;
Would I were eagle,
Or yet a beagle
Threatened by no architect's tommyrot.

Fortunately, much needed help came from local architects, the Federal Art Project's Index of American Design, university professors and specialists like Lewis Mumford, the Historical American Buildings Survey, and the American Institute of Architects. With their aid and the massive research of project workers, the central office managed to pioneer in a difficult subject and to distinguish between soffit pilaster and flush peristyle.[22]

However, in its desire to provide thorough essays, the Washington staff tended at times to overlook the basic objective of the American Guide Series—to guide tourists. Alsberg and some directors like Fisher and Santee preferred to focus on lengthy essays, without realizing the importance of the tours, which could offer an opportunity for creative writing as well. The Idaho director had written only about subjects that interested him until Washington saw his galley proofs and insisted that tours be inserted in that guide. Other project executives asserted that it would be more feasible to concentrate on the important highways and the larger cities and towns. Massachusetts's Clifford Shipton was positive that, in contrast to the Commonwealth, the "ordinary towns" in the Midwest had nothing of topographical and very little of historical interest.[23]

Only the determination of the tour editor, Katherine Kellock, led to an organizational framework covering the *entire* country in a uniform and entertaining style. "K. K." almost single-handedly undertook a presumably dull task which no one else wanted or could manage and

[22] Fisher to Seidenberg, Apr. 10, 1936, Box 11, FWPN; Nancy Telfair (Louise DuBose), "At Midnight," KK papers, LC; Seidenberg interview.

[23] Kellock interview, June 23, 1967; Shipton to Alsberg, Dec. 2, 1935, Box 18, FWPN.

derived from it imaginative and comprehensive final copy. She insisted that the guides satisfy all travelers, whether drivers on interstate highways or hardy trail explorers, and that they cover every mile of the country.[24]

Formidable difficulties arose in the course of covering this part of the guides. Snow and ice blocked travel in Montana, Utah, and Wyoming for months. Great distances between cities hampered regular coverage until workers obtained free railroad passes, official cars of the National Park Service, and even an automobile captured from Mississippi bootleggers. Very bad stretches of dirt road in Texas, old Nevada cow trails, and notorious Wyoming side paths made checking a dangerous task at times. Areas without roads or trains had to be covered by foot, horse, sled, or boat. One writer had to brave the perils of a flight up Glacier Bay aboard a freight plane laden with dynamite and cookstoves for Alaskan gold prospectors. Extensive construction in Oklahoma, Tennessee, and Nevada required new copy to take into account newer and shorter routes.[25]

Other hazards could not be foreseen. A story on modern cowpunchers would be boring, thought an Arizona project employee, until bullets from a .45 sent people ducking for safety at a cattlemen's hotel meeting; his report concluded: "What will happen when I go after some of those smuggling stories?" A teetotaler assigned to write on Bellevue's alcoholic ward thought it wise to experiment along the way; he arrived drunk, was assigned to a bed, and subsequently became a dipsomaniac. One Manhattan worker had a mortal fear of the two-mile ferry trip to Staten Island, and he remained certain that mad dogs would devour him when he reached that destination. On the verge of being fired, he obtained a letter from his physician: "This man has a one hundred per cent case of hydrophobia—fear of dogs and water. Please assign him to another project."[26]

Kellock found it especially difficult to teach the mechanics of tour form to the various projects. She had suggested that descriptions of

[24] Kline interview.

[25] McConkey to Miller, Oct. 12, 1936, Box 92, FWPN; Colby to Alsberg, July 19, 1937, Box 62, FWPN. Another unique hazard—dust on previously inaccessible records in the basement of a Manhattan post office—led to an epidemic of skin rashes and lung infections until WPA furnished workers with coal mine respirators. *New York Times*, July 13, 1936.

[26] Mangione, *Dream and Deal*, p. 87n; Harry Roskolenko, *When I Was Last on Cherry Street*, p. 165.

picturesque cities or towns be placed in the cities section so that the traveler need not leaf through several pages to pick up the thread of the main route. But, as some workers slowly discovered, this categorization did not necessarily follow population figures. Many of the larger towns, originally placed in the cities section, had little history and few points of interest ("POI"). The POI section had been organized to handle special sights found along a main highway; such sights otherwise situated were to be put at the end in an independent side tour. In revising copy, however, Washington editors regularly discovered that points of interest had a habit of disappearing or metamorphosing into gasoline stations, parking lots, and swimming pools. Except for such masters as Ohio's Hatcher, New Jersey's Irene Fuhlbruegge, and Louisiana's Saxon, FWP workers rarely achieved a quick grasp of the forms of tour description and routing. Only after much effort did correct cross-references find their way into city and tour copy.

The tour editor's attempt to give uniformity of direction to the tours, copying the north-to-south and east-to-west standard used by airlines and compasses, met with strong challenges in a number of states. The idea represented a basic change from the European guidebooks like the Baedekers, known for their loop tours starting from capital cities, and was consistent with Kellock's wish to cover an uncharted country in thorough fashion. A number of project directors argued, however, that reading tours in reverse would be both confusing and senseless in their states. For example, both Vardis Fisher and the state automobile association pointed out that 80 per cent of the travel in Idaho flowed in a south-to-north direction. Massachusetts's Ray Billington also wanted that arrangement because he assumed that most people would begin from Boston. Eventually, Fisher went along with Kellock's rule so that his guidebook could see early print, but Gaer permitted Massachusetts to return to the loop system it favored (after the tour editor had reversed it) to speed up that volume's publication.[27]

The tours sections carried an amazing range of material. Controversial subjects could be placed in them. Mining strikes in Harlan, Kentucky, thus found their way here, as did company villages, lynchings, demagogues, and the Donner Pass story of cannibalism. Correction of the success stories which dominated the telling of America's past could

[27] Kellock interview, Aug. 18, 1968.

also be provided. People who had guessed wrong, such as the Maine sea captain who outfitted a sloop to rescue Napoleon from St. Helena or the local bankers who believed that Baboon Gulch would be Idaho's leading city, were now rescued from oblivion.

On the other hand, this dumping ground, as it were, had to be cleared of thousands of words which resulted in disorganized, duplicated, or useless copy. Section A of Wyoming's Tour 71 "won the baby's rattle," in the words of the state editor, with some 20,000 words covering the Indian campaign along the Powder River, the Cattle War of 1812, Teapot Dome, the Salt Creek oil discoveries, and a few other matters. More than 10,000 words, comprising genealogies, detailed county and parish histories, and summaries of county products had to be cut from Virginia's tours.[28]

"Paper tours" and gross errors eventually came to light and underwent drastic alteration. In one curious instance, Katherine Kellock finally discovered that the WPA cars once confiscated from bootleggers during Prohibition registered absurdly low mileage figures; she arranged for different automobiles. But boondoggling inevitably led to obvious mistakes. The Pennsylvania project, which had covered only 10 per cent of the state's vast complex of roads by 1939, proved particularly untrustworthy, and in Delaware, two tour checkers looking for a bridge marked "POI" discovered that it had been washed out nine years earlier.[29]

To the professional writers on the project, the tours section represented an anathema, about which the "Psalm of Touring" could be dictated: "Tell me not in mournful numbers / That a tour is but a dream; / That the highway never blunders / And maps are just what they seem." They found its rules difficult to grasp and the assignment uncreative. The following observation, à la Gertrude Stein, indicated the general dissatisfaction with this type of work: "A tour is a tour is a tour is a tour. To go on a tour is to be on a tour is to stay on a tour is not so bad as to write a tour is not to get a headache on a tour. A tour is a main tour, a side tour, a well-paved tour, a graveled tour—is a tour. . . . Tours are made for men, cabins are made for tours and made for

[28] Stahlberg to Alsberg, Mar. 14, 1939, Box 24, FWPN; Kellock to Gaer, memo, Mar. 23, 1939, Box 51, FWPN.

[29] McKinzie, "Writers on Relief," p. 82; Kellock to Alsberg, Mar. 7, 1939, Box 2447, WPA; Selnikoff to Alsberg, May 22, 1939, Box 1037, WPA.

business are made for the chambers of commerce are made for fun. One can have fun without going on a tour.''[30]

In an effort to combat this resentment and avoid a needlessly dry and pedantic flavor, the central office either asked for or injected reams of visual description. Buffalo ranges, Kansas wheat fields, and portraits of agricultural life began to appear in second drafts. Roadside stands, dance halls, and pool parlors took on new vitality as Fisher, Hatcher, Bell of Kentucky, and others tackled dull manuscripts in neighboring states. These professionals, imparting snap and sting, produced the best writing in all the guidebooks.

The careful attention of the District of Columbia staff lifted the guidebooks from the level of mere travel directions to that of sensitive and authentic writing. The staff's search for the unique and vivid made readers see that ''Kansas'' signified more than a prairie and that ''New York'' meant something besides Greenwich Village. In the process, they began to discover that the whole country had a rich variety of folk and folklore only now awakening to rediscovery.

III

The amassing of a wealth of material and the subsequent writing of the various subjects for the Guide could not have been executed by the federal writers alone. Realizing this limitation, Alsberg fortunately came to an early agreement with Aubrey Williams permitting the use of National Youth Administration students for ''leg work'' and research. Because of the project's educational value, Williams agreed that NYA funds would pay for these services (an example followed by Minnesota's commissioner of education for the state's high school pupils). Projects in West Virginia, New Hampshire, Ohio, Louisiana, Massachusetts, and Kansas found NYA'ers extremely helpful in checking and uncovering countless sources. Exams and quizzes interrupted such work, however, and the best-qualified students received assignments in universities not eager to release them. And NYA directors, often resentful of the project's authority, withdrew their charges when relief cuts befell the FWP.[31]

[30] Davis to Alsberg, May 26, 1938, Box 2367, WPA; Stella Hanau papers. See also Don Farran, ''The Federals in Iowa: A Hawkeye Guidebook in the Making,'' *Annals of Iowa*, Winter, 1973, pp. 1190-96.

[31] Alsberg to Ulrich, Nov. 23, 1935, Box 20, FWPN.

Soon after the project began, Alsberg sought other help by appealing to the public for suggestions, family records, and factual material to supplement its work. Questionnaires to all public schools in Nebraska brought 9,000 replies. Postmasters in North Carolina aided the local project and were equally successful. Letters arrived at the central office from these self-appointed "volunteer associates" sharing a family memory about Lincoln's assassination or citing some diary for a lead to the phrase "it's a long time between drinks." Carl Sandburg provided the source for an item about the impaling of heads on pikes after a slave revolt in Virginia. State highway departments and motor clubs checked on tour mileage; railroad and bus companies provided private information. Government bureaus proved essential. The U.S. Information Service supplied the services of its chief still photographer, W. Lincoln Highton; the Historical Records Survey, the Library of Congress, and the National Archives put their records at the project's disposal.[32]

Occasionally, the project was refused assistance. The Presbyterian church in Washington hesitated to provide private records because one official feared, in part, that such information would be used to levy high taxes on ecclesiastical properties. Elderly Republican ladies in Carlisle, Pennsylvania, refused to grant interviews about their (long-dead) fathers' aid to fugitive slaves before the Civil War. As one put it: "How did I know they weren't from the government trying to find out things about Father to get us in trouble? I wouldn't put such a thing past that Roosevelt. . . ." The Nashville chapter of the League of American Pen Women agreed that the project's work had decided value, but deplored the fact that it wasted time in research dealing with "the lower classes."[33] These views did not represent those of the populace at large, however.

The work of the volunteer associates often proved useful when it came to covering outlying localities and towns with populations of less than 10,000. These contributors also garnered community support for the project. The quality and dependability of their research did not, regrettably, match their enthusiasm. The project's reliance on "volunteer consultants" brought forth much more rewarding results.

[32] Bjorkman to Alsberg, May 29, 1937, Box 113, FWPN; Sandburg to Baker, Mar. 24, 1936, Box 462, WPA.
[33] Evans to Baker, May 21, 1936, Box 19, FWPN; Mangione, *Dream and Deal*, p. 117; McDaniel to Alsberg, Mar. 3, 1939, Box 44, FWPN.

Many local authorities donated their time gratis to the preparation and checking of essays. James Wilson, founder of the *Virginia Quarterly*, the historians E. M. Coulter and Roland Harper, newspaper editors, and museum directors submitted essays on literature, history, flora, and other specialized subjects. The contributions of the Universities of Virginia and North Carolina so impressed Donald Davidson of Vanderbilt University that he organized some of its faculty "to save the day" for the Tennessee guidebook. The Mississippi State College for Women gave credit for English and geography class assignments relating to coverage of towns for the state guide.[34]

Such assistance had particular value in the handling of the contemporary essays in the guides. These essays offered the greatest creative challenge, for they had to fulfill the guides' basic purpose: to create the desire to visit a place. Most state copy, unfortunately, drifted into vague impressionism, with color substituting too readily for fact.

The central office finally turned to professionals outside the project and received a number of worthy contributions. Thus, although neither Booth Tarkington nor Meredith Nicholson would do Indiana's foreword and Ernest Poole wanted $500 to write New Hampshire's essay, the public eventually did read some fascinating, truly distinguished pieces from the pens of Dorothy Canfield Fisher (Vermont), Jonathan Daniels (North Carolina), William Allen White (Kansas), and Douglas Southall Freeman (Virginia).[35]

There were a few drawbacks to the use of these voluntary consultants. A professor from Ohio State spent two years and lots of money for travel and film, and still did not submit an architecture essay. When consultants did hand in articles, their work often proved too pedantic for tourist purposes. An eye for the significant could not be found in a 10,000-word article on Georgia Indian mounds or in a history essay of sixty-seven pages from a faculty member of the University of New Mexico. Finally, after the academic jargon ("to facilitate the study of") had been cut from copy, directors had to face the ordeal of returning heavily edited essays to their original creators. Though Florida's Carita Corse recalled the professors as "worse than movie prima donnas,"[36] most specialists were sustained in their willingness to

[34] Kellock to Alsberg, Aug. 8, 1937, Box 31, FWPN.

[35] Laning to Briggs, May 13, 1938, Box 13, FWPN; White to Cronyn, Sept. 3, 1937, Box 10, FWPN.

[36] John T. Frederick, June 16, 1939, report, Box 465, WPA; Corse interview.

contribute to the Guide Series by an appreciation of its pioneering nature. Their efforts helped the FWP achieve considerable success.

IV

The strength or weakness of all guide copy ultimately rested on the project's state editors. In most state projects, professional writers on non-security wages served as assistant supervisor, associate director, or state editor and cut down hundreds of pounds of copy to a finished version of the guide. For many who ended up writing much of their guidebooks, including Merle Colby (Massachusetts), Opal Shannon (Iowa), Louise DuBose (South Carolina), and Alice Corbin (New Mexico), the salaries represented small remuneration. Some of these indefatigable writers later became the directors of their state projects.

Editors overextended themselves to help bring the guides to light. Faced with a lax and inefficient director, as well as boondoggling and cynical ex-newspapermen, Rebecca Pitts wrote nearly all the essays for the Indiana Guide. The poet Grace Stone Coates did not even buy a copy of the Montana volume: "I think I knew all of it by heart." Vincent McHugh rewrote most of the New York City volume. Editors from Tennessee and Montana who supervised Alabama, Utah, and Wyoming copy at the request of the central office found it expedient to rewrite it entirely.[37]

Changing technical requirements at times proved irritating to these hardworking professionals. When the central office, which had previously used the Government Printing Office manual to assure uniformity, switched to the use of the Funk and Wagnall's dictionary, then to the Chicago *Manual of Style* and Webster's dictionary, uncertainty arose regarding italics and numerals. The problems created by this inconsistent procedure received canonization in an ode, "Punctual Editor Lapses into Coma for Short Period," which read in part:

> If I should tour Fifth Avenue
> But call said st. 5th Ave.
> Would Harris, Reed his eyebrows lift
> And say I misbehave?
> If I should drive on U.S. 10

[37] Rebecca Pitts to author, Jan. 12, 1969; Grace Stone Coates to author, Mar. 11, 1968; Thompson interview.

> And write it just as US
> Would slighted periods call a halt
> And maybe wreck my bus?
> Is 1 mile proper or one mile?
> And when it comes to fractions
> There seems to be a battle waged
> Twixt ½ and one-half factions.

And concluded:

> When are the natives simply (pop.)
> And when the population?
> I've closed my eyes or maybe I's
> Awaiting arbitration.[38]

Further confusion arose out of conflicting instructions emanating from 1500 I Street and then the Ouray Building on G Street, successor to the McLean mansion as the FWP's home office. Contradictions in editorial review were inevitable, because many Washington editors could not possibly read all parts of guide copy. As a result, they failed to see that information whose absence from one place they deplored could be found elsewhere. Although Alsberg would later be praised for having the "courage" to scrap previous style manuals for a uniform master outline in June, 1936, the fact remained that for almost a year the state projects found it impossible to obtain lucid instructions.[39]

State offices received tart letters and editorial comments from central headquarters. Luckily, one member of the Technical Projects Division deflected the following shaft before a colleague sent it flying to the Wisconsin state office: "The consistent lack of apostrophe in possessive nouns in Milwaukee may be part of the cultural progress described in one of the essays. The central office suggests that on such points Milwaukee pause, in charity, until the rest of the Nation catches up, including the GPO." A parenthetical statement derogating Conrad Aiken's superb piece on Deerfield for the Massachusetts guidebook was also squelched. Although the project's central administrators, dependent as they were on cooperation, often leaned over backwards in phrasing their critiques, their comments proved too severe for a

[38] Cited in Harris to Baker, Mar. 26, 1936, Box 50, FWPN.

[39] Kerr interview, July 7, 1968. Finding confusion rather than specific directions in them, Vardis Fisher decided to ship the daily bulletins directly into the furnace. Taber, "Writers' Project in Pacific Northwest," p. 133.

number of distraught directors, especially during the first year of the project's existence.[40]

Experts in various fields corrected the Washington office on many points. South Dakota's assistant director, a former sheepherder, pointed out the error of changing "band" of sheep to "group." "Honest" and "gentleman" were not synonymous epithets for a gambler in New Mexico and Colorado. State specialists informed the central office that the Socialist party government in Milwaukee did not lay foundations for the later state-wide Progressives.[41]

Washington's quest for uniform standards, some state executives believed, resulted in the sacrifice of creativity and color. Santee informed Cronyn that terms familiar to cowboys and the Southwest, like "watered out," "stud," "browse," and "gentle a horse," had been removed from his guide copy. (The phrases were reinserted in the final version.) And when Vermont's Doten eventually did receive praise from Lawrence Morris for his preface to that state's guide, he replied: "After 3 years of struggle with utilitarian prose (in re yours of the 18th emphatically urge quota revision sort of thing) to be told one has a style is quite an intoxicating experience . . . words such as yours will keep our thin blue line of writer-bureaucrats intact and moving forward, content in the knowledge that, behind all the clamor and confusion, there is someone who understands."[42]

In their annoyance, state directors and editorial staffs often failed to understand that Washington's instructions had to be overrigorous and pedantic. The complete novelty of the situation, the uneven caliber of the federal writers, and the vast quantity of guide material pouring in from state offices—all this would have engulfed the central staff had not manuals, instructions, and daily letters been sent out to amateurs and professional writers alike. "Few people," noted the tour editor toward the end of the second congressional appropriation, "realize how

[40] Cronyn to Craun, Feb. 15, 1937, Box 132, FWPN; Apr. 16, 1937, report, Box 97, FWPN.

[41] Lyons to Alsberg, Aug. 26, 1938, Box 88, FWPN. The Nebraska project was particularly fortunate to have Loren Eiseley, who was on the staff for four months before embarking on a career as an author and anthropologist, write parts of the essays on paleontology and archaeology for the state guide. Mangione, *Dream and Deal*, p. 109.

[42] Santee to Cronyn, May 22, 1937, Box 78, FWPN; Doten to Morris, Apr. 15, 1938, Box 25, FWPN. Santee subsequently wrote a friend that he kept his name off the Arizona Guide in protest, feeling that "a lot of bastards, . . . I mean the Brass in Washington who have their names in front in very broad type," did not belong in the guidebooks. Comment found in rare book catalog belonging to Eleanor Powell. Powell interview, Nov. 14, 1968.

shockingly small our staff is; we're trying to check and edit around 12 million words of copy with little over a dozen editors."[43]

Delays had an inevitability about them, but they often arose as a result of the high standards initially set and maintained by Alsberg and his subordinates. Purple phrases ("The oil of human kindness gushes forth from the hearts of these people on the island"), incorrect syntax, and incomplete information all caused weary readers at 1500 I to wonder about yesterday's high hopes.[44] As most state projects shared an unawareness of the difference between condensation of material and indiscriminate excision, Washington constantly had to reinsert picturesque copy. Notwithstanding the complaints of a few directors, good writing did get through the Washington office unharmed. Speed was sacrificed to achieve accuracy and good English whenever a choice in priorities became necessary. The national office succeeded admirably in correcting its first technical errors, as a comparison between the tours in the Idaho Guide and those in later volumes proves. Nebraska's state editor subsequently wrote that the Technical Project's supervision "was of the highest quality";[45] the same could be said for supervision in the other states as well.

As the guidebooks reached completion, they received even more critical treatment to make them as nearly accurate and as stylistically superior as possible. Increased demands were so commonplace that Alsberg could write Pennsylvania's director: "We must apologize for making further changes, but perhaps the State editors would be alarmed if a manuscript were returned without any new suggestion."[46]

In the last analysis, the superior guidebooks produced justified the close review given thousands of pages of manuscript. The central staff sought "an appreciation of the value of facts, an unbiased point of view, a sense of organization of material, and a gift of style." It knew that future judgments of the guidebooks would take into account not only the circumstances under which they had been produced, but also their quality. As Cronyn put it, these volumes represented "not temporary displays of talents on relief, but permanent printed records of

[43] Kellock to Kellogg, May 8, 1937, Box 50, FWPN.
[44] McConkey report, Feb. 11, 1936, Box 60, FWPN.
[45] Rudolph Umland to author, May 28, 1968.
[46] Alsberg to French, Oct. 21, 1938, Box 121, FWPN.

work done.''[47] The guides would be exposed, then, to critical scrutiny for all time. Thanks, though, to its own devoted efforts and those of project workers, gifted state editors, and volunteer associates, the central office had need for few misgivings.

[47] Cronyn to Cronin, Oct. 26, 1936, Box 461, WPA.

Censorship

CENSORSHIP WAS THE GREATEST DANGER faced by the Federal Writers' Project. Long before the creation of Federal #1, when the custodians of culture had urged that the government of the United States emulate other governments in supporting the arts, the painter John Sloan had replied in dissent: "Sure, it would be fine to have a Minister of Fine Arts in this country. Then we'd know where the enemy is." The Soviet Commissariat for Education and, later, the German Ministry of Propaganda and Public Enlightenment required that the creative artists and writers they subsidized compromise their talents for ideological ends. It remained to be seen, therefore, whether the federal writers' art would be similarly prostituted for propaganda purposes or allowed unfettered expression.[1]

The guidebooks had been chosen at the outset as the FWP's main purpose because, among other reasons, Washington officials thought them "a terribly safe thing to do." The project's executives quickly discovered, however, that they had to beware of controversial material for which the administration could be held responsible. At the same time, although Washington had inaugurated the American Guide Series to provide jobs, the project had to preserve what Alsberg termed "the integrity and independence" of its employees.[2] The fundamental issue at stake was this: could the State pay the piper but not call the tune?

This problem was double-edged. "The State Guides," wrote George Cronyn to Texas's director, "may be as ambitious in scope as common sense and state enthusiasm will dictate." These were ambiguous guidelines, however. The central office exercised control over all state copy, just as every private and public agency regulated the work of its

---

[1] George Biddle et al., "The Government and the Arts," Harper's 187 (Oct., 1943):427-34; Grace Overmyer, Government and the Arts, chap. 4.

[2] Cahill Memoir, p. 445; Henry Alsberg, "Writers and the Government: Federal Writers' Projects," Saturday Review of Literature 13 (Jan. 4, 1936):9.

own employees, but from the beginning, certain of the office's discretionary powers had to be limited. The state and national units, as
agents of the government, became equally subject to the rules governing all producers of federal publications.[3]

The Washington office imposed specific limits on factual coverage.
With almost no exceptions, living people could not be named. Family
feuds, some of which had been going on for 100 years or more in parts
of the South, had to be treated with extreme care. Revisions were made
in copy to eliminate possibly controversial statements about Calamity
Jane and Klondike Kate in South Dakota and Oregon copy. The
research editor of the District of Columbia Guide asked E. S. Corwin to
review the piece on the Supreme Court before publication "because of
the touchy nature of the subject matter."[4]

The District of Columbia office carefully checked a variety of subjective claims. Because the prevailing labor situation remained a ticklish
one in Santa Fe and the New Mexico editorial staff found itself divided
between spokesmen for the mine owners and the United Mine Workers
of America, Washington received all data collected on the subject for
final arbitration. The copy about that state's Penitentes, a religious
brotherhood noted for seeking atonement through physical suffering,
had to be handled gingerly, especially since the local Catholic church
frowned upon the sect. A personal judgment about TVA was removed
from Tennessee copy, and Connecticut's labor essay lost detailed
excerpts from reports and the testimony of strikers. The assertion that
"the divorcee will be the center of interest as long as her money holds
out—essentially an admission that she is thoroughly exploited as one of
Nevada's unnatural resources" contained substantial truth, but it could
not endear the state to the reader and, therefore, was cut from Nevada's
contemporary essay.[5]

A number of editors objected to this control, especially when it
interfered with their creative efforts. The first and most prolonged
flare-up occurred with Idaho's Vardis Fisher. After praising the draft of
Fisher's history essay as "this gem of purest ray serene," Cronyn had
added the stipulation that it "be read coolly prior to publication."
Overlooking the qualification, Fisher was shocked at the associate

[3] Cronyn to Davis, Nov. 4, 1935, Box 45, FWPN.

[4] Guinzberg to Corwin, Nov. 27, 1936, Box 26, FWPN.

[5] Cunningham to Alsberg, June 22, 1936, Box 60, FWPN; June 8, 1937, report, Box 106,
FWPN.

director's critique a month later, which pointed to bias "almost to the point of viciousness" and to the lack of appreciation of Idaho's progress in a number of social and economic respects. The guide, Cronyn insisted, could not serve as a forum for retrying a case, some three decades past, involving a bombing attempt by radical laborites in which the former governor, Frank Steunenberg, had lost his life. The associate director was candid enough to declare also that the printing of such statements "might conceivably lead to the boycotting of the Idaho Guide by the organized labor movement of the State."[6]

Throughout the latter part of 1936, Fisher and Cronyn traded accusations. Fisher admitted that, purely from the point of view of principle, Washington's position remained invulnerable. Practically, however, "there is no detachment in a book but only in some books the impression of it." Fisher promised to try to delete or severely temper statements that might have repercussions. However, he wanted the volume's introduction to indicate that the federal government bore no responsibility for opinions expressed therein. Cronyn immediately took issue with this request, and Alsberg refused to sanction a statement on the title page that the guide was "based on materials, etc." from the writers' project. As revisions progressed, Fisher objected to the apparent exercise of "autocratic power" on Washington's part, its "flat contradictions," and its mandatory changes. Cronyn, in turn, insisted that greater leeway had been given the Idaho director than any of his colleagues, and that Fisher had shown himself to have been under a misapprehension about the final character of the work by treating his share of it "as a personal and private enterprise."[7]

In addition Alsberg pointed out to the rebellious director that the Idaho copy suffered from derogatory remarks which, if not corrected, would subject the government (far more so than a private publisher) to dangerous criticism. That the State Fish and Game Department was "vitiated by politics" and that a certain resort charged "extortionate rates" for what looked like "abandoned hen coops" became more than indiscreet commentary. Fisher went too far for even Alsberg's taste when he compared Mt. Borah—"fat and flabby"—to its political namesake. When the associate director abruptly demanded the deletion

[6] Cronyn to Fisher, Aug. 20, 1936, and Sept. 19, 1936, Box 87, FWPN.

[7] Fisher to Cronyn, Sept. 29, 1936, Box 87, FWPN; Fisher to Cronyn, Oct. 20 and 21, 1936, and Cronyn to Fisher, Oct. 22, 1936, Box 11, FWPN.

of ninety-nine lines from the once-lauded history essay, Fisher shot back: "Cronyn's skin is so tender that he has cut out everything except the innocuous—and sometimes he seems even afraid of that." The debate on questions of control and policy finally came to an end only after Cronyn flew out to Idaho in the beginning of November and made most of the changes demanded by Washington.[8]

The real danger of copy emasculation arose not from Washington, however, but from outside the project. After the national director had invited the cooperation of chambers of commerce, these groups began pressing state units to emulate write-ups of the promotional type characteristic of commercial travel brochures. Alsberg cautioned a field representative to the Salt Lake City regional project conference in June, 1936, to explain to the assembled directors that simple and realistic treatment alone could counter the "definitely reactionary" social viewpoint prevalent in the West—"dominated by a few large corporations." The American Hotel Association even objected to the listing of hotels in the state guides for fear that this would ruin the sales of its *Red Book* directory. Confronted by such organizations, workers hesitated to turn in some copy, including the true story of "trained thermometers" in Florida (trained not to register over 84°).[9]

When, as will be related in the next chapter, the central office and WPA evolved a policy of sponsorship to get the guides published, more formidable difficulties arose. Local chambers of commerce displayed their wariness of and antagonism toward any program advanced by an outside agency. And demands arose in well-established areas for protracted history sections that would include biographies of all conceivable prominent persons of the past.

Directors eventually found that local sponsors would rather forego the benefit of a guidebook than accept one containing any controversial material. Work on a local guidebook to the Ozarks came to a halt when the sponsoring Springfield, Missouri, Chamber of Commerce discovered that project writers had identified the relative of a leading citizen as a bank robber and bandit. The Washington Progress Commission eventually dropped its sponsorship of the state guide after failing to

[8] Alsberg to Fisher, Oct. 29, 1936, and Fisher to Alsberg, Nov. 1, 1936, Box 11, FWPN. For Fisher's final consent, see chap. 6 below.

[9] Alsberg to Miller, June 30, 1936, Box 1, FWPN; Kellock to Alsberg, July 6, 1937, Box 58, FWPN. As a federal agency, the FWP could not rate or recommend hotels or restaurants.

receive assurances that final copy would contain no mention of strikes or labor troubles; the politically conservative commission believed that such descriptions would alarm industry that might otherwise be attracted to its borders.[10]

The first clear sign of what might be in store for the project once the guides were published came with the printing of *Your New York*, the initial effort of the New York City unit. Upon its appearance, Cronyn took director Orrick Johns to task for putting out a pamphlet "afflicted with the cheapest sort of ballyhoo," with its "lurid intimations of Chinatown dens, the come-on stuff of the tourist barkers." Johns replied that it had proved generally very popular with the American Hotel Association and the Delaware and Lackawanna Railroad. From the attack which developed a few months later, however, it became clear that not all groups shared this view.[11] The heads of dozens of civic societies petitioned Roosevelt and Hopkins to halt publication and destroy as many of the 45,000 copies as could be recalled. *The Villager*, in particular, protested this eighteen-page "foretaste" of the New York City Guide; a Greenwich Village throwaway sheet aimed to catch the real estate agent and Wanamaker advertising, it could not sanction copy referring to the plotting of "free verse, free lives and a free world" on the checkered tablecloths of quaint retreats, around which could also be found artistic criminals, exiles from fallen monarchies, gangsters, and playboys.[12]

Defenders of *Your New York* pointed out that its descriptions coincided rather remarkably with those of many pre– and post–O. Henry authors and noted that the average visitor would certainly prefer these attractions to the Minetta Brook, statues of General Sheridan and Garibaldi, and the Sixth Avenue El. *The Villager*, in turn, insisted that 4,000 flowering windowboxes in the summer did not reflect "a community of criminals." In spite of the fact that the pamphlet had appeared eight months previously, and that no copies had been distributed in more than three months, petitioning Village residents were not content with the written apology of the assistant administrator of WPA.[13]

[10] Winkler to Cunningham, May 18, 1938, and Edmonds to Alsberg, Aug. 26, 1936, Box 22, FWPN.

[11] Cronyn to Johns, Aug. 25, 1936, and Johns to Alsberg, Aug. 26, 1936, Box 50, FWPN.

[12] *The Villager* file, Box 2114, WPA.

[13] *New York World Telegram*, Mar. 26, 1937; *The Villager*, Mar. 25, 1937; Apr. 9, 1937, memo, Works Project Administration file, Box 13, OF-444C, Franklin D. Roosevelt papers (hereafter FDR papers), FDRL.

Only Hopkins's expression of regret, in April, 1937, satisfied *The Villager* and petitioning Village residents. The *New York Sun* crowed: "The leaders of the fight for vindication deserve congratulation, and Greenwich Village is to be congratulated on having such leaders." Writing to a friend, Harris dismissed the attack: "By the way, does anyone read *The Villager*?"[14] But, coming at the end of the second congressional appropriation, it raised a disturbing question: If an insignificant booklet received such treatment from the local citizenry, what would occur when entire guidebooks saw print, especially if similar barrages were unleashed by sponsors themselves?

II

As the Massachusetts Guide was about to appear, Alsberg arranged a reception to celebrate this first New England guidebook.[15] In front of local sponsors, WPA officials, and the press, the national director stood ready to present a leather-bound copy to Governor Charles F. Hurley, but his supervisor, Ellen Woodward, snatched it away and did so herself. She later regretted this grab at publicity, for the meeting did not insure the scotching of unfair attacks on the project as Alsberg had intended. Upon receiving the first copy on August 17, 1937, Governor Hurley said he would be pleased to recommend that the volume be placed in every library and school in the commonwealth. Yet within twenty-four hours he issued a blast against the book and the project's administrators for what one local paper called "slipping a fast one"—filling the guide with personal interpretations of fact injurious to the state's reputation. These included discussions of the Sacco-Vanzetti case, the Boston police and Lawrence strikes, and the child labor amendment and related material (including a reference to Labor Day in the list of official holidays). Seeking to suspend further printings of it by the state librarian, the governor immediately attempted to have the Houghton Mifflin publishing company delete all passages that tweaked Boston's blue nose.[16]

[14] *New York Sun*, May 1, 1937; Harris to Thompson, Sept. 13, 1937, Box 34, FWPN.

[15] The Idaho and Washington, D.C., guides preceded the volume on Massachusetts by a few months. The next chapter describes these two pioneering efforts within the larger context of publishing the American Guide Series. The public reaction to the Massachusetts guidebook has been taken up at this point because its publication brought the first and most serious threat of censorship from sources outside the project.

[16] Alsberg to Gaer, Aug. 7, 1937, Box 59, FWPN; Gaer to Alsberg, Aug. 27, 1937, Box 99, FWPN; *Boston Traveler*, Aug. 19, 1937.

Local spokesmen swiftly joined the governor in upholding the state's honor. Headlines across the front page of Boston's newspapers came out for the "purging" (a common word in the thirties) of any questionable material. A municipal court justice was photographed tossing the book where he thought it belonged—into his wastebasket. Former Governor Joseph B. Ely said that the volume ought to be burned on the Boston Common. ("Rhetorically speaking," he later added.) U.S. Senators David I. Walsh and Henry Cabot Lodge, Jr., called for investigations, and Congressman John McCormack asked that a second printing be held up.[17]

Certain emphases seemed especially prevalent, in the prosecution's opinion. "Is it a Guide to Massachusetts or a Guide to the Sacco-Vanzetti case?" asked the *Boston Record*, pointing to the forty-one lines given to the latter, in contrast with none for the Boston Tea Party, five for the Boston Massacre, less than one for Justice Brandeis, and less than one-half a line for Oliver Wendell Holmes. Enraged financial and industrial leaders took exception to the absence of an equalizing chapter relating to the state's advances in industry and agriculture. Critics pointed out that no mention had been given to the bombings carried out against Sacco-Vanzetti jurors or Justice Webster Thayer.[18]

The connection made between the writers of the guide and left-wing radical movements, one that would gain increasing popularity as the project's work went on, is particularly noteworthy. The author of the Massachusetts teachers' oath bill pointed to the volume as another case of professors (in this case, especially director Ray Billington) ridiculing the state which paid them, and concluded: "This has justified my stand against subversive communistic propaganda for the past 3 years." In fact, a few months before the crisis, an exasperated project worker had complained to Hopkins that Billington had "apologized for the Revolution, told a Kiwanis club audience that Paul Revere shivered and cringed on the occasion of his memorable ride; [thrown] a sneer or two at George Washington."[19]

Outside agitators received increasing blame. No doubt existed for the *Boston Post* that "certain radicals" in WPA outside of Massachusetts were "deliberately plotting to discredit the State." Representative

[17] *Boston Traveler*, Aug. 18, 1937; *Boston Evening American*, Aug. 19, 1937. I am indebted to the late Bert Loewenberg for allowing me to examine his collection of these newspapers.

[18] *Boston Daily Record*, Aug. 20, 1937; *Boston Transcript*, Aug. 26, 1937.

[19] See chap. 9 below; *Boston Traveler*, Aug. 19, 1937; McDonald to Hopkins, Dec. 4, 1936, Box 1528, WPA.

Edward Sirois of Lawrence, a member of the Massachusetts legislative committee to investigate Nazi, Fascist, and Communist activities, suggested that the state police seize all copies of the book. Governor Hurley, an American Legionnaire, told a cheering convention of his brother members, "If these men don't like Massachusetts and the U.S., they can go back where they came from." This amused project officials, who noted that the other assistant director, Merle Colby, hailed from old New England stock and had written a book about the westward migration of New Englanders.[20]

Governor Hurley and his supporters found champions in other parts of the country. The *Columbus Dispatch* equated the Massachusetts Guide with the theatre project's "living newspaper" and the art project's murals in being "more inflammatory than educational." This seemed not surprising to the *Detroit Free Press*, since the FWP had "obligations" to a New Deal administration which afforded it the opportunity to "slip over quite a lot of propaganda against American institutions."[21]

The guidebook had its defenders as well. The prevailing criticism was "misguided," in the opinion of the *New York Times*. That newspaper sensed the danger that the volume, "whether it be dedicated to the Sacred Cod or Karl Marx," would have to receive the stamp of an official censor. In a time of much talk over government censorship, it seemed ironic that here arose an attempt to censor the government. The governor called on the President to intercede, thus showing, in the view of one correspondent, "to what lengths the suppressors of freedom would go, if they had one of their number in the White House." The conservative *Baltimore Morning Sun* pointed out that even a Brahmin might overlook the disputed passages, particularly by recalling that most of what Massachusetts recognized as her historical glories, such as the Suffolk Resolves, had been regarded as offensively radical in their own day.[22]

---

[20] *Boston Post*, Aug. 21 and 25, 1937; *Boston Globe*, Aug. 21, 1937; *Boston Transcript*, Aug. 21, 1937.

[21] *Columbus Dispatch*, Aug. 24, 1937; *Detroit Free Press*, Aug. 21, 1937.

[22] *New York Times*, Aug. 22, 1937, IV, p. 8; Roback to Hopkins, Aug. 20, 1937, Box 1529, WPA. Georgia's Governor E. D. Rivers, wanting revenge for Hurley's criticism of Georgia's penal system and his refusal to extradite an escaped Georgia convict, gleefully announced a state appropriation to purchase the Massachusetts Guide for local schools. He also hoped to persuade producers to dramatize the Sacco-Vanzetti episode for stage and screen in retaliation for *A Fugitive from a Chain Gang* and *Tobacco Road*. (As a basis for peace negotiations, a Maryland

Hurley's course of action seemed peculiar. The most curious fact about the entire episode was that the governor had raised his objections after first approving the book. Numerous consultants and the Houghton Mifflin company had given the volume enthusiastic support before publication, and the *Boston Herald* had at first expressed interest in using it for a subscription campaign. First the manuscript in its entirety and then the page proofs (except for the index) had been submitted to the secretary of state, who had agreed to sponsor the volume. The publisher then received the manuscript with the sponsor's approval, and so it secured the governor's approval as well. After his sudden attack, newspapers reported that Hurley had said that neither he nor the sponsor had seen the book before publication. Within a day another statement was attributed to him, declaring that he and the sponsor had viewed the manuscript, but that changes had been effected by the central staff after that time. He soon was reported to have altered this accusation to one that the emendations had been accepted by Washington and his office.[23]

The guidebook's sponsor, the secretary of state, informed the press that he had received the proofs but had not been given enough time for a thorough investigation, and calls for censorship arose. The administrator of the Lawrence Public Library refused to buy the guide for its shelves, and Congresswoman Edith Nourse Rogers of Lowell maintained that there should be censorship of *every* book that came out of WPA. The governor himself promised to get the names of the "2 or 3" men who wrote the chapters which "maliciously besmirch the proud record of Massachusetts" and demand that Hopkins remove them from the WPA payroll.[24]

Those most responsible for the volume hurried to its defense. Billington noted, as a teacher of history, that a moderate tone marked the volume; Assistant Director Bert Loewenberg, that the manuscript was

---

paper suggested that both embattled executives join in an attack on California for that state's treatment of Tom Mooney.) *Baltimore Evening Sun*, Aug. 22, 1937, and October, 1937, *Magazine*, p. 11.

[23] Gaer to Alsberg, Aug. 27, 1937, Box 99, FWPN; *Boston Herald*, Aug. 19, 1937.

[24] *Boston Evening Transcript*, Aug. 20, 1937; *Boston Daily Globe*, Sept. 3, 1937. The governor never got the names. Bert Loewenberg interview, Apr. 30, 1968. It was to avoid this problem (in addition to the difficulty of choosing which persons should be included in credit lines) that Alsberg decided to have anonymity in the guides. Harris interview.

"a good piece of work" and "courageous." Hopkins cleverly dismissed the row as perhaps the secret publicity stunt of the book's publishers and blasted all expectations that he would hold up current printings.[25]

The opposition failed to see that the writers of the guidebook did not intend either to please the sedate or amuse the irreverent. As Professor Arthur M. Schlesinger of Harvard remarked, the volume succeeded in giving as fair a brief statement of the Sacco-Vanzetti case as could be made about "a complex situation." The authors, in stressing certain matters pertaining to economic development, reflected their own liberal-labor sympathies. Such a viewpoint could not please Hurley and other Massachusetts stalwarts who, while calling for factual information, wanted the guide to be confined to achievement alone.[26]

While Hopkins and other important officials treated the controversy as minor, a few of the project's central staff had themselves taken issue with the liberal orientation of some essays. Three months earlier, Cronyn and E. M. Williams, the history editor, had pointed out the need to avoid overemphasizing the Draft Riots and striking Boston policemen to the detriment of the more creditable Massachusetts Civil War record and the Boston tercentenary. Katherine Kellock subsequently related that she had cut one reference to Sacco-Vanzetti from tour copy so as not to "rub people's noses in it over and over," and had unsuccessfully advised Alsberg to omit other emphases.[27]

Most book reviewers did not think that the book's interpretive slant marred its value. On the contrary, the interposition of Governor Hurley, in Harry Hansen's opinion, was to be appreciated for directing immediate attention to "this fine, original Guidebook." He viewed its absence of eulogism as "an auspicious start" for the American Guide Series. The director of social studies in Brookline recommended use of the guide in all grammar schools. *Publishers Weekly* selected the volume as the third most distinguished book published in August, 1937, and the editors of the *New Republic* included it on their list of 100 notable books for that year.[28]

[25] *Boston Herald*, Aug. 20, 1937; *Boston Transcript*, Aug. 26, 1937.

[26] *Boston Traveler*, Aug. 19, 1937.

[27] Cronyn to Billington, May 26, 1937, Box 53, FWPN; Kellock interviews, June 23 and Aug. 18, 1968.

[28] *New York World Telegram*, Aug. 21, 1937; Cowley to Woodward, Dec. 13, 1937, Box 1529, WPA.

Because project officials hoped to secure Hurley's continuing support, they agreed to make some changes, with the mutual agreement of the secretary of state and the Houghton Mifflin company, for a second edition. The sponsor told project administrators off-the-record that he legally had no right to stop further publication (especially since the plates had been paid for), but had not raised this issue because he came under Hurley's pressure. At first, the governor made no formal complaint or request for arbitration, and the matter rested for a month. Finally, the state librarian submitted a list of suggested revisions to Houghton Mifflin. These included an essay which paid more attention to the state's present industrial record and less to Sacco-Vanzetti. The central office refused to make all the proposed changes. Such firmness, it reasoned, would also dissuade the sponsors of other projects from demanding concessions to local pride and prejudice at some later date.[29]

At last, toward the summer of 1938, a series of compromises settled the first major crisis regarding censorship. Although under no obligation to do so, the publisher would pay for policy corrections in the second edition, with the factual corrections charged against future royalties. To save face for all parties concerned, Houghton Mifflin released a letter saying that the pressure of publication had prevented the new, combined industry-labor essay from being included in the 1937 edition, "as originally intended," and that "duplicated passages" would be eliminated as well. The new director, Muriel Hawks, and the regional director, Frank Manuel, supervised the editing of the second edition, and Alsberg persuaded Merle Colby to have his name retained in the preface.[30]

The guide, even in a new edition, represented no whitewash, but the entire episode left an imprint which would affect the FWP permanently. The President chose to ignore the episode, as when he visited Alsberg's office, drawled, "I understand you had quite a bit of trouble over this book," and laughed uproariously; but as a result of the publicity received, additions were made to the central staff to prevent the occurrence of phrases such as those to which Massachusetts's governor had

[29] Alsberg to Woodward, Oct. 14, 1937, Box 56, FWPN; Linscott to Cook, Feb. 21, 1938, Box 99, FWPN.

[30] Linscott to Alsberg, Apr. 25 and May 4, 1938, Box 97, FWPN; Alsberg to Hawks, May 28, 1938, Box 99, FWPN.

objected. Charles Wood, a lawyer from the Information Service, was appointed special editorial counsel for this purpose. In a move of even greater significance, the director of the Women's and Professional Projects Division, Alsberg's superior, installed as reader for policy Louise Lazell, an associate who had worked for the Democratic National Committee in preparing official papers. The scrutiny of these new appointees would prove valuable but would also become a nuisance. The changes made in the Massachusetts Guide did not fundamentally alter its point of view, but they had been carried out despite Alsberg's strong reluctance to accept them. Perhaps more important, the vehemence of the attacks against the guide appeared "more sinister than ludicrous," for all the bywords of reaction had been employed against the volume as a product of a Communist and/or "big government" undertaking. Josef Berger of the local Provincetown unit worried that this attempt to stamp out Sacco-Vanzetti and other sensitive topics might easily lead to book burning and further suppression, as in contemporary Hitler-ruled Germany.[31] The following months would make clear, though, that this was not even a remote possibility.

III

The attack upon the Massachusetts Guide directly affected other state projects. Only an assurance from Vermont's director that nothing controversial could be found in his projected guidebook stilled the suspicions of a Burlington paper that that volume had been held up for some revision in final copy. As a result, too, of the Massachusetts controversy, the governor and his council delayed approval of the New Hampshire Guide to give them a chance to "read it with a microscope." Local consultants urged that the less said about the AFL-CIO controversy in Kansas the better, leading the chief editor of that guide to object that his director emasculated copy about railroad strikes and Workers' Alliance relief demonstrations to satisfy the project's sponsors. Although literary groups in that state downgraded William Allen White's importance and classified him as a "pseudo-liberal," project

[31] Mangione, *Dream and Deal*, p. 220; Alsberg to Woodward, Sept. 14, 1937, Box 56, FWPN; Morris to Woodward, Oct. 25, 1937, Box 461, WPA; Berger interview.

executives deemed it advisable to avoid saying anything derogatory about the author of the state guide's contemporary essay in return for his continuing help.[32]

Some project officials drew their own curbs. California's acting director omitted Tenrikyo Church, seat of the ancient Shinto religion, from Sacramento copy since the shrine could be found in the heart of the red-light district. To get the approval of his sponsors, Wisconsin's Leo Lyons carefully deleted any phrases that might seem controversial. He also included two passages dealing with the views and positive achievements of Governor Robert La Follette's opponents to offset any general criticism that the political essay reflected propaganda for Progressivism.[33]

The central office realized the need for additional care in curbing possibly controversial material. Louise Lazell, the new policy reader, substituted "celibacy" for "chastity" in the final proofs of the Maine guidebook. Since labor conditions would be improved with passage of the pending wages and hours bill, she also eliminated a comment regarding lower wages ("reflecting the rise of the Southern cotton industry") from a New Hampshire tour. Among other deletions was a paragraph in Duluth copy drawing attention to the local pollen count.[34]

The Washington office devoted the same scrutiny to local guidebooks and other project publications. Alsberg suggested that "How New England People Live" would be a better choice than "The Condition of the Working Classes in New England" for a regional volume. Lyle Saxon had to leave out a line concerning miscegenation in a poem for the New Orleans Guide and to tone down his enthusiasm and nostalgia for the old quadroon system and the red-light districts. Although Alsberg informed his superiors that "Landsmannschaften of New York" had been edited by a number of persons who read Yiddish and who advised him that the work involved no question of policy, they preferred to have it read by an outside authority just to make sure.[35]

Certain proposals could not see print because of policy considera-

[32] *Burlington Free Press*, Sept. 9, 1937; White to Gaer, Sept. 27, 1937, Box 54, FWPN; Evans to Alsberg, Aug. 5, 1938, Box 83, FWPN.

[33] Johnson to Alsberg, Jan. 14, 1939, Box 80, FWPN; Lyons to Alsberg, Nov. 16, 1938, Box 131, FWPN.

[34] Alsberg to Linscott, Nov. 3, 1937, Box 96, FWPN; Lazell to Barrows, Nov. 5, 1937, Box 106, FWPN.

[35] Alsberg to Gaer, Sept. 22, 1937, Box 59, FWPN; Lazell to Barrows, Nov. 16, 1937, Box 95, FWPN; Morris to Woodward, Sept. 21, 1938, Box 111, FWPN.

tions. The central staff withdrew permission for a book on labor history after it discovered that the sponsor was the militant Tacoma, Washington, Central Labor Council. Although eligible to serve as a sponsor, a CIO unit in Minnesota likewise was refused approval to sponsor a history of labor because of possible controversy. Publication of a bulletin for schools entitled "Florida's Sugar Bowl" drew to a halt, for its emphasis ran counter to the President's tariff program and to a congressional act dealing with sugar cane. New York City's acting director had to drop a pamphlet favoring social security, despite his copious use of legitimate source material taken from medical journals, congressional hearings, and public health reports.[36]

State project personnel raised a number of complaints against the stronger curbs imposed by the Washington office. "Are the Guides to be concerned only with sweetness and light?" asked Connecticut's director upon being told to remove references to beer hall entertainment, the Ku Klux Klan, and Colchester's large Jewish population. Pennsylvania's Paul French protested "stupid censorship" of statements in the Philadelphia Guide explaining the purpose behind the framing of the Constitution and the establishment of the Supreme Court (statements which closely resembled the President's position at the time) and of others describing the control of South Philadelphia by the Vare machine for the twenty-five years preceding Al Smith's capture of the Democratic presidential nomination in 1928 and substituting "troop movements were confused by a dense fog" for "persons were reputedly drunk" in a Revolutionary battle. Chattanooga's district supervisor was prepared to discuss such aspects of life in his city as the high rates of murder and illiteracy, the abundance of sweatshops and unsanitary tenements, the presence of "a veritable army of prostitutes," and the embezzlement of funds at the courthouse. "But such passages," he said, "would be properly blue-penciled."[37]

At times even some members of the central office questioned the efficacy of the policy review. Ellen Woodward, the director of the Women's and Professional Projects Division, insisted that galleys for every volume be reviewed by Louise Lazell before her final approval could be obtained. But the chief policy editor, in the desire to prove her

[36] Alsberg to Egan, Apr. 20, 1938, Box 2733, WPA; Alsberg to Corse, July 7, 1939, Box 84, FWPN; Malmberg interview.

[37] Morse to Alsberg, n.d., Box 54, FWPN; French to Alsberg, Nov. 20, 1937, Box 130, FWPN; Bratton to Elder, Feb. 21, 1937, Box 124, FWPN.

worth, often adopted too narrow a point of view. Lazell questioned the advisability of including in the New York City Guide the story of Tammany Hall, its use of the immigrant vote, and of the machinations of the Tweed Ring, even though the guide's treatment of these matters appeared discreet compared with that in various reputable histories.[38]

Alsberg tried to improve the situation. He had written to Hopkins prior to the Massachusetts crisis that the substitution of one national body for numerous state sponsors would greatly eliminate a large amount of work and difficulty. A year later, with cries of "censorship" from supporters like Bernard DeVoto, the national director felt compelled to ask his superiors to weigh the necessity of a letter from a sponsor for approval of each publication. This requirement, he argued, made the central office's task "almost impossible." He also now suggested that each guide include a prefatory statement that opinions expressed therein did not necessarily represent the opinions of WPA or sponsoring agencies, thereby allowing for freer interpretations in the essay section. Unfortunately, Alsberg's proposals failed, and attempts began in congressional quarters to curb the project's freedom of phraseology still further.[39]

Under the impression that her authority over policy issues was being undermined by state and Washington editors, Louise Lazell, in November, 1938, took her suspicions to a special committee of the House of Representatives investigating un-American activities.[40] Among other matters, she discussed the pro-labor slant being taken in the New Jersey Guide, with derogatory allusions to Mayor Frank Hague of Jersey City and to the purchase of tear gas by a commercial organization as protection against possible strikes. Both the publications editor, Florence Shreve, and her assistant agreed with this testimony and also noted editorializing in the Montana Guide copy. Their

[38] Woodward to Morris, Oct. 18, 1937, Box 2498, WPA; Morris to Woodward, July 1, 1938, Box 2115, WPA.

[39] Alsberg to Hopkins, Apr. 27, 1937, Box 55, FWPN; Alsberg to Woodward, May 25, 1938, and Alsberg to Morris, June 9, 1938, Box 57, FWPN. It will be recalled that Alsberg had refused Fisher a similar request at the close of 1936.

[40] This was not the first time that the zealous worker had challenged her immediate superiors. Holding herself above any authority which existed in the Women's Division of the Democratic National Committee had caused her to be dismissed from that organization two years earlier. Dewson to Roosevelt, Aug. 7, 1936, Box 1375, Series 100, ER papers, FDRL. After she resigned from the FWP, Lazell defended her action in correspondence with the First Lady. Lazell to Roosevelt, Oct. 11, 1938, Box 1465, Series 100, and Mar. 1, 1939, Box 1510, Series 100, ER Papers, FDRL.

statements convinced Chairman Martin Dies of the merit in Lazell's suggestion that Viking Press be subpoenaed to turn over the galley sheets for these volumes.[41]

Dies proceeded, for the benefit of his colleagues, to pick a few extracts from these galleys "to show the types of statements that are placed in publications supposed to be impartial." These included (in New Jersey copy) references to labor massacres in Newark and Bayonne during 1915–16 and to the La Follette Committee's 1938 report concerning corporate expenditures for strike breaking, munitioning, and similar activities. Montana galleys, the chairman noted, discussed the sympathy shared by the state's citizens for labor's point of view, as well as their willingness to experiment with "isms" in the face of "great exertions made by corporate power in civic affairs." Dies also pointed to statements criticizing the passage by the 1937 Montana legislature of the so-called "Hitler Bill," which gave the governor the power to hire and fire all appointive state employees, and those telling the story of Congresswoman Jeanette Rankin's vote against a war declaration in 1916. Chairman Dies did not call for comment from anyone present.[42]

The attention given the New Jersey and Montana guides, in particular, did not take into account that the Washington office or local WPA officials had ordered deletions and revisions in the preliminary drafts of both. The central staff had insisted that such phrases as these be dropped from Jersey City copy: "Practically every important public position in the City and County is held by a follower of Mayor Frank J. Hague"; "Structures squat amid chaos, skeletons of buildings crumble at a touch, sardine-packed residences are only supported by their neighbors." The history essay could not retain the assertion that the Pennsylvania Railroad Corporation "succeeded for the next generation in taking the entire state for a ride across the tracks." Despite the objections of the New Jersey Guild Association, the guide's sponsor, references to trichinosis in a vast local piggery and the use of tear gas against striking workers were removed.[43]

Montana Guide copy, too, had been slated for revision prior to the

[41] U.S. Congress, House, Special Committee on Un-American Activities, *Hearings on H.R. 282*, 75th Cong., 3d sess., 1938, IV, pp. 3111-12. For other matters discussed by this committee relating to the project, see chap. 9 below.

[42] Committee on Un-American Activities, *Hearings on H.R. 282*, IV, pp. 3132-38, 2645-55.

[43] Wood to McConkey, Jan. 3, 1938, Box 107, FWPN; Barrett to Alsberg, Jan. 13, 1938, Box 108, FWPN.

Dies hearings. That state's WPA administrator had insisted that the realistic picture of Billings's South Side, with its pigsties and flophouses, be tempered. A discussion of Butte labor troubles and the assertion that "Helena is a small city with a small-city air" came under similar attack. The sterilization of these "unguarded statements" led the local Professional and Service Projects director to suspect that most of the originality had been ironed out by editing. She warned that " 'he who has no enemies has few friends,' and that may also apply to books and their purchase."[44]

Despite various attacks, the New Jersey volume did not undergo the extensive revision which would have fully satisfied the Dies Committee. True, the counsel to the New Jersey sponsor failed to get the mention of the use of tear gas in the Consumers' Research and Seabrook Farm strikes reinserted in Tours 10 and 33. But no one felt the need to eliminate any of the passages in the New Jersey Guide cited by the committee's chairman. That this was so may be largely accounted for by the fact that the controversial items had been based largely on the reports of conservative newspapers and of professors at Princeton University who had served as consultants to the state project.[45]

In the case of the Montana Guide, however, some changes did take place after considerable contention. The sponsor (director of publicity for the state's Department of Agriculture) threatened to withdraw unless certain deletions were made. Alsberg, who believed that the project had to keep its self-respect, found these requests unacceptable, and at one point WPA's regional director, Florence Kerr, recommended that a new sponsor be found. Eventually, with the help of Senator Burton K. Wheeler's daughter, an understanding took place. In the rapprochement, such sentences as those about the "Hitler Bill" and Montanans' acceptance of foreign "isms" in the face of corporate power disappeared from the first edition.[46]

The Dies hearings had apparent effect on other state projects as well. California Guide copy, which had received a brief mention in Florence

[44] Fowler to Crane, May 11, 1938, Box 104, FWPN; Breshahan to Alsberg, Feb. 9, 1938, Box 24, FWPN.

[45] Epstein to Alsberg, Nov. 31, 1938, Box 27, FWPN; Winser to Alsberg, Jan. 4, 1939, Box 109, FWPN. Mayor Hague exerted pressure so that no state official would serve as sponsor and the state director resigned, but the Newark Public Library eventually helped sponsor the guide, which was published in August, 1939. *New York Times*, Nov. 30, 1938.

[46] Babb to Alsberg, Jan. 18, 1939, and Alsberg to Isham, May 25, 1939, Box 1799, WPA.

Shreve's testimony, came under the careful review of its sponsor, the state librarian. "Vigilantism" was excised by the project director from write-ups of Santa Rosa, Westwood, and Sacramento labor disputes. The policy editor called for some specific changes in the preface to the Alaska Guide: "Drinking time" as a designation for the period following the close of the fishing season had to be cut to avoid the possible resentment of moralistic groups, and the opposition of the Harding administration to conservation had to be indicated less bluntly. Georgia's director, in opposing the use of the term "concentration camps" as the designation for the areas in which workers were interned during a 1934 textile strike, noted that the term now carried implications to the average reader "beyond mere statement of fact."[47]

Some censorship did occur in the guidebooks. As a government agency, the project inevitably had to undergo microscopic inspection and policy changes in copy. Yet the writers' project remained remarkably free of federal or state control in literary matters. A close examination of the guides shows that they suffered from none of the customary stigmata of government enterprise. Coverage of the most delicate topic in these volumes, that of industry-and-labor relations, presented fairly the strife in such towns as Bisbee, Ludlow, Gallup, Gastonia, and Harlan. The fact that flaws were not glossed over impressed critics both here and abroad. D. W. Brogan, writing later in the *London Spectator*, expressed his hope that the British government would follow WPA's example and "dare" to sponsor similarly critical and outspoken aesthetic appraisals of Birmingham and his native Glasgow. With one exception, as will be shown later, the treatment of the Negro in the guidebooks also reflected a relative freedom from censorship. Despite all the cuts and rephrasing to tone down copy, the Nez Percé war, the Tweed Ring, and the "Somebodies and Nobodies" of Atlantic City found their place in the publications of a government-sponsored agency. Nor did local project staff always meet the requests for changes made by the central office and guide sponsors.[48]

Most significantly, a study of the four principal cases involving the threat of censorship reveals that the guides in question finally saw print without evidence of a censor's heavy hand. Despite Vardis Fisher's

[47] Hopper to Alsberg, Mar. 7, 1939, Box 938, WPA; Colby to Alsberg, Mar. 13, 1939, Box 133, FWPN; Tupper to Alsberg, July 13, 1939, Box 1139, WPA.

[48] D. W. Brogan, "Inside America," *London Spectator* 167 (Nov. 28, 1941):507-8. For an analysis of guide copy relating to the Negro, see chap. 7 below.

resentment against the central office's alleged emasculation of copy, far more than the innocuous filled the pages of the Idaho Guide. For all of the commotion over the Massachusetts guidebook, that volume (even with a separate essay devoted to industry for the second edition) discussed Sacco-Vanzetti as well as the Lawrence and Boston police strikes. The changes which took place in Montana copy because of the Dies hearings did not result in chamber of commerce twaddle. The descriptions of Jersey City's grimy buildings, the power of Frank Hague, the Passaic and Closter strikes, and Roebling's company slum houses all remained in the New Jersey Guide, as did the various passages cited by the Dies Committee. And although the committee hearings led to some emendation in volumes that followed, "railroad and banking interests" did not replace the "Southern Pacific Railroad" and "San Francisco bankers," nor were Tom Mooney and Harry Bridges dropped from California's guidebook. [49]

The Washington office, while aware of the need to temper copy, made "a deliberate attempt to counteract the bias of ill-informed popular sentiment." In so doing, to be sure, it had no intention of granting complete license to the editorializing of even its best writers. But its hold on the reins was sufficiently loose to allow, for example, Vardis Fisher to explain the rural West's opposition to the "effete East," where "entrenched politics seemed to have supplanted the heritage of genuine popular sovereignty." [50]

Considering both their interests and the limitations of working as members of a federal agency, the personnel most responsible for the American Guide Series struck a successful balance between radical propaganda and chamber of commerce boosterism. The guides were the product of people who generally shared New Deal, pro-labor sympathies. As such, these volumes did draw attention to machine politics, injustices to both black and white sharecroppers, and various strikes and unionization developments throughout U.S. history. In the course of massive and comprehensive research for the guides, workers also uncovered forgotten episodes which, in the words of one reviewer, supplied "a terrible and yet engaging corrective to the success stories that dominate our literature." Yet a candid exposition of the country's

---

[49] June 30, 1938, report, Box 107, FWPN.

[50] H. C. Nicholas, "The Writer and the State," *Contemporary Review* 155 (Jan., 1939):89-94; Fisher to Alsberg, Dec. 9, 1937, Box 87, FWPN.

flaws, as readers noted, did not require that achievement be over-looked. Indeed, their constant search to find something to say about every community led FWPers, facing and absorbing all facts, to "stumble almost unwittingly into history."[51] Failure and success were recorded as found across the land, and the American Guide Series would reflect reality in its directions. In sum, the FWP's prime movers, without either debunking or embalming, presented fellow Americans with a judicious portrayal of a nation in its continuous process of discovery and realization.

It is this critical approach to the celebration of America which distinguishes the FWP from other manifestations of "cultural nationalism" at the close of the 1930s. At a time of dislocation and disorder, when "a swelling chorus" of affirmation and praise in American culture zealously reasserted traditional values and reinforced conformity, the project's guides (and subsequent auxiliary publications) did not simply represent a constricting search for unity in the collective national past.[52] A careful reading of the work produced by the FWP sharply challenges the view that the "innocuous and non-controversial" or a "hothouse Americanism" pervaded its writings. Rather, the balanced portrait that emerges from these pages is of a people—giving meaning to Roosevelt's "forgotten man"—and a land rediscovered in all of their diversity. Thus, the project's effort indicates innovation, both in approach and in final result, which students of the decade have yet to fully appreciate.[53]

[51] Robert Cantwell, "America and the Writers' Project," *New Republic* 98 (Apr. 26, 1939):323-25; Alfred Kazin, *On Native Grounds* (1952 ed.), p. 391.

[52] For the first incisive analysis of "cultural nationalism," see Kazin, *On Native Grounds*, chap. 15. Kazin's observations have subsequently been refined, notably by Warren Susman, "The Thirties," in Stanley Coben and Lorman Ratner, eds., *The Development of an American Culture*, pp. 179-218. Susman, in turn, influenced Richard H. Pells's *Radical Visions and American Dreams: Culture and Social Thought in the Depression Years*, pp. 310-29. Also see Alfred H. Jones, "The Search for a Usable American Past in the New Deal Era," *American Quarterly* 23 (Dec., 1971):710-24. None of these studies, however, notes the distinction made here between the FWP's publications and other intellectual and artistic currents of the Depression years. For an examination of auxiliary project publications, see chap. 7 below.

[53] "Innocuous and noncontroversial" manuscripts is the conclusion drawn by Taber, "Writers' Project in Pacific Northwest," pp. 175-76. This study, limited to three states in one region, also overemphasizes the difficulties of federal red tape and local pressures faced by the FWP during its existence. "Hothouse Americanism" was how a creative writer on the project dismissed the FWP's achievements years later, because the project was not formulated and administered by writers for true professionals to further the cause of the art of writing in America. See Harold Rosenberg, "Anyone Who Could Write English," *New Yorker* 49 (Jan. 20, 1973):99-102.

The FWP's achievement becomes all the more conspicuous when contrasted with what a contemporary observer called ''government interference with the arts on a heroic scale'' in Europe. At a time when the legendary Baedeker had to substitute ''Adolf Hitler Platz'' for every ''Kron-Prinzen Strasse'' in his guidebooks, the writers' project and its guides faced no massive suppression. This freedom reflected conditions in the country as a whole, as well as the appreciation of its citizens for the value of free inquiry. Notwithstanding the influence of William Randolph Hearst, Bernarr MacFadden publications, the American Liberty League, the DAR, and the American Legion, a Gallup poll of whether schools should teach the facts about Socialism, Communism, and Fascism, taken in May, 1936, mustered an affirmative vote of nearly two out of three responses.[54] In this setting, the project was generally able to function with minor hindrance even in controversial matters, and the American public would appreciate the candor, as well as the excellence, of the guides.

Jerre Mangione's informal reminiscence, *The Dream and The Deal*, hardly analyzes the project's output. My conclusions in this chapter, as well as those in chaps. 4 and 7, were argued further in ''The Federal Writers' Project and 'Cultural Nationalism': A Critical Celebration of America,'' a paper presented by the author at the convention of the Organization of American Historians, St. Louis, Missouri, Apr. 8, 1976.

[54] Overmyer, *Government and the Arts*, p. 244; Wecter, *Great Depression*, p. 196.

THE CENTRAL STAFF, AFTER DEALING with problems relating to the writing and censorship of the state guides, finally had to focus on the issue of publication. Work on a guide to Washington, D.C., provided its members with their first experience in this area. The choice of the nation's capital arose from the knowledge that the book would cover one of the most popular tourist areas, while all research and writing could be done in Washington. The financial officer for Federal #1 saw it as "an experiment to justify the program"; the D.C. guidebook would serve as a model for all future state guides. The volume reflected a politically astute selection as well, he noted, for it alone could have gained the support of Congress when funds became necessary for subsequent publication. By presidential letter on August 7, 1936, $14,000 became available for that purpose through the Emergency Appropriation Act.[1]

Theoretically, as in the case of the state offices, the D.C. Guide project was to consist primarily of "writers" on relief. Here, too, however, the writing and editing of the guide became the province of nonrelief personnel. While legmen brought in everything from quoits to quintuplets for a script on sports and recreation, editors had to prune copy, undertake new research, or answer "innumerable foolish questions" from scribes whose only qualification consisted of having learned how to write while serving as shipping clerks. The real work for the guide had to be shunted to men such as Benjamin Guinzberg, who had met Alsberg while covering the 1920 Riga Conference for the *Chicago Tribune* and had got on the editorial staff only after "knocking vainly at many doors" in Washington. Guinzberg, an assistant editor

[1] Alsberg to McMahon, Mar. 12, 1936, Box 28, FWPN; Ozer interview; Harris to Morris, May 12, 1937, Box 52, FWPN. The Government Printing Office, assigned to publish all material of a federal nature, estimated that about $9,000 would be necessary; an additional $2,000 was to cover distribution for reviewers in newspapers and periodicals. Harris to Morris, Apr. 26, 1937, Box 55, FWPN.

of the recently completed *Encyclopedia of the Social Sciences*, wrote about most of the government agencies; specialist editors like Roderick Seidenberg, Sterling Brown, and Katherine Kellock handled the essays and tours. Federal bureaus contributed valuable information— about the 1,800 varieties of flowering plants and ferns in the vicinity, for example.[2]

For nearly a year, twenty workers (ten writers among them) labored on the D.C. Guide, accumulating over 1,000,000 words of copy. Editors finally boiled these down to about 450,000 words, with an index listing over 5,000 items. Accounts of government buildings and institutions amounted to one-third of the book.[3]

For various reasons, the volume could not serve as a model for others. Because Washington, D.C., is unique, in that its main industry is government, no other guidebook would resemble this offering. Editors, moreover, had not blue-penciled enough copy, perhaps because of the novelty of the enterprise. Most important, because the D.C. Guide came under federal jurisdiction, the decision regarding its format fell entirely into the hands of the Government Printing Office (GPO), a fact which did not serve the interests of the project. The GPO, which did $18 million worth of government printing annually, specialized in putting out small pamphlets, primarily for congressional use. In addition, it did its work "more slowly than any good commercial shop even when charging 20 per cent extra for alleged speed," and the entire process cost as much as 40 per cent more than it would have through outside printers. Harris's wish that the layout department and other "progressive forces" be given a greater say in publication, to avoid the "standards of 1895," went unfulfilled; the GPO held the D.C. Guide for over five months.[4]

The central office suffered constant frustration over publication by a federal agency. GPO printing meant, among other things, one format, no color, uniform binding, unvarying body type, heavy ink, and coated

[2] Staples, Mar. 27, 1936, report, Box 50, FWPN; Benjamin Guinzberg interview, Aug. 26, 1968.

[3] Harris to Lee, Feb. 20, 1937, Box 55, FWPN.

[4] Cedric Larson, "Uncle Sam, Printer, Publisher and Literary Sponsor," *Colophon* 1 (1939):83-90; Harris to Alsberg, Jan. 7, 1937, Box 55, FWPN. A month's delay also occurred when the central office had to secure the approval of the calligraphic section of the Library of Congress to employ L'Enfant's "handkerchief plan" of the city for the guide's flyleaf. Kline interview.

paper. Cronyn's hope that the Baker and Taylor Company might handle national distribution failed to materialize when it became evident that the margin allowed distributors would be small. Because the Superintendent of Documents had no services of this kind, project officials thought that the volume would have to be distributed as U.S. Savings Bonds, through national post offices. No copies could be given on consignment, a procedure necessary for proper marketing and standard with commercial publishing houses.[5]

The physical appearance of the guide supplied the most dramatic proof of the inadequacies of such a publishing arrangement. With 1,160 pages of coated paper, the volume was almost three inches thick and weighed 5.5 pounds; it surpassed in thickness and weight such contemporary best sellers as *Anthony Adverse* (1,234 pages and only slightly less than three pounds) and *Gone With the Wind* (1,037 pages, 2.14 pounds). The project's public relations director clearly had not reckoned with the GPO when he had forecast a pocket-size book of 600 pages. Though the FWP could be praised for offering the public a fine volume at the low cost of 54 cents per pound, the *New York Times* noted that Samson himself would have hesitated to go sightseeing with such a burden. Alsberg himself confessed to Louisiana's director that this represented "a case of the mouse producing a mountain." FDR, presented with the first copy off the press, had his secretary digest it to one page for him and then reportedly said, "Now we'll use it for a door-stop."[6]

Despite the book's heft, critics heralded it as a possible forerunner of guides which, when taken together, might "enable us for the first time to hold the mirror up to all America." A cross-section of the city that included the marbles of the Capitol and disease-infected alley tene-

[5] Cronyn to Corrigan, n.d., Box 51, FWPN; Harris to Woodward, Feb. 5, 1937, Box 55, FWPN.

[6] Greene to Markel, Nov. 17, 1936, Box 12, FWPN; Alsberg to Saxon, May 7, 1937, Box 95, FWPN; Cronin interview. The suggestion, from Mordecai Ezekiel of the Agriculture Department, that certain parts be reprinted for tourists was later heeded for the chapters on the White House, the Capitol, and the Negro, which the central office sent free of charge, upon request, to libraries, schools, the DAR, and visiting congressional constituents. In 1939 the central office brought out an updated version of the section on government agencies as *Our Federal Government and How It Functions*. To satisfy the tourist's yen for pictures and simple text, art editors Seidenberg and Kline spent a few months that same year putting together an album entitled *Our Washington*. This offshoot of the first D.C. Guide achieved so much popularity that it went out of print in a year. Ezekiel to Gill, May 3, 1937, Box 50, FWPN; Kline interview.

ments nearby served as clear evidence that Uncle Sam as patron had avoided Baedeker's "highly sensitive neutrality." The architecture essay, with its equal lambasting of the Federal Triangle ("Hoover's Folly") and the New Deal Interior Building, received singular praise. All in all, the huge volume made a tremendous impression in Washington official circles. "I praise it highly," Harold Ickes wrote Hopkins; Jake Baker thought that it "very effectively" accomplished the purpose of the American Guide Series. Senators had to be told regularly that free supplies were limited.[7]

With the central office "appalled at the mess" involved in GPO regulations, Katherine Kellock, knowing that "something had to be done in a hurry," suggested that route guides be rushed through for publication. She first concentrated on the Intracoastal Waterway (a route she knew well), wrote the states for material, and did most of the final editing for that volume. The central office drew funds for its publication from the $80,000 which had been allotted for the original five regional guide volumes mentioned in the presidential letter of August 29, 1935. The water routes in the book, intended chiefly for the small-boat owners who traveled between Norfolk and Key West, were inspected with reference to the *Atlantic Coast Pilot* and with craft freely supplied by the U.S. Light House Service and local yachtsmen. Authorities lauded the book's comprehensiveness and picturesque charm, and they advised that it be put in the locker or knapsack of every voyager expecting to visit the area.[8]

The experience gained in publishing these two guides convinced the Coordinating Project Office that an alternative procedure would be far preferable. The GPO monopoly had to be replaced by a cheaper and faster method, one that would also suit the Washington office's artistic point of view and supply publicity for future sales. As the first of the state and local guides stood ready for print, and administration critics clamored for results, the situation called for a definite ruling about publication.

[7] *New York Times*, Jan. 10, 1937, VII, p. 8; *Newark Evening News*, July 6, 1937; Ickes to Hopkins, Apr. 28, 1937, and Baker to Harris, May 6, 1937, Box 50, FWPN. The first edition of 5,000 had cost about $12,500. An additional 8,000 copies were then offered for general sale (at $3.00), with profits going to the U.S. Treasury. Of the initial printing, some one thousand copies went gratis to congressmen, WPA units, and miscellaneous publicity outlets. Morris to Woodward, Apr. 8, 1937, Box 1052, WPA.

[8] Kellock interview, Aug. 18, 1968; Harris to Morris, May 12, 1937, Box 52, FWPN; *Panama City* (Fla.) *Pilot*, July 15, 1937.

II

Publication by private firms provided the best answer. The awarding of contracts to university presses presented one alternative. President Robert Hutchins of the University of Chicago, for example, was interested in both the Chicago and Illinois guides. But private concerns offered better opportunities from the standpoint of cost, speed, and sales. Houghton Mifflin and Viking Press wanted to undertake production, and Simon and Schuster seemed ''very anxious to become more or less the official publisher'' for the project. Unlike the GPO, these established houses could also pay royalties, an especially important factor when critics of the project were calling for cuts in federal costs. They could also offer a standard 40 per cent reduction to private dealers, compared to the GPO's 25 per cent discount. The issue of copyright had to be considered as well; the security of copyright was not available for federal publications. The government, moreover, could not publish books on a commercial scale, nor did the project have the opportunity to offer subsidies or guarantees to interested but wary private firms as an inducement to enter a relatively uncharted field.[9]

The unique concept of ''sponsorship,'' arrived at by the WPA Legal Section and the Procedures Division toward the close of 1936, permitted the FWP to enter the world of private industry. In a 1934 letter to Baker, Hugh Harlan, now supervisor of the Los Angeles project, had suggested that business and semipublic organizations supply funds to publish the research findings of a proposed Writers' Bureau. The first legal ruling on project publications allowed for a subdivision of the government or a tax-supported institution (such as a university or library) to obtain its manuscripts, copyright them, and make arrangements for publication on a nonprofit basis. If necessary, the sponsor would arrange to guarantee the costs of production as well; all receipts could be used to make revisions or finance further activities of the project, with any money left over to be returned eventually to the U.S. Treasury.[10]

Sponsors could not readily be obtained for the project's guidebooks, especially since financial guarantees (almost always a requirement)

[9] Harris to Alsberg, Mar. 31, 1937, Box 50, FWPN; McDonald, ''Federal Relief,'' pp. 409-10.

[10] McDonald, ''Federal Relief,'' pp. 728-29; Cronyn to Fisher, May 21, 1936, Box 11, FWPN.

became inextricably linked with state politics. The editor of the *Conservationist* had to withdraw his guarantee of $3,000 worth of Minnesota Guide copies, since, with a new governor in office, he did not want to jeopardize his position on the state's Conservation Committee. Due to the indifference of its legislative sponsor, the Alabama Guide bill failed to pass in the June, 1937, session. Severe cuts in Georgia's legislative funds forced the issue to be temporarily dropped there. When the chairman of the statewide Board of County Commissioners met defeat in his bid for renomination, he promptly lost his interest in the North Carolina Guide.[11]

Directors of local bodies faced similar considerations. Salt Lake City's Chamber of Commerce refused to sponsor the guide to Utah on the ground that its funds had to cover the promotion of its livestock interests and other concerns. State historical societies were "not anxious to buy a pig in a poke," preferring to wait until final copy came in.[12]

Sponsorship became possible in a number of forms once commercial publishers and sponsors arrived at certain understandings. Private firms agreed that, in order to issue books as large as the state guides at a reasonable price, their initial editions had to be large enough to bring down the cost of material and labor. Thus, the first editions of the New England guides consisted of 10,000 copies. If a publishing house knew that it could be assured of an initial sale of 2,000 copies or more, it usually assumed responsibility for the rest of the edition. Fortunately, after some hesitation and false expectation, a good many sponsors consented to purchase 2,000 copies each.[13]

A number of factors led sponsors to assume this gamble. Sometimes, energetic and respected project directors like Minnesota's Mabel Ulrich and Ohio's Harlan Hatcher produced the desired result. The governor

[11] Mangione to Alsberg, June 14, 1937, Box 100, FWPN; Bjorkman to Alsberg, Nov. 15, 1938, Box 36, FWPN.

[12] Backman to Howe, Jan. 26, 1937, Box 127, FWPN; DuVon to Alsberg, Aug. 15, 1936, Box 90, FWPN.

[13] Since most guides sold for $2.50–$3.00, this amounted to an outlay of $2,000–$4,000 at the 40 per cent regular bookdealer's discount; the sponsor then regained his money by selling the volumes through channels other than bookstores. This was the most popular arrangement, although some sponsors preferred to guarantee the publisher that copies would be purchased (at the wholesale price) after eight months, if a loss were sustained, for an amount up to about $2,500. Alsberg to Chandler, July 29, 1937, Box 94, FWPN; Alsberg to Frederick, n.d., Box 88, FWPN.

of Illinois lost his skepticism after he and consultant Paul Angle had read copy for a half-hour. Others accepted financial responsibility purely on their assumption about the Guide's tourist value and its consequent sales and possible profit. By encouraging such assumptions, Vardis Fisher achieved a considerable triumph in obtaining the sponsorship of Idaho's secretary of state. State governors, boards of education, historical societies, and advertising and development commissions all served as sponsors, quite an achievement for the project during that period of political mud-slinging against WPA. The Milwaukee Guide received a record subsidy (only matched by the state volume) of $7,500. By 1939, sponsors had guaranteed costs to the amount of $400,000 for project volumes already published; an additional $600,000 had been assured to cover publications under way or contracted for. While it is true that sponsorship had its disadvantages, particularly in the editorial sphere, this support far outweighed the inconveniences.[14]

Sponsorship, besides being a commitment of duly constituted state or local agencies, was also assumed by ad hoc groups formed solely to facilitate publication. They had been created under the initiative of Alsberg and the state directors to gain flexibility while complying with WPA regulations. The first of these organizations was in the New York City project, which "needed prestige desperately." Alsberg and others on the New York project had originally contemplated a proposal to offset the specter of controversy surrounding that local unit; the president of the Carnegie Corporation suggested that either Alvin Johnson or Henry Seidel Canby head a sponsoring committee. Upon the advice of attorney Morris Ernst and columnist Franklin P. Adams, a dummy corporation called the Guilds' Committee for Federal Writers' Publications, Inc. was established. Primarily, the committee existed to contract for the New York City Guide, a volume which the Authors' League had refused to sponsor because of its objections to WPA relief regulations as they affected the project.[15]

The Guilds' Committee, despite some weaknesses, served the FWP well. According to Ernst, its directors ("FPA," Lewis Gannett, Margaret Marshall, Bruce Bliven, and Travis Hoke) did not want to see

[14] *Chicago Tribune*, July 1, 1940; Lyons to Alsberg, May 20, 1937, Box 49, FWPN; Jan. 5, 1939, report, Box 1, LC FWP. For more on sponsors and editorial review, see chap. 4 above.

[15] Thompson interview; Keppel to Alsberg, Oct. 29, 1936, Box 31, FWPN; chap. 3 above.

"such fine material" gather dust on the shelves of the Library of Congress. Bliven admitted, at the time, that the corporation's precise function seemed nebulous even in his mind, and he thought the committee would promptly dissolve with the signing of the New York City Guide contract. Years later, Bliven aptly termed the ad hoc group a "window-dressing operation." It should also be noted that Ernst (his services given free of charge) handled a number of contracts, and that "FPA" wrote some prefaces to project books. The guilds' example led to the formation of the Poor Richard's Associates (Massachusetts), the New Jersey Associates, and the Bret Harte Associates (California).[16]

Inherent in this type of sponsorship was the danger that any royalties accruing to sponsoring agencies could remain in their hands. This possibility resulted from the decision, included in the new Federal #1 operating procedure for 1938, to make funds easily available for further project publications. Unfortunately, it led to the creation of some ad hoc organizations in which state and project executives exercised personal financial interest and control. The director of a state corporation known as Nevada Unlimited sought sponsorship so that the project could be "the tail to his kite." One project supervisor, who was working on the Tampa Guide, succeeded in setting up his own West Coast Progress Association for a time.[17]

The most flagrant case of divided interest occurred in the William Penn Association, which actually published a number of project volumes. Its founder, the director of Pennsylvania's project, had been recognized in the FWP's early months by one of the Washington staff as "not a very good editor, but a very able businessman and very ambitious." Paul French apparently believed that the association would become a big publishing venture to which he could turn if the project closed down. Alsberg did order French to resign from the association in September, 1937, but the director continued to sign checks as its president, and he published the Philadelphia Guide without even going through the requirement of open bidding. These facts were brought to the notice of Postmaster-General James Farley—along with charges from a project employee that, one, the association had bought a local paper with the idea that it would afford employment if the project closed and, two, workers were required to buy shares in the group. Farley

[16] *New York Sun*, Nov. 25, 1936; Bruce Bliven to author, June 27, 1967.

[17] Williamson to Alsberg, Nov. 10, 1937, Box 106, FWPN; Harris to Morris, Nov. 4, 1937, Box 1054, WPA.

immediately relayed this information to Alsberg's superior. Another project worker pointed out that as late as March, 1939, no accounting of the considerable profits accruing to the association had been given.[18]

An investigation by the WPA Finance Division revealed considerable truth behind these accusations. Among other irregularities, travel vouchers of nine employees had been padded, and one worker had made two trips on behalf of the association—all with French's knowledge. This supplemented the central office's negative estimate of his directorship. Although the Pennsylvania director insisted on obtaining the facts behind his eventual dismissal in August, 1939, he did not respond to WPA's offer to present his case to the Finance Division.[19]

This informal method of accounting, "confusing and inadequate" in the case of the Guilds' Committee, led the Treasury Department's Julius Davidson to suggest at a later date that all monies be turned over to WPA for the Special Deposit Accounts section of the Treasury's Disbursing Office. Though arguing that "there is no evidence of financial irregularity or any reason to suspect it," the former financial officer for Federal #1 quickly added that, on the other hand, "positive assurance of financial responsibility, which the Federal Government in its fiscal relations rationally requires," was decidedly absent. It is noteworthy that his overall figures, showing that royalties to sponsors remained relatively insignificant, did not include the Pennsylvania project and the William Penn Association. Toward the end of June, 1939, the project began an attempt to provide for direct negotiations with private firms, with the consent of the General Accounting Office and the GPO. The close of Federal #1 in July of that year aborted this move, however. From then on, publication officially rested in the hands of the new sponsors, now exclusively agencies of their respective state governments.[20]

III

Eager to publish the first state guidebook and not having been told by the Washington office, as late as May, 1936, how to release federal

[18] Harris to Alsberg, Mar. 31, 1937, Box 50, FWPN; Farley to Williams, Mar. 11, 1938, Box 463, WPA.

[19] Farley to Williams, Mar. 11, 1938, Box 463, WPA; Buffum to Alsberg, June 15, 1939, Box 2446, WPA; Kerr to Boland, Sept. 11, 1939, Box 2447, WPA.

[20] McDonald, "Federal Relief," pp. 411-12.

copy to a private publisher, Vardis Fisher persuaded a local firm to undertake publication of the Idaho Guide. His singular success in doing so can be ascribed to the fact that the managing director of Caxton Printers was a friend; neither expected to profit on this first venture. Fisher's advanced plans caught Cronyn and Alsberg completely by surprise. He projected an initial library edition (using finer materials to give the guide "dignity and beauty"), to be followed by a cheaper tourist edition sponsored by chambers of commerce, with changes in format and material to be decided later. In his haste to publish, he had type set which, when subsequently reviewed by Cronyn and others, had to be redone entirely at considerable expense to the publisher. Deletions and countless corrections "completely demoralized" the firm's publishing schedule.[21]

"The bureaucratic bastards in Washington," Fisher reminisced years later, tried to stop publication of the guide. Alsberg had told him repeatedly that for Idaho to be the first state volume would be "a dreadful embarrassment." When the national director failed to convince the salty individualist that the guide to the capital and then some of the larger states should come first ("petty jealousies be damned," Fisher retorted during one telephone conversation), Alsberg sent Cronyn out with instructions to delay Fisher's book in any way possible. Knowing of the associate director's appreciation for whiskey, Fisher and his publisher served their guest one drink after another while imbibing whiskey-colored water themselves. Unaware of this stratagem but determined to follow Alsberg's directive, a woozy Cronyn began throwing photographs of Idaho potatoes about the room with the comment: "There will be no hyperboles in these guides. Idaho has boasted so much of its potatoes that Idaho potatoes have become, to put it simply, a frightful bore." Finally, to prevent Caxton's total withdrawal and Fisher's resignation and to insure that the volume would greet congressmen at the opening of the seventy-fifth session, all parties agreed to a number of compromises. The guide was printed in January, 1937, a few weeks before its D.C. counterpart.[22]

[21] Fisher to Lockridge, Feb. 8, 1937, and Fisher to Cronyn, May 6 and Nov. 24, 1936, Box 11, FWPN; chap. 4 above. Later, in gratitude, Fisher dedicated his Pulitzer Prize–winning *Children of God* to Caxton's managing director.

[22] Fisher to author, June 20, 1967, and May 19, 1968; Taber, "Writers' Project in Pacific Northwest," p. 141; Fisher, *Orphans in Gethsemane*, pp. 749-55; Fisher to Cronyn, Nov. 24, 1936, Box 11, FWPN.

Critics welcomed this first state guide with lavish praise. The *Saturday Review of Literature* summed up the general view: "In the main, it succeeds overwhelmingly, far better than we had any right to ask for or reason to expect." Fisher's unmistakable, vigorous style could be discerned in the guide's account of the exploitation of Indians and fur-bearing animals, as well as in its fine essays on flora and other topics. Thus the guide's very first lines about the popular image of the last frontier and its "shoddy sawdust counterfeits":

> The lusty and profane extremes of it still live nebulously in the gaudy imbecilities of newsstand pulp magazines and in cheap novels, wherein to appease the hunger of human beings for drama and spectacles, heroines distressingly invulnerable are fought over by villains and heroes and restored to their rich properties of mine or cattle ranch; and the villain if left unslain, passes out of the story sulking darkly; and the hero, without crackling a smile, stands up with the heroine clinging to his breast and addresses the reader with platitudes that would slay any ordinary man.

Even a New Deal opponent went so far as to say that, if the Eastern states could do as well, "it will be admitted that this WPA project has much to commend it." Hopkins's gift of a copy "delighted" the President. In its first few months, sales of the guide reached 1,800 copies.[23]

Neither the central office nor Fisher felt entirely satisfied with the volume, however. The Coordinating Project Office had made concessions to raise the standard price to $3 for a heavy 6″ × 9″ book (rather than the preferred 5¼″ × 8″). Tour treatment and particularly indexing suffered in the rush to publish. On the other hand, Caxton's tight finances prevented advertising, and led to the mistaken use of $600 worth of WPA franking privileges which only a private settlement between the central office and Postmaster-General Farley corrected.[24]

The advertising and distribution programs of local printers proved

[23] *Saturday Review of Literature* 15 (Feb. 27, 1937):8; *Idaho: A Guide in Word and Pictures* (Caldwell, Idaho, 1937), p. 17; *Baltimore Sun*, Feb. 28, 1937, III, p. 2; Hopkins to LeHand, Jan. 18, 1937, WPA file, Box 12, OF-444C, FDR papers, FDRL.

[24] McDowell to Davidson, June 27, 1937, Box 11, FWPN. In addition, a raise of $45 per month had to be given Fisher (which he quietly transferred to Caxton) to cover the 150 copies sent to consultants and other state directors. This became necessary because the General Accounting Office had ruled that no authority existed to "dispose of Government property by gift." Fisher to Alsberg, Jan. 31, 1938, Box 11, FWPN.

equally troublesome in the Dakotas. Their directors, Lisle Reese and Ethel Schlesinger, somehow convinced the state legislatures, plagued though they were with local problems of drought and grasshoppers, to advance $3,500 and $2,500 for this end. Schlesinger had actually braved one of North Dakota's worst snowstorms in a small plane equipped with skis to secure funds from the state's finance committee, but the governor withheld approval until the last day of the session just to needle this long-time acquaintance for being a Democrat. The victory of both directors (the two youngest on the project) rested, however, on the condition that printers in their states be given the contract. As a result, these two books hardly showed the professionalism that marked the other guides. South Dakota's volumes had to be sewn and glued one at a time. A second edition and national distribution became an impossibility, however, after North Dakota's printing house broke up its type (no plates had been made); South Dakota's Guide Commission refused to sell unbound sheets for fear of competition. (A similar difficulty occurred on St. Patrick's Day, 1937, when a fire destroyed the plates for the Idaho Guide, thus preventing a tourist edition.)[25]

Fortunately, larger firms undertook publication of the other state guidebooks, thereby insuring better typography, publicity, royalties, and expanded sales. Realizing that the project's involvement with local printing had proved a "rather unfortunate" experience, Alsberg decided to follow the advice of both a D.C. staff member and the editor of *Publishers Weekly* and open the volumes to bidding. Letters were sent to some fifty publishers, and the publication process received additional care from Jerre Mangione, who had been appointed coordinating editor to establish contacts with various houses, draw up contracts, and insure their fulfillment. Ruth Crawford of the New York City project served as the liaison between the central office and its publishers (particularly Viking and Random House), corrected galleys, and supervised all matters involving photography.[26]

Houghton Mifflin became the first firm to make a successful multivolume bid. It agreed to publish the six New England guides without

[25] Reese to Alsberg, June 16, 1938, Box 1296, WPA; Schlesinger to Alsberg, Oct. 26, 1938, Box 115, FWPN; Mangione, *Dream and Deal*, p. 232. These various dangers had actually been foreseen by Jonathan Daniels (among others), when he suggested that Congress create a permanent commission to hold the publishing rights to the guides and see to their publication and distribution. Daniels to Alsberg, Oct. 15, 1936, Box 36, FWPN.

[26] Alsberg to Woodward, Nov. 22, 1937, Box 56, FWPN.

royalties on the first 10,000 copies of each; the sponsor was to receive a 10 per cent royalty on the retail price beyond the first edition. For the prized guides of the Mid-Atlantic states, Washington finally effected a compromise between Random House and Viking Press. The former took New York City (a 10 per cent royalty per copy for the first 10,000 and 10 per cent beyond that edition, with a rare $500 advance), and the latter got the New Jersey, New York State, Pennsylvania, Delaware, Maryland, and West Virginia guides. Sparsely populated areas, with few bookstores and fewer readers, offered a special challenge. In a record contract, the volumes for Tennessee, Arkansas, Wyoming, Montana, Kansas, Nebraska, Mississippi, Iowa, and Minnesota went to Viking, the only publisher to put in a bid for all. Oxford University Press secured many Southern volumes, with offers of 10 per cent royalty after 5,000 copies and 12½ per cent after 20,000.[27]

The largest number of guides eventually went to a fledgling company, Hastings House of New York. Walter Frese, its director, had begun his interest in "telling the world about America" in early 1936 with Samuel Chamberlain's *A Small House in the Sun*. He managed to get numerous contracts for the guides on the basis of the ability of his outfit (unlike the larger firms) to make quick decisions and as a result of Hastings's pioneering use of sheet-fed gravure for illustrations. He, too, was obliged to take "loss leaders"—such as a local guide to the Mission of San Xavier in order to get the Arizona volume.[28]

Publishers took the state guides for both prestige and profit. Random House put in a massive bid for the guides, even writing the President to intercede with Alsberg in its favor. Macmillan, which had originally been alarmed that the writers' project sought to kill private publishing, took the biggest chance of all on the Alaska Guide, with a 10 per cent royalty on the second 10,000 copies. Such firms realized that only the federal government, through this relief project, had the resources to cull the vast information necessary for these books, and that its activities were also capable of stimulating a great deal of business.[29]

Despite this interest, not all went as smoothly as Washington wished.

[27] Alsberg to Manuel, Mar. 29, 1939, Box 97, FWPN; Alsberg to DuVon, July 16, 1938, Box 90, FWPN; Alsberg to Richardson, Feb. 8, 1939, Box 128, FWPN.

[28] Walter Frese interview, Sept. 13, 1967. The idea of having the guides published by national companies seems to have first been suggested by Louisiana's Lyle Saxon. See Clayton, "Writers' Project in Louisiana," pp. 168-70.

[29] Cerf to Roosevelt, Aug. 4, 1937, WPA file, Box 14, OF-444C, FDR papers, FDRL; Putnam to Alsberg, Jan. 30, 1939, Box 133, FWPN.

Viking withdrew from a combined contract for the Arkansas–Texas–New Mexico guides on the ground that delivery dates had not been met. Alsberg believed, however, that the company had taken advantage of a technicality to avoid a marketing loss in that part of the country. No happy "days of grace" existed in this sphere of work. The unexpected publication program for the New England state guides led Houghton Mifflin and regional editor-in-chief Joseph Gaer to demand that all but essential Washington changes be cut to meet production deadlines. Other directors, on the other hand, raised complaints against publishers who chose to rearrange tours and tamper with facts or format. Houghton Mifflin procrastinated four months with the Vermont Guide, in State Director Dana Doten's opinion, because of its desire to bring out all the New England volumes together and "bunch" publicity and advertising; the rush of galley schedules brought inevitable errors.[30]

Considering the risk involved in this new venture, the efforts of publishers on behalf of the state guides are noteworthy. They did demand and receive the right to raise guide prices to meet rising costs. At the same time, to satisfy sponsors not legally empowered or willing to assume the financial responsibility in a standard libel clause, firms like Viking and Oxford consented to amend the clause so that any court costs could be charged against royalties. Many attempted to enhance the project's work by proposing names for vacancies in executive positions and by writing congressmen in protest against cuts on FWP rolls. Quincy Howe of Simon and Schuster warned Senator Robert Wagner that relief slashes in December, 1937, would "squander our most precious national asset: trained intelligence." At the same time, Harold Guinzburg of Viking Press informed the President of the "seriousness, ability and devotion" of the project's workers. Having taken the gamble to publish, these commercial houses worked incessantly to transform guide manuscripts into galleys and galleys into books.[31]

IV

The New England guides, first to be completed as a regional unit, received almost unqualified praise. The reviews of the Massachusetts

[30] Alsberg to McKown, Mar. 24, 1939, Box 850, WPA; Doten to Alsberg, Sept. 2, 1937, Box 46, FWPN. Such pressure once resulted in Katherine Kellock's redoing the entire index for the California Guide at Alsberg's request in two days. "It was one of the craziest things I ever did in my life," she recalled years later. Kellock interview, June 23, 1968.

[31] Howe to Wagner, Dec. 17, 1937, and Guinzburg to Roosevelt, Dec. 18, 1937, Box 461, WPA.

volume, aside from the issue of propaganda, set the tone for those of its counterparts. One critic praised the photographs and the art-architecture essays of the other volumes highly, but regretted that the flora and fauna essays were perfunctory and that the single maps left much to be desired when compared with Baedeker's for Paris and London. The *Bridgeport Herald* began with a few slurs and wisecracks against "Roosevelt's Rough Writers," but ended by bestowing considerable tribute on the Connecticut Guide. Dorothy Canfield Fisher sent copies of the Vermont Guide to friends in Europe.[32]

Some of the offerings of the mid-Atlantic states competed strongly for the most favorable reviews. *New York Panorama*, the first volume of the New York City Guide, received special plaudits. The reviewer for the *New York Times* expressed his wonder that the color, squalor, and vitality of the city could have been so well captured in one volume. If this guide represented a sample of government boondoggling, the *Nashville Tennessean* declared, "we could use a great deal more of it." The New Jersey Guide was considered a "genuinely valuable book," and the American Institute of Graphic Arts chose Delaware's guidebook as one of the fifty books of the year.[33]

Guides to the lesser-known states proved a very pleasant surprise. Readers would no longer think of Nebraska as only background material for the novels of Willa Cather, Harry Hansen observed. The New Mexico Guide was "a first-rate job," in Bruce Catton's judgment, and the new guidebook to Iowa, said *Wallace's Farmer*, would help enlighten the local citizenry on their state's interest and diversity.[34]

Objections to the guides did occur. The DAR protested that Vermont's book did not treat the Green Mountain Boys with sufficient respect. Margaret Marshall took issue with the statement in the New York City Guide that since the *Nation* had come under her aegis the literary section had not been consistently liberal, and she asked that her name be dropped from the sponsoring Guilds' Committee.[35]

But such objections resembled voices in the wind. Reviewers never

[32] Page 105 above; *New York Herald Tribune*, Apr. 24, 1938; Derby to Alsberg, May 8, 1939, Box 6, FWPN; Fisher to Doten, Oct. 19, 1937, Box 2670, WPA.

[33] *New York Times*, Sept. 14, 1938; *Nashville Tennessean*, Oct. 2, 1938; *New York Times*, July 5, 1939.

[34] *New York Herald Tribune*, June 30, 1939; *Albuquerque Tribune*, Sept. 14, 1938; *Wallace's Farmer and Homestead*, Oct. 22, 1938.

[35] *New York World Telegram*, Nov. 4, 1937; Marshall to Shaw, Sept. 21, 1938, Box 38, FWPN.

tired of speaking about the high quality of the guides, and Harry Hansen even argued that they "contain more thrills to the page than any historical novel of the hour." Their thoroughness and "tang of the countryside" led the *New Republic*, the *Nation, Time*, and the *New Yorker* to include the first volumes of the American Guide Series among the best books of 1938. The guidebooks "make it hard to stay home," concluded the *Baltimore Sun*.[36]

The rediscovery of America, a note running through much of the literature of the late thirties, provided most critics with their prevalent theme in reviewing these volumes. Lewis Mumford termed the conception and execution of the state guides a great patriotic effort. "Centuries after Columbus' famous voyage," proclaimed the *St. Louis Post-Dispatch*, the country was being found anew. Foreign correspondents praised the critical studies as reflecting "the self-determination to restore America to herself." The *Journal of the National Education Association*, noting the project's concern with natural history and folklore that otherwise might have disappeared or remained unexplored, termed the guidebooks "a genuine folk movement." Van Wyck Brooks wrote Alsberg that every college in the country should give him a Ph.D. for his success in carrying out an "impossibly difficult job" with "astonishing" skill, taste, and judgment.[37]

While all the guides received the praise of reviewers, the best volumes came from those states which were blessed with an abundance of professional talent. Deerfield, "a beautiful ghost," tells readers of its guide: "I dared to be beautiful, even in the shadow of the wilderness," but also, "and the wilderness haunts me, the ghosts of a slain race are in my doorways and clapboards, like a kind of death." By contrast, at Coney Island, "riders are whirled, jolted, battered, tossed upside down by the Cyclone, the Thunderbolt, the Mile Sky Chaser, the Loop-o-Plane, the Whip, the Flying Turns, the Dodge, Speedway, the Chute-the-Chutes, and the Comet. Above the cacophony of spielers, cries, and the shrieks and laughter, carrousel organs pound out last year's tunes, and roller coasters slam down their terrific inclines. In

---

[36] *New York World Telegram*, May 9, 1938; *Baltimore Sun*, Apr. 3, 1938.

[37] Lewis Mumford, "Writers' Project," *New Republic* 92 (Oct. 20, 1937):306-7; *St. Louis Post-Dispatch*, Sept. 8, 1938; H. G. Nicholas, "The Writer and the State: The American Guide," *Contemporary Review* 155 (Jan., 1939):89-94; *Journal of the National Education Association* 27 (May, 1938):140-41; Brooks to Alsberg, Sept. 8, 1938, Box 460, WPA. For the relationship of this theme to the literature of the 1930s, see chap. 5 and conclusion.

dance halls and honky-tonks, dancers romp and shuffle to the endless blare of jazz bands.'' As for Chicago, ''. . . in and around the Loop, rising high about great museums housed in vast marble piles, looms a serrated mass of towers, spires, shafts, and huge cubes, a jagged mountain range of brick, stone, steel, concrete, and glass. To the south, beyond the busy docks along the Calumet River, are great black mills, factories and furnaces, filled with the roar and rumble of machinery, their gaunt stacks belching black clouds by day, red flames by night.''[38]

States with fewer professionals produced competent but duller books. The guide to the Cornhusker State gave superficial and fleeting treatment to the impact of slavery upon Nebraska's antebellum history, William Jennings Bryan's importance in the 1890s, and Tom Dennison's long reign as political boss of Omaha. Kansas's offering could have done better by such colorful Populist orators as Mary Elizabeth Lease and Jerry ''Sockless'' Simpson. Occasionally, though, as when viewing residential Minneapolis by plane, the reader got a fresh perspective: ''. . . a forest dotted with houses, threaded with the blue of lakes that loop the town from the Mississippi to the Minnesota River like a chain of beads each in a green velvet setting, and crossed by dozens of straight white lines which lead with scarcely a curve or angle into the city's business heart.'' From the ground, Butte lay ''against a bare southward sloping hillside, like a vast page of disorderly manuscript, its uneven paragraphs of buildings punctuated with enormous yellow and gray copper ore dumps and with the gallows frames that mark mine shafts.'' Most of the lesser volumes lacked such spirited prose, and yet this shortcoming did not invalidate their coverage of forgotten boosters, courageous pioneer women, Kansas ''Exodusters,'' and the exploits of Febold Feboldson and of Paul Bunyan's blue ox, Babe. They did not overlook the government's sordid treatment of the Cherokee and the Sac and Fox, and they gave various nationalities due recognition for their contributions to the country's settlement.[39] In

[38] *Massachusetts, a Guide to Its Places and People* (Boston, 1937), p. 233; *New York City Guide* (New York, 1939), pp. 473-74; *Illinois, a Descriptive and Historical Guide* (Chicago, 1939), pp. 189, 302. Superior results were also achieved in the Idaho and Alaska guides, written mainly by Vardis Fisher and Merle Colby, respectively.

[39] *Nebraska, a Guide to the Cornhusker State* (New York, 1939); *Kansas, a Guide to the Sunflower State* (New York, 1939); *Minnesota, a State Guide* (New York, 1938), p. 167; *Montana* (New York, 1939), p. 136; *A Guide to South Dakota* (Prairie, S.D., 1938), pp. 80-82; *Tennessee, a Guide to the State* (New York, 1939), pp. 40-42.

so doing, these guidebooks, together with the best of the series, could claim a significant share in rediscovery and restoration.

Publicity helped bring the guides' importance to millions of Americans. H. R. Greene, previously promotion manager for the *New York Mirror* and the *New York Times*, joined the central staff as coordinating editor in charge of public relations. He began his task by issuing an article, "Have You Discovered America?," to reveal the country's unfamiliar ethnic colonies and to tell of the project's plans. "See America First" received emphasis in conjunction with a currently popular theme, and railroads were contacted for further promotion. With a keen eye for public attention, Washington began advising projects to prepare material for civic festivals and similar gatherings.[40]

"Briefs," news items based on material discovered in the course of research for the guides, went out as fillers to newspapers. They boasted of prize discoveries: the long-lost address delivered by President Lincoln the night after his reelection, the legal paper filed in the Dred Scott case, Robert Morris's will. Workers had come across a variety of other interesting finds, and some, such as the story of Captain John Smith's selling a white boy into bondage, created a stir. ("Handouts" on the facts that Mark Twain opened his wife's letters and Martha Washington used castor oil also received much publicity.)[41]

The project used many other outlets to disperse information and thereby gain recognition and tribute. State directors made radio broadcasts over such stations as WXWJ (Michigan), WRNL (Virginia), KFBK (California), and KGIR (Montana). They also arranged exhibits at the New York Public Library, the Smithsonian Institution, the *New York Times* National Book Fair, public schools, national boat shows, and the 1938 Golden Gate International Exposition. Paramount News made a reel of the project's work. Individuals offered suggestions to widen the public's interest. Some of these ideas included picture post cards with guide material, serialization by *Cosmopolitan* of volumes not yet published, and the giving away of state guides to buyers of extra

[40] Special articles file, Box 74, FWPN.

[41] *New York Times*, Feb. 12, 1936; *Denver Post*, July 1, 1936; Harris to Byrd, Feb. 28, 1936, Box 47, FWPN; The Massachusetts Guide's attributing "Mary Had a Little Lamb" to Sarah Joseph Hale (a leading nineteenth-century feminist) proved somewhat embarrassing to Henry Ford: he had transported the alleged schoolhouse which had figured in the nursery rhyme from Sudbury, Massachusetts, to his Greenfield Village on the basis of a conflicting claim of authorship by Mary Sawyer. *New York Times*, Nov. 27, 1936.

gasoline. One editor even suggested issuing jigsaw puzzles of the individual states and regions.[42]

The sales of the first state guides reflected the laudatory reviews and the central office's all-out publicity effort. At a time when any publishing house considered itself fortunate to market the 2,500-3,500 copies which paid the cost of printing and distributing such volumes, most guidebooks fulfilled this aspiration and satisfied concerned sponsors. The Vermont book sold 2,000 copies in its first week of publication; by 1940, it had passed 6,000 and its Maine counterpart had topped 7,000 sales. *New York Panorama* sold 3,279 copies in three months. In a period when publishers called a sale of 7,500 copies a pronounced success, the much-debated Massachusetts book escaped the bonfires of zealous patriots and went into a second edition beyond an initial printing of 10,000.[43]

The FWP represented one of the few relief projects whose final product received practically unanimous praise. Arch critics of the New Deal like the *New York Herald Tribune* and the *Baltimore Sun* blasted away at WPA on page one and heaped laurels on this segment of Federal #1 in the book review section. Regarded by one reviewer as "the biggest, fastest, most original research job in the history of the world," the state guides merited such recognition because they helped present the country with its first candid self-portrait.[44] This singular achievement, executed generally with a felicitous style, proved to be one of the most enduring products of WPA.

[42] Alsberg to Manuel, Nov. 8, 1938, Box 99, FWPN.

[43] *New Orleans Item*, Mar. 8, 1941; Newsom to Henderson, Nov. 5, 1940, Box 801, WPA; Kerr to Austin, May 27, 1939, Box 2117, WPA.

[44] *The Pathfinder* (Washington, D.C.), Dec. 17, 1938.

Auxiliary Projects

WORK ON THOSE AUXILIARY PROJECTS which gained the FWP its
widest public support—the city and other local guidebooks—often
began before work on the state volumes and interfered with the necessary concentration on the latter. In many instances, these efforts were
motivated by the local pride and interest of project workers themselves.
The central office also shared responsibility, though, as it had devoted
its first manual to the secondary guides. It was not until the second
manual, relating to the state guidebooks, was issued that the primacy of
the state volumes among the project's priorities became clear.

While the Washington office assigned the city guides a subsidiary
role, it recognized that they served a number of useful purposes. Most
important, the volumes would gain community support for the project,
which might increase the sales of the larger guides when they finally
appeared. Second, the smaller guidebooks would raise morale in a
number of projects whose gifted writers had come to the conclusion
that their work would never see print. For this reason, as Gaer wrote
Alsberg, it became "imperative" that publication of these books proceed without delay. The Pennsylvania unit, eager to display its talents,
rushed through a pamphlet entitled *3 Hikes Thru Wissahickon* to present
the first of all project publications.[1]

Sponsors expressed definite interest in these minor volumes. One
state director thought they saw "the economic possibilities which may
follow the widespread distribution of local Guides." Pride also accounted for this concern, especially when an anniversary celebration
took place. A tercentenary history of Milford, Connecticut, a guide to
Little Rock for the Arkansas Centennial Commission, and a pamphlet
Historical Romney for the 175th anniversary of the West Virginia town
received local support. In North Carolina, the *Charlotte News* pub-

[1] Gaer to Alsberg, Oct. 12, 1936, Box 161, FWPN.

lished segments of the city guide for its fiftieth anniversary edition, and the American Legion backed the entire booklet.[2]

In spite of all their interest, sponsors appeared to be "rare and cagey birds." Directors who spent strenuous days making local contacts often found financial help contingent upon accepting the dictates of these potential benefactors. Even more so than in the case of the state guides, perhaps because the local books would receive special attention, many groups that were approached to be sponsors wanted to reduce the project's activities to little more than advertising campaigns. The local chamber of commerce insisted that a guide to Pittsburg, Kansas, avoid a history of AFL-CIO agitation, and debate about the spot where Travis, Bowie, and Crockett died in defending the Alamo and the number of cannons the fort possessed led to unspecific descriptions in the San Antonio Guide.[3]

Sponsoring agencies occasionally reneged on commitments for local guides. Publication of the San Xavier Guide had to be postponed after the resort season passed and the dudes departed. The Omaha city guide never saw print because the Junior Chamber of Commerce never substantiated its promises. The guide to Tampa suffered the same fate because it mentioned a red-light district, the illegal "Little Chicago" gambling area, and the fact that Cuban Negroes did not speak English in their homes.[4]

Manuscript copy for the local guides had a particularly depressing effect on the Washington office. Midwestern town guides always seemed to begin: "Bottsville, like Rome, was built on seven hills." A draft of the Knoxville Guide drew a simple judgment from one reviewer: "Fooey!" Every section dealing with contemporary Miami suffered from "an excited approach."[5]

Still, the central office tended to give more leeway to the local guides

[2] Montgomery to Alsberg, Sept. 29, 1936, Box 122, FWPN. On the other hand, WPA's administrator in New York, a native Arkansan, took one look at a title and sneered: "Who the hell wants a guide to North Little Rock? Don't you know it's the asshole of the world?" Mangione, *Dream and Deal,* p. 89n.

[3] Northrop to Bjorkman, Sept. 22, 1938, Box 115, FWPN; San Antonio Guide file, Box 106, FWPN.

[4] San Xavier Guide file, Box 826, WPA; Rudolph Umland to author, May 28, 1968; Powell interview.

[5] *The Pathfinder* (Washington, D.C.), Dec. 17, 1938; Frederick to Alsberg, Oct. 24, 1938, Box 124, FWPN; Miami Guide file, Box 85, FWPN.

than to their state counterparts. Savannah copy retained an overabundance of adjectives, even though the Georgia office did correct the use of "huge"—applied to leaves and cannonballs—four times within the same paragraph. The Rousseau County, Mississippi, manuscript made invidious comparisons with North Dakota regarding climate and attractiveness to prospective settlers. The Gulf Coast, Mississippi, and Arrowhead, Mississippi, guidebooks duplicated too much of their respective state guides.[6]

The situation became especially troublesome on the Pennsylvania project. Under the pressure of Director Paul French's plea for immediate action, as well as Gaer's conviction that workers would "gradually" improve their work and "find their best stride," the central office approved many local Pennsylvania guidebooks which had little value and even contained egregious mistakes. French focused on quantity, and at the end of August, 1939, he pointed to his thirty-two books and pamphlets as the largest list issued by any state project. This record came at the expense of accuracy and quality, however; one reviewer dismissed the Philadelphia Guide as being full of "sententious generalizations" and falling "far short of even average acceptability."[7]

Such books achieved recognition through sales. By 1939, the Dutchess County booklet (at $1.25) and *New Castle on the Delaware,* both prepared with the invaluable help of the central office's Philip Coan, had sold 3,000 copies each. The Dubuque and Cedar Rapids booklets (at 15¢) sold over 1,000 each, the Lincoln, Nebraska, city guide (at 25¢) passed 16,000 copies, and the larger Philadelphia Guide sold out a first edition of 2,500 almost before it came off the press. A more expensive city guide, however, did not fare as well: the Augusta Guide (at $1.50) sold slowly because of poor publicity, an inadequate discount to booksellers, and the considerable cost of postage on small mail orders.[8]

At times, exceptionally fine local guides reached print, such as those done by Director Hatcher's Ohio project, one for Cape Cod, and *Old Bellevue,* with its inclusion of excerpts from pioneer Nebraska news-

[6] Dillard to Alsberg, Mar. 20, 1937, Box 86, FWPN; Cronyn to Ulrich, June 2, 1937, Box 100, FWPN.

[7] Gaer to Alsberg, Feb. 27, 1937, Box 119, FWPN; French to Alsberg, June 19, 1939, Box 2447, WPA; *New York Times,* Jan. 16, 1938.

[8] Alsberg to Hopper, Aug. 24, 1937, Box 81, FWPN; Tupper to Alsberg, June 23, 1939, Box 10, FWPN.

papers and from travelers' accounts to enliven copy. The New Orleans Guide, stamped with the expertise and warmth of "Papa" Saxon, represented the best of the local guides. Except for the New York volume, it was the only book to receive a 10-cent-per-copy royalty on the first edition of 10,000 and an advance of $500. Its spoof on the famous statue of President Jackson, its local menus, and its fine sketches of local residents combined to win it such encomiums as "the perfect guidebook." The New Orleans Guide remained on local best-seller lists for six weeks and had sold some 10,000 copies by 1941.[9]

The other worthy additions to the American Guide Series were the transcontinental tour books, begun, as has been seen, with the federally published *Intracoastal Waterway.* Familiar with U.S. 1, Katherine Kellock wrote about the route from Washington to Richmond as a model for this highway guide. The first guidebook to a whole, numbered route (the main link between the original thirteen states and the longest of the North-South highways), *U.S. 1* marked "a stage in American thought." People would no longer think of the country in terms of rivers or railroad lines, one reviewer said. Van Wyck Brooks, who believed the state guides "perfectly thrilling," regarded this volume as "another Bible." It had a supplement in *The Ocean Highway,* so interesting a book that one Florida paper claimed the project provided the government "105% writers-value." The head of the Auto Association of Great Britain recommended both volumes to its 3,000 members.[10]

Trail books followed. They had been suggested by Kellock as a corrective to exaggerated, romantic histories of pioneer days. With the discovery of early Mormon diaries by the Historical Records Survey, information from Van Wyck Brooks, and write-ups from state projects, the tour editor managed to edit *The Oregon Trail* on free weekends. The book represented, one director said, an exemplary "biography of a road."[11]

Thus, auxiliary guides became the first publications to answer

[9] See Chap. 8 below for more on *Cape Cod Pilot; New Orleans Item,* May 27, 1939; *Tulsa World,* June 12, 1938.

[10] Page 120 above; Kellock interview, Aug. 18, 1968; *New York Herald Tribune*, Mar. 5, 1938; Brooks to Kellock, Mar. 3, 1968, KK papers, LC; *Lake Worth Leader*, June 1, 1938.

[11] Kellock interview, Aug. 18, 1968; Alsberg to McDaniel, Mar. 22, 1939, Box 124, FWPN. For information on the survey, see page 52 above. Katherine Kellock's idea for a supplement, "The California Trail," to please a powerful member of the House Appropriations Committee who served as Nevada's lone representative, had to be shelved with the close of the FWP. Kellock to Alsberg, Mar. 25, 1938, Box 461, WPA.

Alsberg's call, in the summer of 1936, for the project to demonstrate that it was producing "useful work." By its very nature, the FWP was unable to show much in the way of tangible results before then. Writing to Cronyn at the time, Fisher expressed his conviction that the state volumes would be long in coming—if, indeed, they ever saw print.[12] Until the primary guidebooks could be completed, at any rate, the local and highway volumes drummed up sponsorship and public interest, kept workers busy and maintained their morale, and made use of material that could never have gone into the more substantial products. Occasionally, these efforts proved not only worthwhile but comparable to their successors.

II

Perhaps the most pioneering of all the project's subsidiary efforts became the black studies, first begun for the state guides and then taken up in their own right. Within their original plans for the five-volume American Guide, Alsberg and Cronyn had included a separate section entitled "Negro Culture in America"; they planned to expand it into a more comprehensive essay later and, possibly, publish it. They soon jettisoned this idea in favor of an essay on black history and lore in each state guidebook, under the editorship of Sterling Brown and his research assistants, Ulysses Lee and Eugene Holmes. Although Brown viewed his appointment as proof of "a serious effort to give qualified colored writers and Negro subject matter fair treatment in the FWP," he succeeded only in doing the latter. His singular achievement in this respect, most noticeable in the state guides, was not attained without considerable difficulty. However, since his superiors refused to bow to myriad local pressures to avoid this most sensitive of issues or at least to treat it in a more gingerly fashion, the larger volumes were consistently objective. They provided the impetus for what the Technical Project called "collateral" publications in the field.[13]

The silence concerning Negroes in city and tour descriptions represented the most common defect in state copy. This absence became

[12] Alsberg to Derby, Aug. 17, 1936, Box 81, FWPN; Fisher to Cronyn, May 6, 1936, Box 11, FWPN.

[13] Cronyn to Baker, Nov. 30, 1935, Box 52, FWPN; Brown to Europe, Apr. 16, 1936, Box 8, FWPN. For information on employment problems, see chap. 3 above.

especially marked in accounts of heavily populated black areas of the South, including Beaufort, Tallahassee, Biloxi, Portsmouth, and the all-Negro town of Blackwell, Arkansas. The professional and business classes, which fell outside the domestic service, farm, and unskilled labor categories, went unnoticed. Miami history copy omitted past regulations governing public transportation, such as: "Nigger, don't let the sun set on you here." "Negroes" was spelled with a lowercase *n*, and in Alabama copy the designation was "darkies." The North Carolina project's slowness in digging out the desired material was attributable largely to the "remarkable ignorance of the white citizenry as to what the Negroes are doing." The Missouri office removed photos submitted by a project worker of rural hovels inhabited by Negro families on relief in Independence. Kentucky blacks who were consulted felt that too much publicity would not be beneficial; the faculty of the State Industrial Institute for Negroes at Frankfort refused point-blank to aid the work.[14]

When states had no choice but to mention Negroes in the separate guide essay, the flagrant use of standard stereotypes proved common. Georgia copy pictured the black as "cherishing only affectionate regard" for his Southern plantation masters. He was "by nature gregarious" in Kentucky, "imitative" in Louisiana, and engaged in "friendly and stimulating rivalry" with whites in Alabama. The South Carolina project's contention that "the Negro, insofar as he rises from sharecropper . . . to ownership status, will have more and more opportunity for advancement" simply meant, as Brown noted, that he would advance if he advanced.[15]

Bias and misconceptions did not confine themselves to Southern projects. Ohio copy blamed Northern climate (rather than marginal labor status and a consequent inability to pay for medical service) for the high mortality rate among Negroes and claimed that "they dominate most other groups in their love for pageantry and fancy dress." The New Jersey project failed to note that, according to the 1930 state census, illiteracy among blacks was much lower than that among whites. Dover, Delaware, copy contended that "Negroes whistle

[14] Oct. 4, 1937, report, Box 85, FWPN; Bjorkman to Alsberg, Dec. 13, 1937, Box 200, FWPN; Beard to Harris, June 15, 1937, Box 102, FWPN; Cordell to Alsberg, June 22, 1937, Box 59, FWPN.

[15] May 27, 1937, report, Box 187, FWPN; Sterling Brown report, Box 123, FWPN.

melodiously.'' Segregation at the University of Minnesota's dormitories and the importance of the slave trade to Maryland's antebellum economy were unnoted in state drafts.[16]

Project directors rushed to defend their guides' treatment of the Negro. Bjorkman emphasized that ''proper balance'' had been observed in the North Carolina Guide copy, while Oklahoma's director objected to a separate essay as ''an infringement from [sic] states' rights.'' Mary Miles of Alabama protested that ''Dr. Brown has a chip on his shoulder.'' She stressed that the guide had to be not merely truthful but agreeable to both blacks and whites: ''Alabamans understand the general Negro situation here better than a critic whose life has been spent in another section of the country, however studious he may be.'' (The studies of white specialists such as Arthur Raper and Howard Odum at the University of North Carolina, upon which Brown relied, were dismissed as representing the viewpoint of ''a Yankee School.'')[17] In the case of the Mississippi Guide, the state project overrode Washington's corrections by submitting an entire draft in a rush and then including some objectional references in the final edition. From the very beginning, one Washington editor had found that that state's writers seemed ''utterly unable or unwilling'' to bring dignified restraint and dispassionate detachment to the subject. Director Eri Douglass insisted that sales of the book would be doomed if a ''sociological treatise'' on ''any of the many debatable phrases of the race question'' were opened, and that the project's editors wanted to tell the true story without playing up any of the state's ''sore spots.'' Though Cronyn warned that no ''aesthetic delicacy'' could serve to eliminate the latter, the book appeared with numerous omissions and distortions and considerable anti-Negro propaganda.[18]

A tone of ''amused condescension'' characterized the treatment of the Negro in the Mississippi Guide. Brown had been able to delete ''the passing of public hanging was, in the eyes of the Negro, a sad mistake,'' but meaningless generalizations, such as the contention that the

[16] Sept. 22, 1937, report, Box 108, FWPN; Brown to Alsberg, June 8, 1937, Box 200, FWPN.

[17] Bjorkman to Alsberg, Sept. 1, 1938, Box 113, FWPN; Thompson to Cunningham, May 16, 1938, Box 117, FWPN; Miles to Cronyn, Mar. 19 and Aug. 26, 1937, Box 77, FWPN; Brown interview.

[18] Ulysses Lee interview, Aug. 12, 1968; Van Olinda to Cronyn, Aug. 15, 1936, Box 101, FWPN; Douglass to Cronyn, July 16, 1937, and Cronyn to Douglass, July 20, 1937, Box 101, FWPN.

black "assured himself of a share in all things good," remained. The Negro affairs editor could only go on record as having criticized and objected to much of the copy in its pre-final state. Alsberg admitted he may have failed to pay "sufficient attention" to Brown's objections, and added, "I certainly don't want this to happen again." Fortunately, it did not; the episode taught Brown and his staff to guard against a repeat performance.[19]

As a result of the combined efforts of Brown, his assistants, and his superiors, the story of the poverty and tragedy of the American Negro received wide audiences for the first time. Charles S. Johnson's contribution "Negroes in Tennessee" for the state guide and the use of studies by Carter Woodson and other revisionist historians helped to change traditional stereotypes. Though not entirely satisfied with the results (as in the case of the Beaufort Guide), Brown later argued that states took blacks more seriously because of the guides and the "collateral" publications which followed. Realizing the quandary in which many Southern state projects found themselves while dealing with the vexed subject of a Negro essay, the central office still maintained that hard facts had to be faced and could be presented "without offending any susceptibilities." Although project workers rarely treated this highly controversial subject with "sincere idealism," as Alsberg had hoped, the results did provide a noteworthy corrective to certain views throughout the country.[20]

The publications which followed the state guidebooks enhanced the revolutionary work initiated in these volumes. The Negro writer Helen Boardman, herself on the New York project, wrote Harris that work in this field for the American Guide should be done by blacks, an idea also endorsed by Louisiana's Saxon and Roscoe Lewis of Hampton Institute. Saxon, with the aid of Lawrence Reddick, set up an all-Negro project at Dillard University which worked on ex-slave narratives and the history of the Negro in New Orleans and Louisiana. In the course of their research, they cataloged the publications of the Louisiana Histori-

[19] May 19, 1938, report, Box 200, FWPN; Alsberg to Brown, May 31, 1938, Box 37, FWPN; Brown interview. Stereotypes regarding slaves and plantation culture persisted in the Louisiana and New Orleans guides, but to a lesser extent. This was largely due to Director Saxon's views, even though the Louisiana executive took a liberal attitude toward blacks in his personal relationships. See Clayton, "Writers' Project in Louisiana," pp. 210-11, 255-69, and chap. 8.

[20] Brown interview; Cronyn to Miles, Aug. 5, 1937, Box 77, FWPN; Alsberg to state directors, June 15, 1937, Box 56, FWPN.

cal Society and indexed parts of the influential antebellum journal
DeBow's Review. Workers turned up interesting material on voo-
dooism and the powers of "Easy Life Powder," "Bend Over Oil," and
"Boss Fix Powder" that was similar to some found in the Florida
project under the supervision of the Negro novelist Zora Neale
Hurston.[21]

Other projects dealt with specific topics relating to the Negro.
Katherine Dunham worked, with extra-project direction from
sociologist Horace Cayton, on a study of Chicago cults (one later
became known as the Black Muslims). Arthur Weinberg, who had lost
his job as a dresser of Hart, Schaffner and Marx mannequins, assisted
her by frequenting the many "store-front" church services around Hull
House and the South Side and then by talking to Negro patients in the
county psychopathic hospital. New York City's black studies unit,
under the supervision successively of Claude McKay, Henry Lee
Moon, Ted Poston and, especially, Roi Ottley, worked on a history of
the Negro there. Fragmentary studies began in Oklahoma, Arkansas,
and Pennsylvania, but they suffered from a shortage of qualified
personnel.[22]

The most original of the collateral black projects, the ex-slave
narratives, dated from 1936, when Florida, Georgia, and South
Carolina project workers began recording interviews. John Lomax,
then the FWP national advisor on folklore and folkways, drew up a
standard questionnaire for the American Guide Manual "to get the
Negro to thinking and talking about the days of slavery." Initially, this
may have seemed like a desire for "human interest," but a more serious
purpose was implied in Alsberg's memo calling for accounts and
documents about the institution of slavery. It emphasized that the
ex-slaves should speak for themselves on such topics as existence
before and after emancipation, songs, slave uprisings, hopes and
realities, and present conditions.[23]

When Lomax left the project in July, 1937, he was succeeded by
Ben Botkin, a specialist in folklore from the University of Oklahoma.
Botkin and Sterling Brown altered the first questionnaire to remove

[21] Boardman to Harris, Mar. 20, 1936, Box 31, FWPN; Feb. 13, 1936, report, Box 59,
FWPN. For more on this project and the loss of its records for an intended study of the Negro in
Louisiana, see Clayton, "Writers' Project in Louisiana," pp. 94-97, 178-82, 301-8.

[22] Arthur Weinberg interview, Mar. 31, 1968.

[23] Page 17 above; Alsberg to state directors, June 9, 1937, Box 56, FWPN.

traces of bias and forestall the artistic flourishes reminiscent of Thomas Nelson Page and Joel Chandler Harris. Nevertheless, those interviewed would often "tell white journalists what they generally wanted to hear." Dialect became "subjectified," to use Brown's term, depending on the interviewer and the ex-slave. Years later, Georgia's director conceded that she felt the project's "greatest loss" was that whites conducted the interviews, but she defended the procedure as at least not being in "the segregated tradition." Reviewing the entire collection for the Library of Congress, Botkin concluded: "Beneath all the surface contradictions and exaggerations, the fantasy and the flattery, there is an essential truth and humanity which surpasses as it supplements history and literature."[24]

The best of collateral black studies and a subsequent classic in its field employed the ex-slave narratives most dramatically. This new historical source had first been used by Ulysses Lee in his research about the portions of the capital near Civil War forts for the D.C. Guide. Compiled with the aid of fifteen black workers and the driving supervision of Roscoe Lewis, *The Negro in Virginia* expanded the technique, telling of indentured servitude and slave revolts from as early as 1687. Liberal though she was, Virginia's Eudora Richardson feared that the book would have an unfavorable impact on both the project and "interracial relations." Sterling Brown did tell the forthright Lewis to make "corrections," but these hardly resulted in the presentation of a bland "good white folks" notion such as was prevalent even among contemporary historians. The ex-slave narratives, used extensively for the first time in one volume of the work, revealed the slave's attitude toward the white man's assumption of superiority and his feelings about freedom and his master's God. Realizing the book's value in educating whites and blacks, the president of Hampton Institute sponsored it and gave the workers office space.[25]

[24] Brown interview; Carolyn Dillard to author, Apr. 28, 1968; Botkin report, May 26, 1941, Box 4, LC FWP. For the fullest edition of the ex-slave narratives, see George P. Warwick, ed., *The American Slave: A Composite Autobiography,* vols. II-XVII. Eugene Genovese's *Roll Jordan, Roll* (New York, 1974) has best utilized these sources. Also see Charles L. Perdue, Jr., Thomas E. Barden, and Robert K. Phillips, eds., *Weevils in the Wheat: Interviews with Virginia Ex-Slaves* (Charlottesville: University Press of Virginia, 1976), which presents previously unavailable interviews conducted by the Virginia unit, the only project where former slaves were interviewed solely by blacks.

[25] Lee interview; *The Negro in Virginia* (New York, 1940); Richardson to Alsberg, Dec. 8, 1938, Box 47, FWPN.

Another, more questionable, volume dealing with blacks in particular was *Drums and Shadows,* compiled by Mary Granger of the Georgia project's technical staff. This attempt to connect coastal Negro folkways with those of Africa represented, Brown later wrote, "a hodgepodge of chit-chat and gossip, with leading questions and often misleading answers." In spite of Brown's adverse view and that of Howard University's sociology faculty, other specialists, like Melville Herskovitz and Guy Johnson, supported the contentious study, and it eventually did get published.[26]

Other projects enjoyed less fortune. Brown's idea for a "Portrait of the Negro as an American" could not be carried out because of his full-time teaching at Howard University and the close of the FWP. The proposed work would have revealed the black as a participant rather than a separate "problem" in American life. "Go Down Moses," a study of the anti-slavery movement suggested by Brown and Lee, eventually had to be dropped as well. Inferior project studies, such as an analysis of the Negro in Philadelphia, required extensive revision and a general rewriting. Publishers might have been reluctant to gamble on state manuscripts (as has been charged in the case of the New York City book). Also, even the better efforts existed only in rough draft at the time the federal project came under congressional pressure to close or limit its activities.[27]

The FWP pioneered in giving a fairer appraisal of the Negro's role in American history through the guides, specialized volumes, and valuable ex-slave narratives. In addition, the files for the New York City manuscript went into Roi Ottley's *New World a-Comin'* , and Chicago's found their way into St. Clair Drake and Horace Cayton's *Black Metropolis.* Arna Bontemps and Jack Conroy, who had been working for the project on a volume about the Negro in Illinois, eventually polished up the rough drafts and brought out *They Seek a City.* They later updated the book, with Conroy taking the contemporary chapters, and retitled it *Any Place but Here.* Ottley's success convinced their publishers to go ahead with the venture.[28]

Even more important, the FWP gave gifted Negro writers on its rolls

[26] *Drums and Shadows: Survival Studies among the Georgia Coastal Negroes* (Savannah, 1940); Brown to Botkin, 1940 report, Box 201, FWPN.

[27] Brown interview; *The Negro in New York,* preface by James Baldwin. But also see Gilbert Osofsky's review in the *New York Times,* June 25, 1967.

[28] Bontemps interview.

confidence in the value of this material for blacks. The project's work influenced Henry Lee Moon's later publication of *The Balance of Power,* a study of the black voter. The necessity of actually reading documents about court trials, black folklore, and even Stokes's iconography regarding slavery gave "density" to young Ralph Ellison's sense of the American experience. Ted Poston discovered that "a hell of a lot of insurrections" had occurred in the course of American history and that W. E. B. Du Bois had used the phrase "Black Power" as editor of *The Crisis.* Negro intellectuals found the thirties most important because they received a more realistic "social understanding" than that conveyed in the "Harlem Renaissance" of the 1920s.[29] The Federal Writers' Project, in rejecting the message of that renaissance, abandoned the exotic and the primitive to sharpen its readers' concern for and understanding of the Negroes' past. Together with the explosion in the social sciences during this decade, the FWP black studies showed the way to a better comprehension of the country's racial dilemma.

III

The project's work in folklore also had significant value. As with all other proposals, ideas for a WPA program in this field had predated the FWP. One Savannah resident submitted a plan for 6,400 men (preferably married) to cover the entire country and produce a folklore history of the Depression. His estimate of $8,500,000 must have dismayed some WPA officials in Washington, but such authorities as Jean Thomas, founder of the American Folk Songs Society, seconded the need for such work. Alsberg himself wanted the balladry and folklore of the Kentucky mountain regions covered as a unit, but deferred this to concentrate on the Guide Series.[30]

Fortunately, the project secured the help of experts in this area. For about a year, John Lomax served as an advisor on folklore while

[29] Brown interview; Ralph Ellison telephone conversation, May 30, 1968; Ted Poston interview, Dec. 4, 1967; Bontemps interview. Also see Bontemps's comments in *Negro Digest* 8 (June, 1950):43-47, about the social consciousness of the "WPA black writers' school." It should be noted that only at the start of the decade had the *New York Times* (Mar. 7, 1930) called for the use of "Negro" henceforth: "It is not merely a typographical change; it is an act of recognition of racial self-respect for those who have been for generations in 'the lower case.'"

[30] Page 17 above; Balinger to McClure, June 24, 1935, Box 461, WPA; Alsberg to Vinson, Dec. 5, 1935, Box 15, FWPN.

continuing his journeys through the South to make records for the Archives of American Folk Song. Asked to evaluate the increasing amount of material gathered by state projects while researching for guides, as well as to make suggestions for the FWP's enlargement, he proposed a large collection of ballads, poetry, and tales to arouse interest in the project's other work. Lomax's ideas were particularly helpful in the guide folklore essay, and his manual of instructions for collecting primary sources proved very useful to Ben Botkin, who took over these responsibilities in 1938. Botkin, the editor of *Folkways* and author of *Folk Say*, had been an early advocate of exploring the diverse folk groups within a given region. Following individual interests, he proceeded to expand his predecessor's emphasis on the South to include the predominantly urban and industrialized areas of the nation.[31]

Botkin's more comprehensive approach did not solve all the problems involved in such work. As he and Lomax found out, workers could rarely cope with this specialized material and, in place of first-hand experience, copied from secondary or unreliable sources. In writing to Saxon that less-qualified personnel could be used as field workers to gather "word-of-mouth" folklore for Botkin's proposed "American Folk Stuff," Alsberg demonstrated that even he did not fully grasp these difficulties.[32]

The new approach, however, had a significant effect on the New York City and Chicago projects. Fortunately, the New York unit had qualified personnel who, under the supervision of Alfred Hertog and Nicholas Wirth, began studies of folklore according to occupational groups. Work on this "living lore," suggested by the "Lexicon of Trade Jargon" being done for that project, resulted in a vast collection of Americana and employed many trained writers to record characteristic speech rhythms and vernacular. In Chicago, under the direction of Nelson Algren, a series of "industrial tall tales" about Slappy Hooper, "the world's biggest, fastest and bestest sign painter," and "Hank, the Free Wheeler" introduced contemporary coloring to a historical genre. The latter story, modeled on Henry Ford's success with "flivvers," concluded with the dead hero awakening to upbraid his six paid pallbearers: "What the hell is this? You call this efficiency?

---

[31] Lomax to Alsberg, July 13 and 25, 1936, Box 61, FWPN; Ben Botkin interview, Mar. 28, 1968.

[32] Alsberg to Saxon, June 8, 1938, Box 15, FWPN.

Put the thing on wheels! Lay five of these birds off, and cut the other one's wages 'cause the work is easy and the hours ain't long and the pace is slow.'' The historical collection ''A Tall Chance of Work,'' was never published, but some samples later found their way into Botkin's *A Treasury of American Folklore*.[33]

Few other efforts dealing with folklore had much value. Though Oregon ''webfoot whoppers'' merited space in *Frontier and Midland,* most other attempts, such as *Old Newberry Tales, Hoosier Tall Tales,* and a host of Nebraska pamphlets for schools, proved decidedly inferior. Difficulties arose even in the writing of the ''whoppers,'' since the Oregon editor changed ''By God'' to ''By Doggy'' and refused to accept ''bastard'' and ''son of a bitch'' even when quoted.[34]

Special studies relating to Indians and their culture failed to realize their potential. Minor school bulletins on Indian legends in South Dakota, New Mexico, and Arizona represented the most that could be done after the path-breaking state guide essays on Indians were completed. Lack of information and the bias of project workers militated against further study. Relief cuts terminated a fieldwork project carried on among several tribes under the outside supervision of Franz Boas and Ruth Benedict. In Trenton a state official refused to sponsor a series of Indian school bulletins because the first one had dealt with an Indian legend of creation and he feared youngsters would begin to ask about childbirth.[35]

Despite these varied problems, the project's pioneering work in folklore won the esteem of professional groups. Originally skeptical of the FWP, the American Folklore Society adopted a more positive attitude after one of its professional members became folklore editor. Alsberg could be satisfied that the project's work had helped promote a folklore revival in the United States. The guides and collateral publications, along with the unpublished files, presented what Botkin later termed the ''grassroots and basic oral culture'' of the country's heterogeneous populace for the first time. The regional sociologist Howard Odum expressed his enthusiastic approval of these endeavors and suggested that a folklore guide be published under Botkin's direc-

[33] McDonald, ''Federal Relief,'' pp. 846-50; Ben Botkin, *A Treasury of American Folklore* (New York, 1944), pp. 524-54.

[34] Winslow file, Box 6, FWPN.

[35] Kellock to Alsberg, Jan. 26, 1936, Box 58, FWPN; Harris to Morris, June 5, 1937, Box 56, FWPN; Fuhlbruegge to Alsberg, May 19, 1938, Box 107, FWPN.

tion. The Joint Committee on Folk Arts, organized to coordinate the work of all Federal #1 projects, eventually sponsored the Southern Recording Expedition for the Library of Congress and other compilations.[36]

The work of the Folklore Section became closely linked to the social-ethnic studies under the direction of Morton Royse, a specialist in minority groups. Adopting a functional approach that stressed cultural backgrounds and activities rather than peculiarities and "contributions," Royse sought to produce intensive studies on single groups and cross-section analyses of whole communities. As with all other collateral studies, material for these had already been amassed from work on minority groups for the state guides.[37]

In its first supplementary instructions, the Washington office had called for a file on racial groups, heritage, and culture; certain projects set up "racial groups" to facilitate this task. Work for the New York City Guide soon revealed that 90 per cent of basement ice dealers came from Apulia, Italy, almost all of the city's window washers from Ukrainian stock, and most of its shoeshine men from southern Italy. Amora White of the New Mexico project translated the first play presented in the United States, *Los Moros y Christianos*. Foreign-born workers translated records of the Swedish Lutheran churches at Raccoon and Penn's Neck, New Jersey, to commemorate the 300th anniversary of the arrival of the Swedes and Finns in the area. Data uncovered on the Turks of Sumter County, South Carolina, the Cajuns of Louisiana, the Greek sponge fishers of Tarpon Springs, Florida, the Russians of Brookside, Alabama, and the Swiss of New Glarus, Wisconsin, led the central office to suggest articles for a projected volume, "Pockets in America." Though refused by the Dodge Publishing Co., the material became available for future scholars.[38]

As was inevitable, files provided sufficient material for a few pioneering studies. As a natural consequence of all the research done

[36] McDonald, "Federal Relief," pp. 853-87; Botkin interview; Odum to Alsberg, Aug. 26, 1938, Box 462, WPA.

[37] Morton Royse in Caroline F. Ware, ed., *The Cultural Approach to History* (New York, 1940), p. 87. Ray Allen Billington asserted, in the same work (p. 80), that the project contributed to the rise of "the modern school of social history."

[38] *New York World Telegram*, July 23, 1936; *Los Moros y Christianos* file, Box 110, FWPN; McClure to Mangione, Sept. 1, 1937, Box 32, FWPN.

for the guides, the New York project began working on a book about Italians and Jews in the city to be subtitled "from shofar to swing." *Armenians in Massachusetts,* which appeared in December, 1937, was the first of a series of nationality survey books and was followed by *Italians in New York* (in English and Italian). *The Armenian Mirror* praised the former as the product of "a liberal and far-seeing administration." Materials published later included *The Jewish Landsmannschaften of New York* and *The Albanian Struggle in the Old World and New.*[39]

The racial approach did not satisfy the director of social-ethnic studies, and he proceeded with a new emphasis. However laudatory the reviews of these books, the material had been written from the point of view of contributions and individual personalities, rather than with an emphasis on participation and acculturation. Royse substituted the "social-ethnic" for the "racial" approach and, from the time of his appointment in April, 1938, he applied this method to intended studies of the foreign language press in America and of specific minority groups. The central office supplied files for a volume of studies about acculturation that was subsequently published under the editorship of Ralph Linton. A few project workers initiated a study of Chicago neighborhoods, in conjunction with Louis Wirth and two of his colleagues at the University of Chicago, to cover ethnic groups and foreign community newspapers. Analyses of Utah Mormons, Pennsylvania Mennonites, Oregon Lithuanians, and Minnesota Irish were also begun, although the central staff turned down a proposal to cover German-Americans from an anti-Nazi point of view as being too controversial for the project.[40]

The highly ambitious program fell short of expectations for a number of reasons. Even more than the folklore studies, it required specially trained personnel. At times Alsberg and Royse quarreled over methodology. Another problem was that Royse, who was traveling about the states, could not keep up with the material pouring into the central office. Then, too, both the folklore and social-ethnic studies

[39] Nelson Frank interview, Feb. 20, 1968; *The Armenian Mirror* (Boston), Dec. 15, 1937. The files of the New York City project dealing with Jews can be found at the Municipal Archives and Records Center, 23 Park Row, New York City.

[40] McDonald, "Federal Relief," pp. 862-63; Benedict to Alsberg, Oct. 21, 1938, Box 32, FWPN; Alsberg to Shaw, Feb. 2, 1938, Box 31, FWPN.

were slighted by various state units eager to publish and not interested in mastering specialized techniques for books accorded secondary importance by the Technical Project.[41]

The most noted of these conflicts of interest occurred in the South, where the innovation of the "life-history" approach forged a link between the folklore and social-ethnic collateral projects. William Couch, then the associate director of North Carolina's project, resisted the introduction of social-ethnic studies in the South; he felt they were inappropriate in a region where immigrants had assimilated thoroughly. More interested in finding out about the daily lives of Southern workers, he sent a woman who worked in the textile mills of Greensboro to gather interviews. Couch submitted an outline for an expanded study based on her material to Washington. Alsberg and Kellock were wary, especially after the violent Gastonia strikes, but Couch went ahead and asked neighboring projects to send him similar copy. Within two weeks replies had come in, especially from North Carolina and Tennessee. Totally committed to the possibility of transforming case histories into readable documentary narrative for immediate publication, Couch grew impatient with the folklore editor's requests to send samples for a tentative anthology of creative writing. "I confess I'm bewildered by Botkin's plans," he wrote Tennessee's director: "Every time I discuss the subject of folklore he refers to just about any and everything." Couch's project seemed to contain too many "brutally frank" stories for his immediate superior, who was very much concerned with their effect upon his typists, who were all young, unmarried women, and the state director doubted the wisdom of including such stories among the thirty-five accounts which made up the collection.[42]

However, the chorus of hosannahs which greeted the publication of *These Are Our Lives* proved these fears illusory. A reviewer for the *New York Times* considered the book one of the most important works

[41] McDonald, "Federal Relief," pp. 863-64; Mangione, *Dream and Deal,* pp. 280-82.

[42] Couch borrowed from Plutarch's *Lives,* the contemporary studies of sociologist John Dollard, the documentary *You Have Seen Their Faces,* and especially his concerns about the different levels of life in the South to develop the "life history" technique. Couch interview, Jan. 21, 1968; Couch to McDaniel, Apr. 8, 1939, Box 1, LC FWP; Bjorkman to Couch, Jan. 13, 1939, Box 77, FWPN. Couch's insistence on total freedom of expression during the interviews halted work on a second study of families in federal farm villages, where managers' approval was first required, William T. Couch Memoir, COHC, pp. 338-39.

written "since the cultural renaissance dawned below the Potomac." Rupert Vance concluded that Emile Zola and Arnold Bennett would have liked these realistic sketches of tenant farmers and day laborers.[43]

These Are Our Lives was a pioneering venture because it provided the reader with faithful representations of living people. Although Couch limited his selection of the oral histories to workers and allowed FWP interviewers to prove themselves as writers at times, the volume contains valuable insights about a certain anonymous group of Southerners in the Depression years. Sketches based on personal interviews covered such diverse matters as family, education, income, politics, religion, medical needs, diet, and the subject's use of time. A black worker in the cotton mill villages since she was nine decides to "keep on a-gummin, as one can't afford false teeth at $50." The wife of a white farm laborer gives up hope for real lace curtains. A Negro odd-job worker realizes that "white folks ain't goin' to let a nigger starve when he mind [*sic*] his manners and keeps his place." This realism established a new form of historical research and, by so doing, the project achieved a remarkable combination of literary worth and valuable social documentation.[44]

Projects in the New England states began collaborating on studies bearing some resemblance to Couch's work. Under the direction of Frank Manuel, work started on "Living Lore in New England" and "Yankee Folk," the latter an experiment in monologue form. A few hand-picked informants talked freely about themselves and their work without the use of questionnaires. Drawn up by Botkin and Manuel, the new plan divided the area into three regions and chose twenty ethnically different workers who would "idealize" their occupations and nationalities. This sharp break from the traditional approach to old Yankee stock would have revealed ethnic and racial interrelationships which, until then, had gone unnoticed. Regrettably, congressional

[43] *Boston Evening Transcript,* June 10, 1939; *New York Times,* May 21, 1939. Lewis Gannett insisted that members of Congress should read this unbiased selection, which mediated between "drearily impersonal" sociology and fiction. *New York Herald Tribune,* May 20, 1939. For Couch's views on contemporary sociological and fictional views of the South, see the fine analysis by Jerold M. Hirsch, "Culture or Relief: The Federal Writers' Project in North Carolina, 1935-1942" (M.A. thesis, University of North Carolina, 1973).

[44] *These Are Our Lives* (Chapel Hill, 1939), pp. 153, 335, 358, 120; William Stott, *Documentary Expression and Thirties America,* pp. 204-5. Also see Bernice K. Harris, *Southern Savory,* pp. 181-205, for a novelist's reminiscences about collecting the life histories.

plans for the project halted this work. Another promising study, "Living in New England," failed for other reasons.[45]

While neither the folklore nor the social-ethnic studies realized their full potential, they did (as did the black studies) make substantial contributions to their respective fields. Botkin, who published some of the vast material collected after the project closed (ex-slave narratives in *Lay My Burden Down* and folk tales in *A Treasury of American Folklore*), later expressed his gratitude for the opportunity to extend his research from the regional to the national level. The project's findings, he noted, signified "the nearest thing we've had to a national folklore." Other volumes in folklore and social-ethnic studies were published by the project's successor after 1939, and although Nathan Asch, writing for the Foreign Language Information Service, exaggerated in his claim that "the FWP does justice to the Nationalities that make up America," the project did break new and fertile ground in this area as well. The approximately 14,000 manuscripts of folklore, 3,000 ex-slave narratives, and 1,000 social-ethnic manuscripts that were turned over to the Library of Congress project by Botkin and Royse in September, 1940, varied in quality, but they provided a wealth of information for future scholars that has yet to be fully appreciated.[46] They represented another illustration of the fact that the Federal Writers' Project could be credited with far more than the seminal state guides.

IV

The FWP made significant contributions in a wide variety of areas besides black, folklore, and social-ethnic studies. In 1927, the U.S.

[45] Manuel to Alsberg, Aug. 4, 1938, Box 97, FWPN; chap. 9 below, *n* 8. For other suggestions in this field, see Lewis to Cronyn, Nov. 19, 1935, and Wise to Niles, Jan. 24, 1939, Box 31, FWPN.

[46] Botkin interview; Nathan Asch press release, Oct. 24, 1938, Box 28, WPA Division of Information files, Works Projects Administration records, Record Group 69, National Archives, Washington, D.C.; Apr. 2, 1941, report, Box 211, FWPN. *Gumbo Ya-Ya,* published in 1945 by Lyle Saxon and Robert Tallant, reflected Saxon's primary interest in and appreciation of Louisiana antebellum plantation life. For a discussion, see Clayton, "Writers' Project in Louisiana," pp. 223-40, 255-69. The more than one thousand life histories produced by the FWP are mostly to be found in the Southern Historical Collection (University of North Carolina, Chapel Hill), with another group deposited in the Library of Congress. They were the subject of a session entitled "'You're Getting Paid to Be Nosey?': The Federal Writers' Project Southern Life Histories Program, 1938-1939," held at the convention of the American Historical Association, in Atlanta, Georgia, on December 28, 1975. The observations of Jerold M. Hirsch and Tom Terrill, who presented papers along with me at that time, are much appreciated.

Geographic Board had expressed the hope that state boards would be created to compile gazetteers of place-names, and the Minnesota legislature began this work with the help of the local project ten years later. Vardis Fisher had included a list of place-names in the Idaho Guide and followed it up with an expanded booklet; projects in Utah, South Dakota, Oregon, and Nebraska followed suit. This particular concern with America's past had been suggested to Alsberg by a New Mexico resident shortly after the project began, and it reflected contemporary, more extensive studies by John Rees and Will Barnes.[47]

Certain publications soon found their way into schools across the country. Idaho became the first and only project to put out a state encyclopedia, which was larger than any other volume except the D.C. Guide. This time, the director first prepared an outline for Washington's perusal, so that Cronyn would not jump on him and say, "Fisher, this will never do." *Tours in Eastern Idaho* went to various schools to enliven geography classes, as did other project pamphlets. The best of these were the school bulletins, pioneered by New Jersey's project and distributed gratis, which covered peaches, Stephen Crane, and numerous other subjects. They achieved a total circulation of more than 200,000 and were copied by the Florida, New York City, and Cincinnati units. The Adult Education Project in South Carolina used *Palmetto Pioneers* to "show traits worthy of emulation" and to combat an alarmingly high rate of adult illiteracy.[48]

Other publications demonstrated the project's diverse activity. The largest first edition of any project publication (10,000 copies) covered the history of Johnstown's eighteen floods, which entitled the Pennsylvania community to the dubious sobriquet "Flood City." Their respective presidents sponsored histories of the Universities of Kentucky and Louisville, and the Dartmouth Historical Society financed a compendium on New England's whaling masters for library reference use. Requests flooded the Washington office after the *History of Fire Prevention in Portland* had been printed and distributed at the National Fire Chiefs Convention in Salt Lake City during September, 1938.[49]

The FWP also contributed its services to a number of miscellaneous projects. Upon the suggestion of Mayor Fiorello La Guardia of New

[47] Minnesota miscellaneous file, Box 20, FWPN; Alsberg to Otero-Warren, Dec. 26, 1935, Box 28, FWPN.

[48] Fisher to Cronyn, Mar. 5, 1937, Box 11, FWPN; Alsberg to Newman, n.d., Box 48, FWPN.

[49] *Johnstown Democrat,* May 2, 1939; Griffith to Alsberg, Dec. 19, 1938, Box 39, FWPN.

York and the U.S. Conference of Mayors, a municipal government subproject collected more than 2,000 documents on public safety, city finances, civil service, and the like. In return for the use of its files, the TVA received the temporary help of a Chicago editor to write up publicity on recreational resources in the Southern highlands. State offices supplied material for papers and graduate theses on Mexicans in Colorado, the Brooklyn Bridge, and the Florida boom. The FBI received a list of all union organizations in Montana and Idaho to aid it in distributing circulars to solve a kidnapping.[50]

Under certain circumstances, the project was not free with its files and workers. It refused requests for information on "the mystery of Hamilton's marital life," a historical account of the government's participation in the larger American expositions for the World's Fair Corporation, and speeches on "the regulation of big business." Employees could not donate valuable time for Swedish translation work for the Federal Housing Administration or contribute to an analysis of some 1,200 cases of attempted suicide among records of the Boston City Hospital.[51]

In the course of its diversified work, the project had to face competition and many attacks from private concerns. Alabama's governor delayed sponsorship of the state guide because of the efforts of the state archives department to get a different volume approved as the state textbook. A former worker on the New Jersey project removed some controversial points about Philip Freneau's death, crap shooters, and the Klan and published her own book on Matawan. (The project offered an unexpurgated edition free.) The publishers of the *Marvelous Minnesota Manual* for tourists objected to Houghton Mifflin's getting the Minnesota Guide. And a Mrs. Humphries, who had sued the Macmillan Co. and Margaret Mitchell for allegedly plagiarizing her book on the Ku Klux Klan for *Gone with the Wind*, threatened to bring similar charges against the Mississippi Guide.[52]

[50] Harris to Cole, Apr. 7, 1937, Box 82, WPA Division of Information files; Anderson to Alsberg, Feb. 10, 1938, Box 24, FWPN.

[51] Gray to Alsberg, Mar. 1, 1937, Box 43, FWPN; Fuhlbruegge to Alsberg, Jan. 20, 1938, Box 26, FWPN; Loewenberg to Alsberg, Aug. 21, 1936, Box 99, FWPN.

[52] Miles to Alsberg, Aug. 13, 1937, Box 78, FWPN; Fuhlbruegge to Alsberg, Dec. 23, 1936, Box 108, FWPN; Harris to Douglass, June 23, 1937, Box 22, FWPN. Accused of using high-pressure tactics to sell a souvenir map for economic gain, Vardis Fisher recalled the Boise attorney who got married and joined a church: "On his first visit, he looked around him and said, 'Not a single damned fee in the whole house.'" Fisher to Boise Merchants Bureau, Mar. 21, 1938, Box 11, FWPN.

Yet the FWP continued to offer its services in ways which reflected a breadth not originally foreseen by the project's planners and administrators. The project indexed the newspaper files of the Dubuque Library, several of Cleveland's newspapers from 1819 on, the hearings of the La Follette Civil Liberties Committee for the National Labor Relations Board, and the feature sections of the *Daily Oklahoman*. The first volume of an index to the history of the motion picture (including 9,000 book and magazine references) "brought order to the chaotic state of its literature," in the opinion of the president of the Museum of Modern Art, its sponsor. One worker was assigned to the department of sociology at the University of Chicago to examine and inventory some 3,000 maps, another edited a newspaper at the Clemson College Opportunity School (South Carolina), while a third taught journalism in a New York City neighborhood center. Workers placed thousands of historical markers on sites in Texas, West Virginia, and Indiana with information supplied from state project files. Photos went to the Museum of Modern Art for its exhibit on New England scenes at Paris's Jeu de Paume Museum and to the Metropolitan for its "300 Years of Life in America."[53]

The writers' project also developed strong ties with various government organizations. New York City's Racial Group Section helped supply Italian, Spanish, and German translators for the Federal Theatre's *It Can't Happen Here*. The FWP verified data on the art project's New Mexico mural "Los Moros y Christianos" and checked historical information for the theatre project's Yorktown pageant. Workers in Ohio and New York helped Constance Rourke's Index of American Design with other research matters. In return, the project got information on the Moravians' first printing of Bach music (in Bethelehem, Pennsylvania) from the music project and received advice from the art project on jackets for the Montana Guide and posters for other volumes. Other federal agencies received aid, including the Central Housing Commission and WPA's Recreation Division, whose puppet shows in North Dakota were based on themes taken from local project field material.[54]

With the success of its local and route guides, the black, social-

[53] Saposs to Alsberg, Feb. 23, 1938, Box 53, FWPN; Schlesinger to Alsberg, July 12, 1938, Box 68, FWPN. For numerous translations by the Louisiana project alone, see Clayton, "Writers' Project in Louisiana," pp. 297-300.

[54] Gaer to Alsberg, Mar. 10, 1938, Box 53, FWPN; Schlesinger to Alsberg, July 12, 1938, Box 68, FWPN.

ethnic, and folklore studies, and the varied contributions made in other areas, the FWP possessed a diverse record of accomplishment that went far beyond its primary concern, the state guidebooks. Like the other divisions of Federal #1, it could now give "public performances" of its talents. Critics, waiting with confessed skepticism for "something out of Nazareth," had to admit that the delay proved worthwhile. Bulging files represented mines of information for books and pamphlets of all sorts, ranging from local oddities to *Who's Who in the Zoo,* a delightful guide to New York City's zoological parks (in seventeen sections, one for each animal order). The material gathered for its Baedekerizing of the nation's highways could also be placed at the disposal of various organizations and individuals. For these reasons, the FWP's final product differed widely from that of most other relief agencies.[55] And, as was not the case with many WPA construction jobs, the fruits of the Federal Writers' Project would be of enduring significance.

[55] Alsberg to Woodward, Jan. 5, 1937, Box 55, FWPN; Hettwer interview.

THE GREAT DEPRESSION DID NOT SPARE established writing talents. Robert Carleton Brown, despite having published fourteen books, ended up badly in debt and wrote Alsberg that he was "willing to work anywhere." Manly Wade Wellman, a noted detective story writer, could not "struggle along" on his own beyond January, 1936, and also applied to the FWP. Because the Hitler regime had confiscated the German editions of his books, Nathan Asch was forced to apply for a project post. Max Nomad could not even buy groceries with returns from his books, and his savings were almost gone when the FWP opened. Having published in magazines and worked for the MGM scenario department in New York, a broke John Cheever assured Alsberg that he could handle the English language with "clarity, ease and meaning." His Guggenheim fellowship about to expire, Jack Conroy sought an editorial position to support his wife and three children.[1]

The hated requirement of relief certification proved especially onerous to many professionals who, swallowing pride, attempted to obtain work on the FWP. Worried lest the guides be written by "unemployed plumbers or men of any other qualification," Josef Berger added, "This seems doubly unfair, because the writers have waited so long for their one opportunity." Even after taking the bitter pill and going on relief, "thinking that would stir 'em up," Nelson Algren found that his gesture did not "especially bother" WPA officials and speed up his request for a position.[2]

Under difficult circumstances, subterfuge and adroitness were some-

[1] Brown to Alsberg, Nov. 4, 1935, Box 31, FWPN; Wellman to Alsberg, Jan. 6, 1936, Box 36, FWPN; Asch to Alsberg, Jan. 25, 1937, Box 29, FWPN; Nomad to Alsberg, Oct. 18, 1935, Box 33, FWPN; Cheever to Alsberg, Sept. 25, 1935, Box 31, FWPN; Conroy to Alsberg, Oct. 29, 1935, Box 23, FWPN.

[2] Berger to Vorse, Dec. 17, 1935, Box 18, FWPN; Algren to Johns, June 19, 1936, Box 31, FWPN.

times employed to land a job. To meet the two years' residence requirement in New York, as Anzia Yezierska discovered, "the best people" used ink eradicator to substitute their own names on envelopes addressed to friends. Merle Colby proved more politically astute than most. Afraid that all jobs in Boston would be taken by the time he reached the head of a line of prospective applicants, he scribbled on a note "Take care of Merle Colby," signed it with the first Irish name that came to mind, and had it sent to the WPA interviewer. He was hired within a few minutes, after proving that he was both eligible for relief and a published novelist.[3]

Since the heaviest concentration of needy writers could be found in large urban centers, these cities claimed the most impressive talent. The New York City project possessed the largest collection, including Asch, Maxwell Bodenheim, Lionel Abel, Harry Roskolenko, Kenneth Patchen, Edward Dahlberg, Vincent McHugh, Kenneth Fearing, Norman MacLeod, Claude McKay, and Philip Rahv. The Chicago unit had Stuart Engstrand, Arna Bontemps, Richard Wright, Algren, and Conroy. The services of Kenneth Rexroth and Raymond Larsson distinguished San Francisco's project rolls. Other state projects could claim fewer but also noted personnel: Conrad Aiken, Berger, Colby, and George Willison were on the Massachusetts project, Weldon Kees and Mari Sandoz on the Nebraska project, and Cheever on the New York State project. Seven of the project's employees were Guggenheim fellowship recipients: Sterling Brown, Richard Wright, Kenneth Patchen, Max Nomad, Josef Berger, Jack Conroy, and Kenneth Fearing. When the project added state directors like Fisher, Santee, Saxon, and Hatcher, it clearly possessed many more talents than could be counted on the fingers.[4]

Having faced mounting economic hardship, professionals first viewed any position on the project as "a God send."[5] This initial

[3] Yezierska, *Red Ribbon on a White Horse*, pp. 152-53; Mangione, *Dream and Deal*, p. 101.

[4] The last assertion is in Robert Bendiner's *Just Around the Corner*, p. 195. Other professionals included Harry Kemp, Frank Shay, Sol Funaroff, Willard Maas, John Hermann, Parker Tyler, Dorothy Van Ghent, Miriam Allen de Ford, Alice Corbin, Opal Shannon, William Pillin, Rebecca Pitts, Adrienna Spadoni, and John Morosso. Contrary to some sources, e.g., Wecter, *Great Depression,* John Steinbeck was never on the FWP.

[5] Rothermell to Alsberg, Oct. 11, 1935, Box 30, FWPN. Despite all the difficulties that he would subsequently encounter on the Massachusetts project, Conrad Aiken could later praise it as "a splendid idea, invaluable," and one which ("as I was totally broke at the time") kept him alive. Aiken to author, Oct. 20, 1967.

enthusiasm often waned, however, after a few months on the FWP. The confusion that prevailed in the New York City project permitted the bohemian Harvey Breit to adopt a ''don't-give-a-damn'' attitude. When Norman MacLeod found he ''couldn't possibly manage to keep busy past 11 A.M.,'' he solved the problem by drinking beer with some of that unit's supervisors before lunch. Those professionals who submitted worthwhile work to state offices regularly discovered that the editing which followed seemed ''something rare and peculiar.'' The poet Parker Tyler had little interest in subprojects about foreign newspapers and vitamin research when it seemed they just existed to provide employment. Henry Lee Moon put it most simply in recalling that he had two ambitions on the project. They were: ''Stay on as long as you had to and get off as quickly as you could.''[6]

Editing poorly written manuscripts led to exasperation and boredom. Kenneth Rexroth went over ''some of the most atrocious prose'' he had ever read, including ''the wooden hills appear to be holding in close embrace the mountain that was god.'' This volatile storyteller found some comfort in field trips to collect data on California's flora and fauna for the guide until the ''tragic charade'' of Munich left him ''too politically disgusted to be on any government payroll,'' and he resigned in 1939. John Cheever disliked people in Washington always dressing alike and talking about their civil service classification. Available women, touch football, and a little writing on the side did not compensate for mundane assignments. He offered his resignation to Alsberg when the tasks assigned to him ''seemed neither interesting nor useful,'' but agreed to help with the final editing of the New York City Guide. As soon as that work neared completion, and still uneasy about the disgrace he had brought upon his anti–New Deal family by accepting a project post, Cheever left the FWP to resume his professional career.[7]

The requirement of anonymity inevitably put an additional damper on the project writers' enthusiasm. For example, the jazz critic Charles Smith, who had complete charge of all reading materials for children prepared by the project, received no credit for some 150 publications completed by the time it terminated. Reviewers pointed to this ''serious

[6] Breit interview; Norman MacLeod, *You Get What You Ask For*, p. 79; Parker Tyler interview, Feb. 27, 1968; Henry Lee Moon interview, Dec. 7, 1967.

[7] Rexroth to Hopper, n.d., Box 81, FWPN; John Cheever to author, July 3, 1967; Mangione, *Dream and Deal*, pp. 134, 103.

drawback on the full-blooded functioning'' of the project as the reason why writers could not be blamed if they failed to take great personal interest in its work.[8]

The disillusionment of some professionals resulted from their experience with state project executives. James Aswell and Edward Bunce found Tennessee's director "singularly blind" to vigorous prose. Norman MacLeod (fortunate to be transferred to the New Mexico project after the New York director objected to his drunken sprees and insubordination) could not accept the editing of good copy by New Mexico's Ina Cassidy; he finally resigned. His frustrations with the battles of ideological factions in New York and ineptitude in both projects received fictionalized treatment under the title *You Get What You Ask For*. The other novel about the FWP, *Lamps at High Noon*, was based on Jack Balch's encounter with state politics on the Missouri project.[9]

The situation in the Missouri unit became so intolerable that, for the only time in the FWP's history, the professional writers called a strike in an attempt to get a replacement for their director. Until the end of 1936, the central office believed Geraldine Parker's glowing accounts of her work and that of an editorial staff which included Balch, Conroy, Jean Winkler, and Vance Randolph. (In fact, the Kansas City office, manned by political lackeys of the Pendergast machine, served as a gambling center for horse races, and film for the guide was used for pornography.) The state project head made her first effort to impress Alsberg by inviting him to a luncheon in his honor at the beginning of 1936. Funds for this gathering were collected from project employees, but Parker deferred payment to the Park Plaza Hotel in St. Louis because it was "secondary" to other project expenses. Her incompetence might have gone unnoticed except for the fact that Wayne Barker, a party member in charge of financial records who had organized most of the local professional writers into a union, found discrepancies in the records and got word to Washington. The director and local politicos made sure that he was fired (on charges of peddling smut postcards) for his efforts.[10]

---

[8] Smith to Newsom, Sept. 3, 1939, Box 1967, WPA; Charles Glicksberg, "The Federal Writers' Project," *South Atlantic Quarterly* 37 (Apr., 1938):157-69.

[9] Aswell to Aswell, Mar. 16, 1938, Box 44, FWPN. (The regional director succeeded in removing the Tennessee executive in question.) MacLeod, *You Get*, pp. 157, 167; Jack Balch, *Lamps at High Noon*.

[10] Kellock interview, June 23, 1968; Jack Balch interview, Jan. 19, 1968.

The events that followed Barker's dismissal fused his colleagues into revolt and made national headlines. The former staff employee convinced his left-wing friends that he had really been fired for union activity and for writing in the *New Masses*. The professional editors, under the impression that Alsberg would stand by them, quickly replace Parker, and return Barker to the project, immediately struck. However, the Washington office found itself in "an awful bind," since Alsberg had to think of the Kansas City machine's national political power and of the ensuing danger to the FWP and the entire WPA. The more militant professionals chose not to wait for negotiations, and they picketed the state headquarters. When fourteen received dismissal notices from that office during the strike and picketers were arrested, a number of irate Writers' Unions on other projects wired the central office in protest against Parker's apparent suppression of unionization.[11]

A thorough investigation of Barker's activities and the facts behind the dismissal of the strikers revealed another side to the case. In mid-November, worried by the possibility of increased adverse publicity, Alsberg sent Harris to review the entire issue and clean up the dangerous mess. After careful study and consultation with WPA's state administrator and the vice-president of the Newspaper Guild (who arbitrated the dispute), Harris concluded that Barker had not been fired for either of the reasons for which he had persuaded the local Writers' Union to champion his cause. Alsberg had additional reason to doubt Barker's word after he made unauthorized use of Alsberg's name, while vacationing in Washington, to obtain information about an anti-Semitic organization for the *New Masses*. This unwarranted behavior had nothing to do with his dismissal, according to Harris's report, but, when coupled with Barker's "gross misconduct" and "illegal procuring of federal documents" (obtaining proof of Parker's questionable actions from her private desk), it convinced Washington that he was not "reliable." Of the fourteen dismissed, six had been automatically dropped for "unauthorized absence for more than three days" (a local WPA rule); they received an offer of immediate reinstatement. They included Balch, Conroy, and Jean Winkler, who had been accused by Director Parker of altering Ozark guidebook copy as part of "strike strategy." The others did not receive similar terms, since they had not performed real service for the project and had gone

---

[11] Balch interview; Thompson to Alsberg, Nov. 2, 1936, Box 29, FWPN. For a discussion of these unions, see chap. 9 below.

out on a "protective strike" to save their jobs.[12] In quick fashion, the Washington office settled the embarrassing issue. While the union failed to win its demands, including a 20 per cent increase in wages and Barker's reinstatement, the central office did drop Geraldine Parker (she "resigned" as of mid-December). At long last, too, the luncheon bill for $140 was paid.[13]

At the same time, while Harris succeeded in disclosing some of the union's unjust demands, the dénouement of the episode indicates why some professionals became disgusted with the FWP. Conroy, who the Washington office thought would make an excellent replacement for Geraldine Parker, left Missouri for Chicago's project because "all of us who came back defeated after the strike were penalized in various ways . . . and I was put in a much more menial position." Balch, who had been appointed by Alsberg, eventually left, as the situation "became blander and blander." The person chosen to fill the directorship, a political appointee, proved little better than Parker. Almost two years later, Washington closed the Missouri project. The guide eventually had to be written by Harold Rosenberg of the national office and a few individuals from outside the state.[14]

Balch's disillusionment then found its way into print. He had never approved of Parker, who always sent manuscripts for approval to the Pendergast machine (which had approved her candidacy) before forwarding them to Washington. Silicosis poisoning in mines was thus deleted from copy, and the realism of painter Thomas Hart Benton drew this comment from her WPA superior: "I wouldn't hang him on my shithouse wall. How about writing about our wonderful roads instead?" For a disgusted Balch, the final Missouri Guide was "a whitewash of the state." He decided to convey his recent experiences on the project and a "residual anger" in fictional form, and the result was *Lamps at High Noon.*[15]

Although this project had to suffer an especially heavy influence of

[12] Harris to Anderson, Nov. 25, 1936, Box 55, FWPN; Harris to Hutchinson, Nov. 23, 1939, and Winkler to Cunningham, May 18, 1939, Box 22, FWPN.

[13] Baldwin to Harris, Nov. 20, 1936, Box 31, FWPN; *St. Louis Star-Times,* Nov. 16, 1936.

[14] Harris to Woodward, Dec. 12, 1936, Box 55, FWPN; Jack Conroy to author, Mar. 20, 1968; Balch interview; Harold Rosenberg interview, Jan. 31, 1968.

[15] Balch interview. Geraldine Parker became transformed into a Mr. Thornton C. Hohaley, with James B. Colon, Joe Tremaine, Fred Oneigo, "Hennessey," Lloyd Matson, and Charlie Gest taking the places of Alsberg, Pendergast, Morris, Conroy, Baker, and Balch,

state politics, the problem of local control was also encountered in many other states.[16] It gave professionals another reason to lose interest in their work on the American Guide Series.

II

Most creative writers, in their dissatisfaction with the guides and with the interference of state politics, sought a special program which might cater to their talents. Of a number of proposals to this end, the one that suited professionals best was a subproject enabling them to write in their own homes and then submit evidence of their progress every few weeks to local supervisors. This idea was first suggested by the Writers' Union to the planning division of Federal #1 in the summer of 1934, and the union continued its demand in mid-1936, writing to Alsberg, "We know you agree it is disgraceful to have creative writers waste their talents by reporting on Bronx sewers and Brooklyn bathhouses."[17]

To such requests, the national director replied that plenty of time existed for private creative effort. The project did call for only thirty working hours a week and the completion of a not very difficult assignment—an article of 1,200 to 2,000 words—and workers had weekends entirely free. True, Conrad Aiken was once given twenty-four hours to do a study of Cambridge architecture for the Massachusetts Guide. He learned to stay away from project headquarters and send his wife to deliver his copy—"lest I be dragooned into something further." His brief five months with the project proved "long enough to be overworked by them, as nobody else could write!," and he sailed for England to return to his professional interests. His case was not representative; more often, authors thanked the central office for the assurance of an economic security which enabled them to undertake private ventures, off project time, with peace of mind. The short-story writers John Stahlberg and John Morosso, among others, could now devote "more than the fag ends" of their time and energies to individual interests. Articles by Ralph Henry (Eric Thane) and Genevieve Chandler appeared in the *American Mercury* and

[16] See chap. 2 for more on the local control issue.
[17] Whitcomb to Goldschmidt, Aug. 27, 1934, Box 57, FERAN; Rosenberg to Alsberg, July 15, 1936, Box 34, FWPN. For other suggestions, see p. 13 above. Also, Barrows to Alsberg, Dec. 11, 1936, Box 208, FWPN; Dunton to Alsberg, Apr., 1937, Box 1, LC FWP.

Scribner's. George Cronyn, writing five hours every night, finished *Mermaid Tavern*. Stuart Engstrand completed *The Invaders*, Edward Heth wrote *Told with a Drum*, and Edward Varandyan finished *The Well of Ararat*.[18]

Those who complained about writing for the guides assumed that an opportunity for creativity did not exist in these volumes and that the project should always accommodate them, rather than vice versa. However, as Alsberg pointed out, "a certain rigidity of arrangement" had not interfered with good writing "except where project writers . . . failed to realize the possibilities in this special form." In a number of cases, such mistaken assumptions led professionals to adopt the condescending attitude that guide work was a little beneath their talents. Iowa's director found that one writer "didn't easily respond to any kind of office discipline"; he therefore cut that individual from the project's rolls at the earliest opportunity.[19]

Despite these observations, the national director had a special interest in starting a creative writing program, and he chose employees from New York City for an experiment in this direction. In the fall of 1936 he reached an understanding with New York City's director, Orrick Johns, which permitted Edward Dahlberg, Claude McKay, Maxwell Bodenheim, and four less-known figures to pursue their own interests on the basis of "a special assignment with direct responsibility" to Johns. Dahlberg wrote *Those Who Perish*, Baruch Weinrebe (B. Rivkin) did a study of the main tendencies of Yiddish literature in America, and Bodenheim submitted special narratives for the Reports Project and the piece on Greenwich Village in the guide. In 1937, this group was expanded to twelve, including Richard Wright, Harry Roskolenko, and Lionel Abel and the poets Willard Maas, Sol Funaroff, Helen Neville, and Harry Kemp. Roskolenko produced *Sequence of Violence* and, as a result, got accepted to the writers' retreat at Yaddo on Eleanor Roosevelt's recommendation. Abel translated Rimbaud, Wright began the manuscript which resulted in *Native Son*, and the others wrote poetry.[20]

---

[18] Conrad Aiken to author, Oct. 20, 1967; Stahlberg to Alsberg, May 16, 1938, Box 24, FWPN; Morosso to Alsberg, Aug. 24, 1936, Box 26, FWPN.

[19] Alsberg to Kerr, Mar. 28, 1938, Box 12, FWPN; DuVon to Wittenberg, Dec. 16, 1936, Box 14, FWPN. For information on Alsberg's defense, before a congressional committee, of the creativity involved in writing the guides, see McDonald, *Federal Relief Administration and the Arts*, p. 694.

[20] Johns to Alsberg, Aug. 25 and Sept. 11, 1936, Box 111, FWPN; Roskolenko interview.

This experiment proved extremely difficult to maintain because it lacked the close editorial supervision which was needed to save appointees from "too much daydreaming and procrastination." Writers often handed in material on yellowed paper that had obviously been done a decade ago. Kemp produced little, and another worker submitted one short poem after two and a half months. Bodenheim, who until then had avoided his customary drinking sprees by punctually reporting to work every day, could not cope with the simple requirement of a once-a-week trip to the office. Standing before the office building, the sozzled Greenwich Village poet could not bring himself to enter without a few more drinks at a bar across the street. He eventually staggered in to report with the aid of two friends who had ignored his protests. Considered unsatisfactory because of these and other problems, the New York City creative project was abandoned in the spring of 1938.[21]

The central office approved a few creative project assignments in other states but only sub rosa, as Alsberg told Bert Loewenberg, "lest too many ask to be thus employed." Meridel LeSeuer got on the Minnesota unit to finish a novel while supporting her two children; the playwright Virgil Geddes worked on a book about the Mississippi as a member of the Connecticut project. As a reward for extensive work on the Indiana Guide, state editor Rebecca Pitts received permission to be absent from the local office until the rest of the state guide caught up with her essays and final editing became necessary.[22]

Occasionally, the central office took advantage of professionals in its employ. The classic example was the case of Josef Berger, who, while writing for the Massachusetts Guide, managed to finish a guidebook to Cape Cod in his off-project hours. Drawing heavily on information from local historians and interviews with sea captains, as well as on newspaper clippings, Berger put together a fascinating account of bounty mutineers, "purity posses," clambakes, and dashing army officers who divided their time "between virgin forests abroad and the virgins at home."[23] The copy reached galley proof and the author was looking forward to a well-deserved by-line and royalties when, upon learning of Berger's venture, Gaer and Cronyn insisted that it come out as an FWP publication. Paul Smith of the local Modern Pilgrim Press

[21] Bruere to Kellogg, June 17, 1937, Box 2115, WPA; Thompson interview; Mangione, *Dream and Deal*, p. 160.

[22] Alsberg to Loewenberg, Aug. 1, 1936, Box 99, FWPN; Ulrich to Alsberg, Jan. 27, 1936, Box 21, FWPN; Rebecca Pitts to author, Jan. 2, 1969.

[23] Berger interview; *Cape Cod Pilot* (Provincetown, R.I., 1937).

finally agreed, and Washington representatives replaced the author's foreword with the following statement: "Though a collective task, the editors felt that the folklore and yarns that constitute a major part of the book would be enriched in presentation by the use of the personal pronoun." The preface included a by-line for "Jeremiah Digges" (Berger thought that an English name would better suit the subject) and acknowledged the "editorial and research assistance" of project members. The use of the ad hoc Poor Richard Associates as sponsor enabled Berger to get 10 per cent royalties (paid first to Paul Smith). This procedure would later be copied when the local printer agreed to let Viking Press share in putting out a larger edition to meet increasing demands, after the volume had received favorable reviews.[24]

Cape Cod Pilot drew enthusiastic notices, but the author's identity remained a mystery for some time. Lewis Gannett praised it as "a contribution to American literature as well as to Cape folklore." The librarian of the American Antiquarian Society found the lively volume "delightful" and felt it regrettable that the author had modestly hidden under a pseudonym. However, Harris and Alsberg informed superiors and other state directors that the book's author was "a fictitious character . . . [representing] several writers on the project." When novelist Robert Nathan told the actual author that no major reviewers had received copies, Berger realized that the 150 volumes sent to the central office had probably gone to politicos, and he had to send additional books to newspapers for review. Berger did not gain recognition of sole authorship, and only after his receipt of a Guggenheim (largely on the strength of the book) did Alsberg write his superior: "We've just learned that Jeremiah Digges is Josef Berger. . . ." The volume eventually sold out its edition of 10,000, but Berger refused to sanction a second printing when Viking asked him to take a 50 per cent cut in royalties, and it became a collector's item.[25]

Berger's later work reflected the special interests he further developed while on the FWP. He published *Bowleg Bill*, a series of twelve folk stories based on personal research done before and during the project, and again Viking agreed to include an acknowledgment to the FWP. (105,000 copies were printed for the country's armed forces

[24] Berger interview.

[25] Lewis Gannett quoted in *FWP, Catalogue, American Guide Series* (Washington, D.C., 1938); Vail to Billington, June 14, 1937, Box 54, FWPN; Alsberg to Cronin, Apr. 6, 1938, Box 460, WPA.

during World War II.) In spite of the treatment accorded *Cape Cod Pilot* by the Washington office, the author worked without pay, while beginning research on the Guggenheim, on the chapter of "Living in New England" that dealt with the fishing industry of the area's Portuguese community. (His fellowship study, a history of that fishing community, was published as *In Great Waters* soon thereafter.) His guide to the Cape Cod area led to the proposal of similar treatments of Plymouth, Massachusetts, and the low country of South Carolina.[26]

This personal triumph may well have been what encouraged Alsberg to let a few gifted writers try their hand at other creative ventures. Miriam Allen de Ford received permission to polish up her primary material for a volume of biographical sketches of eminent figures in San Francisco's past, and Kenneth Rexroth put out a manuscript on camping in the Sierras. Caxton Press eventually published *They Were San Franciscans*, but Houghton Mifflin and other firms found Rexroth's book too specialized. Nathan Ausubel's "The Jews of New York," although meriting Alsberg's judgment as "a beautiful piece of work," suffered a similar fate.[27]

With a few notable exceptions, creative projects did not succeed because selection and supervision remained difficult, and the regulations that did exist proved bothersome to the chosen few. Miriam Allen de Ford thought it "unfair and petty harassment" to be forced to follow a new law of the California WPA's timekeeping department that she sign in every morning, instead of sending in her time slip daily. When a supervisor questioned her fight to cover the deportation of Harry Bridges for labor union papers, she got sore and left the project for good. These various difficulties, including the fact that the work of any selected writer could either be "a golden egg or a paving stone," gave Alsberg good cause to abandon his plans for additional work in this direction. He could offer professionals the guide essays and occasional light booklets such as the especially successful New York City *Almanac for 1938* and the San Francisco *Almanac for '39'ers*. Work on folklore was another outlet for creativity: Tillie Olsen for a brief time recorded life stories and songs of Mexicans, Slavs, and Filipinos on the

[26] *Bowleg Bill* (New York, 1938); Gaer to Linscott, June 8, 1937, Box 59, FWPN; Montgomery to Couch, May 18, 1939, Box 2532, WPA.

[27] Miriam Allen de Ford file, Box 81, FWPN; *They Were San Franciscans* (Caldwell, Idaho, 1947); Olsen to Mangione, Mar. 18, 1939, Box 81, FWPN; Alsberg to Strauss, Feb. 7, 1939, Box 31, FWPN.

California project; Algren, Conroy, James Aswell, and Jim Thompson also submitted articles for an intended folk anthology entitled "Nobody With Sense,"[28] but such subprojects did not entirely fulfill writers' creative urges.

Most professional writers worked diligently at their FWP assignments, but the feeling lingered that limited opportunities existed to exercise their talents. Nelson Algren took his supervisory duties relating to Chicago industrial folklore seriously and wrote most of the acclaimed Galena Guide; Arna Bontemps always found him at his desk, hard at work. Yet Algren subsequently dismissed the Illinois unit as "a badly fink-ridden operation" in whose premises he spent less time than in King's Palace (a nearby bar), until he was caught there by a supervisor and fired.

> My move then was to report to the relief office, establish myself as a pauper, and get a free bag of potatoes. This qualified me to get back on the payroll. It usually only took about three days to get back on, so I'd manage to get fired toward the end of the week and get my bag of potatoes on Saturday morning, so I could get back to King's Palace, via the project, by Monday afternoon. This worked out pretty good until the army got me when I wasn't looking. The work habits established by the WPA were by then too strong to break, so I succeeded in spending three years in the service without getting the Good Conduct Ribbon.[29]

Many professionals on the FWP shared an underlying frustration.[30] They could not write novels, plays, and poetry (their real interests) on project time, and they could never completely adjust to the collective authorship of the state guides. Without individual literary outlets, they felt, even their sincerest efforts would be lost in the anonymity of the guidebooks and forgotten in numerous manuscripts which would forever rest in file drawers.

III

Looking upon the guidebooks as "made work for hopeless hacks," a group of professionals took the initiative and established their own

[28] De Ford to Laning, Oct. 21, 1938, Box 81, FWPN; de Ford interview with B. Skydell, Jan. 20, 1969 (notes in possession of author); Tillie Olsen to author, Mar. 4, 1968; "Nobody with Sense" file, Box 472, WPA.

[29] Bontemps interview; Nelson Algren to author, Dec. 6, 1967.

[30] Asked to discuss his experience on the project, John Cheever wrote: "The Washington rooming-houses where one lived, the social and athletic life of the project, the diversity of the

creative ventures. Gifted San Francisco workers were not pleased that the central office, in first concentrating on the guides, had not developed a creative outlet similar to those for other projects in Federal #1. If WPA hoped to rehabilitate the unemployed, it could furnish the means of literary publication just as logically as wall space for a mural or stage area for a play or symphony. Believing that popular magazines were "fake and synthetic" and little magazines frequently short-lived and irresponsibly edited, Lawrence Estavan, a former reporter on the *San Francisco Chronicle*, gathered together the leading writers on the local project to discuss the possibility of an alternative.[31]

An editorial board composed of Miriam Allen de Ford, Leon Dorais, Robin Kinkead, Kenneth Rexroth, and Richard Romain, with Estavan as chairman, elected to write for nothing and save whatever they could from their $65-$95 monthly salaries to pay for the production of a literary anthology. Their enthusiasm and the brashness of youth alone accounted for a remarkably successful first effort. With the cover and name supplied by Rexroth, *Material Gathered* consisted of private pieces, including those regularly rejected by commercial magazines. Every member of the editorial board reviewed the anthology prior to publication. The typing, the cutting and mimeographing of stencils, and the final binding were carried on "before and after hours; the powers that were, winked."[32]

The mimeographed magazine, with a press run of 200, had a commitment to nothing but the chance to act as a quality showcase for unpublished writers (whether unpublished because of the Depression or their refusal to adjust to the left-wing ideology of the contemporary little magazines). Critics seemed to think that it accomplished this objective well. Reviewers in the *New Republic, Prairie Schooner*, and local newspapers came away with very favorable impressions. Stories by Nahum Sabsay, de Ford, Dorais, and Margaret Wilkins and poetry by Rexroth, Estavan, and Raymond Larsson appeared as good as any to be found in *Story, Scribner's, Harper's*, the late *Dial*, and *Hound and Horn*.[33]

---

cast—drunken stringers and first-rate men—the buckling for power, the machinations of the Dies Committee and the sexual and political scandals all make an extremely interesting story but it doesn't seem to be my kind of thing.'' Cheever to author, July 3, 1967.

[31] Lawrence Estavan to author, Dec. 25, 1967.

[32] *Ibid.* I am grateful to Mr. Estavan for copies of *Material Gathered* and *The Coast.*

[33] Estavan to Harris, Nov. 16, 1936, Box 80, FWPN. Reviews can be found in *The Coast.*

The reception of this October, 1936, experiment encouraged the board (now including Ben Hamilton, Dorothy Van Ghent, and Margaret Wilkins) to establish a regularly published literary magazine. Again, the activist Rexroth drew the cover (an outline of the Pacific Coast) and suggested its name. *The Coast* ("A Magazine of Western Writing") appeared in the spring of 1937, at a price of fifty cents to cover part of the printing expenses. This time, to satisfy the central office's original objections that its first effort had given the impression of being an official publication of the writers' project (and hence the government), the board included on the cover of the intended quarterly: "an unofficial cooperative publication of writers on the San Francisco Writers' Project." *The Coast* maintained the high overall quality of its predecessor, but, as the board had no additional funds for a new issue, it died after "one single hour of glorious life." As Estavan later put it, these two offerings represented "a very bright and happy spot in a drab and gloomy decade."[34]

The original hope expressed in the preface of both selections ("the establishment of Federal magazines for creative writers in every locality capable of supporting them"), as well as Estavan's desire for a creative writing project in San Francisco, did not achieve realization. The central office never set up regional magazines as subprojects, and the various state units which attempted to emulate the success of San Francisco's writers produced only feeble facsimiles. They included Vermont's *The Catamount, Prairie Press* and *Over the Turquoise Trail* (both of New Mexico), *'Bama Scripts* (Alabama), *Shucks* (Nebraska), *Manuscripts* (South Dakota), *Forerunner* (Pennsylvania), and *6 × 9* (New Jersey).[35]

The lack of creative talent in most states made regional literary magazines unfeasible as a subproject of the FWP, but a national magazine to serve as a medium for the best efforts of all project employees was conceivable. As had been true with its other undertakings, the central office received this idea from various individuals. The poet Mark Turbyfill and the literary translator Ralph Manheim proposed such an effort, and workers in Phoenix and Puyallup, Washington, suggested one magazine cooperatively owned by its readers and another to include fiction opposed to "morbidity, anti-social deduc-

[34] Lawrence Estavan to author, Dec. 25, 1967.

[35] For critical reviews, see Gaer to Alsberg, Apr. 14, 1937, Box 61, FWPN; Cronyn to Fuhlbruegge, Oct. 30, 1936, Box 108, FWPN.

tions and unthinking Pollyanna-ism.'' The talented writers in the St. Louis office proposed that Jack Conroy's *Anvil* (Conroy, a country boy, thought he had been ''hornswoggled out of his magazine by city slickers Rahv and Phillips'' of *Partisan Review*) be resumed under the project, and promised Alsberg that it would become self-sustaining in a few months.[36]

Some members of the Washington office, Alsberg in particular, were also interested in such a venture, but certain problems seemed insurmountable. They realized that a writers' project without a vehicle of literary publication represented an anomaly. The project had enough fine writers, no American magazine actually devoted itself entirely to belles lettres, and thus (as Alsberg argued) no reason existed why the FWP should not ''move in and take possession'' of the wide-open field. The central office also keenly sensed that anonymity did not prove very satisfying to the project's creative writers. However, a national magazine seemed ''out of the question,'' wrote Alsberg in April, 1936, ''because we're not even publishing a house organ containing comparatively innocuous material about WPA.'' The problem of finding sponsors to finance the venture—which would not make a profit—also presented itself.[37]

For more than a year and a half, Alsberg and the executive board tried unsuccessfully to initiate such a magazine. The national director's call immediately drew a favorable response; Vermont's Doten even suggested that it would represent ''a long step'' in the direction of national support for future literary efforts. To avoid any conflict with government printing rules, the Washington office decided that it would be done by multilith (rather than typesetting) and that it would not be sold. With the publication and favorable reception of *Material Gathered*, the national director's faith quickened that the public would give the project much support, and he suggested $800 as the magazine's monthly cost. However, complications of various sorts arose, including the fact that literary craftsmen expressed their reluctance to forward material when neither payment nor project hours would be granted for producing it.[38]

''As a last desperate remedy,'' Alsberg finally called for contribu-

[36] Balch *et al.* to Alsberg, n.d., Box 460, WPA; Jack Conroy to author, June 10, 1968.

[37] Alsberg to Hopper, June 18, 1937, Box 80, FWPN; Alsberg to Johns, Apr. 4, 1936, Box 31, FWPN.

[38] Doten to Alsberg, Aug. 24, 1936, Box 185, FWPN; ''Report to the City Projects Council,'' Feb. 1, 1937, Authors' League papers.

tions of off-time work for a future anthology (if a sponsor could be found), and a worthy collection unfolded. An editorial board, headed by Vincent McHugh and including Donald Thompson and Travis Hoke, found that contributors to *American Stuff* mainly focused on contemporary social themes. The plight of the Negro received vivid portrayal in Richard Wright's autobiographical segment about the South, "The Ethics of Jim Crow" (which the editors fortunately realized was "the no. 1 piece in the book," despite Alsberg's hesitation over its frank truths). Sterling Brown's poem about the brutality and dearth of hope confronting black children proved a worthy supplement. Harry Roskolenko dwelt on the harshness of industrial environments, and Leon Dorais contributed a piece, taken from *The Coast*, on the anonymity of relief applicants. Edwin Bjorkman and Salvatore Attansio spoke out against totalitarian values and in favor of the democratic ideal. Viking Press thought so highly of the collection that it put out a first edition of 5,000 (instead of the usual 1,500 for such a volume), with a 20 per cent royalty on the wholesale price thereafter.[39]

With the success of *American Stuff*, the national director tried to promote other creative possibilities. He had hoped that the anthology and similar offerings would compare favorably in quality with what had been produced by the other arts projects, and would hence be included in any plans for the perpetuation of Federal #1. He also wanted the literary ferment of a troubled America to find a voice on the project. While attending the 1937 American Writers' Congress as an invited speaker, Alsberg expressed to John Hyde Preston his desire to find as many markets as possible for project writers. Shortly thereafter, Preston informed him that he had begun a new magazine called *Direction* and eagerly sought "thoughtful work that has a social meaning." Having failed in negotiations with *Story* and *American Quarterly*, Alsberg agreed to draw up a contract for two issues. Preston would spend about $950 on the first number, with $500 allocated to the sponsoring body and the rest for printing costs.[40]

To facilitate publication of the national magazine, Alsberg brought

[39] Foreword, *American Stuff;* Harris to Isbell, n.d., Box 185, FWPN; Thompson interview; Stott, *Documentary Expression*, pp. 51-53. While some reviews of the volume reflected a conservative bias (see *Washington Evening Star,* Aug. 28, 1937), more liberal readers found little class hatred or left-wing rhetoric, and some, like Stephen Vincent Benét, claimed that it had enough good work to qualify as "a unique piece of book-making." *New York Herald Tribune,* Sept. 5, 1937, X, p. 1.

[40] Alsberg to Hutchinson, Sept. 21, 1937, Box 37, FWPN; Preston to Alsberg and Morifield, Jan. 11, 1938, Box 32, FWPN.

Harold Rosenberg (an established poet then on the New York City art project) to the FWP as the new editor. To satisfy noisy left-wingers, Fred Rothermell and George Petry were picked as his assistants. After executive members of the project turned down such suggestions for names as "Boondoggle," "We Say," "Procession," and "American Ground," Jerre Mangione and Alsberg persuaded Viking Press that the use of "American Stuff" would not interfere with the sales of its book by that name. Including pieces from *Material Gathered*, a subtle study of Yiddish literature, an ex-slave narrative, and eight prints by the Federal Art Project, the contents showed a catholicity and variety of talent similar to those revealed in the volume's larger namesake.[41]

The feasibility of a permanent national magazine as a subproject of the FWP seemed evident at last, as Alsberg wrote state directors in early 1938, but new difficulties arose. By the end of that year, *American Stuff* (at $2.00) had sold 1,444 copies and the special issue (at 25¢), 3,100 copies.[42] The second *Direction* issue could not be completed, however, because the freedom from constraint of which Rosenberg wrote in his first preface was not extended to the ideological sphere: Rosenberg found that the Communist party members of the American Writers' Union on the New York project (where the magazine was being compiled) sought to frustrate the publication's nonpartisan policy. Delegations constantly came to Alsberg urging that only specific material be published, and party adherents tried to gain control of the editorial board so they could "boast in Moscow that they had a magazine with funds from the U.S. government." When Alsberg visited the New York project, as he often did, these delegations would object that the national magazine was not "democratic," since no votes could be taken on articles finally chosen. It could only be considered anti-Semitic, they argued, because neither of the assistant editors was a Jew (in spite of the fact that Alsberg, Gaer, and Rosenberg were). Party members picketed Rosenberg's office (they thought him a Trotskyite), and the final appearance of the magazine caused the executive secretary of the Federal Writers' Local of the Workers' Alliance to accuse Alsberg of not giving it the "progressive direction requisite to its success."[43]

[41] Rosenberg interview; "American Stuff by Workers of the Federal Writers' Project," *Direction* 1, no. 3 (Feb., 1938).

[42] Alsberg to Corse, Jan. 27, 1938, Box 85, FWPN; Kerr to Austin, May 27, 1939, Box 2117, WPA.

[43] Rosenberg interview; Konecky to Alsberg, Sept. 3, 1937, Box 31, FWPN.

These forces ended all hope for a national project magazine. The delegations became so persistent that Alsberg, "partly to get rid of the noise" and also to have an authority edit the guide art essays, invited Rosenberg to become a member of the central staff. The embattled editor, just then trying to supplement his income with poorly paid reviews of books on art, received the long-distance call from Washington in the offices of a New York publisher. Flinging a badly executed manuscript on the desk of the startled executive who had been trying to persuade him to undertake a rewrite for a pittance, Rosenberg announced his acceptance of "a position with the U.S. Government" and left in a huff. It was suggested that Petry take his place, with Willard Maas or another member of the creative project joining the editorial board, but these plans did not materialize. A projected volume for May, 1938, to include material from Mormon diaries discovered by project workers, samples of New York's "Lexicon of Trade Jargon," a piece on Georgia Coast superstitions, and work by Fearing, Bodenheim, Jim Thompson, and Dorais, never saw print. John Frederick refused to join the editorial board, not wanting to face pressures from New York's radical groups, who were then attempting to use the magazine for their own social-economic point of view. The sponsoring Guilds' Committee did conduct preliminary negotiations in August, 1939, for a second volume to be entitled "New American Stuff," but the project's demise ended this last attempt for a national creative magazine.[44]

The success of *American Stuff* led to special issues devoted to off-project work in a few notable magazines. The idea for the most distinguished of these, the *Poetry* "Federal Poets Number," had been suggested to its editor by Willard Maas. Alsberg convinced *Poetry*'s editor that this special title would result in more publicity and distribution. Maas selected contributions purely on qualitative grounds, and thus received the *Daily Worker*'s criticism for including Trotskyites and "dilettantes" in the issue. In review, John Peale Bishop praised the fact that "both the pallid and the rubicund" had been admitted to an uncensored anthology, and he especially hailed the work of Raymond Larsson and Kenneth Fearing for being concerned with the "depriva-

---

[44] Rosenberg interview; Frederick to Alsberg, Apr. 4, 1938, Box 185, FWPN; Alsberg to Sieve, Aug. 17, 1939, Box 186, FWPN. Kenneth Burke, though not a member of the FWP, was offered the editorship of the magazine to mollify feuding Stalinists and Trotskyites. He turned it down for a teaching position at the University of Chicago, unwilling to become embroiled in what he later called "the combustion of paranoia politica." Mangione, *Dream and Deal*, pp. 102, 249.

tion and doubt'' which formed the actualities of the decade. Two other collections, a brief one in the *New Republic* (edited by Sol Funaroff) and an entire issue in the *New Masses* (edited by Funaroff and Maas), proved decidedly inferior.[45]

The editors of these anthologies sought to create public support for the continuation of the project on a permanent basis, without the hated relief requirement, by means of the pending Coffee-Pepper federal arts bill. Malcolm Cowley, who hoped that as a result the best of the FWP poets would receive permanent aid, emphasized, ''If we want to have poets in this country, we will have to keep them alive.'' Maas pointed out that the special issue of *Poetry* served as an argument that regimentation would not occur under a permanent Federal Bureau of Fine Arts. Funaroff foresaw that ''the literary class of '29'' would come of age, leading to the final emergence of ''a people's literature'' in this country, but the bill met Congress's hereditary opposition to such a scheme, and what Cowley called ''the first of all the literary arts and the key to appreciating the others'' never received federal subsidy.[46]

In his fervent desire to present professionals with additional avenues for creative work, Alsberg suggested that the editor of *Story* sponsor a competition for project employees. A prize of $500 and the publication of his manuscript would be awarded the winner. In early 1938, judges Sinclair Lewis, Lewis Gannett, and Harry Scherman (president of the Book-of-the-Month Club) informed the public that the work of a twenty-nine-year-old unknown named Richard Wright had won first prize in a field of 600 applicants. Meridel LeSeuer's short novel, *The Horse*, took second place.[47]

Wright's talent had been discovered by project officials prior to the contest. When a friend suggested that he leave a post office job to apply for the FWP, the future author took the chance. Work on some ethnological aspects of Chicago's Black Belt for the Illinois project, the

[45] Willard Maas interview, Dec. 11, 1967; Alsberg to Dillon, Apr. 22, 1938, Box 33, FWPN; ''Federal Poets Number,'' *Poetry* 52 (July, 1938); *Poetry* 52 (Aug.,1938):276-83; ''Federal Poets,'' *New Republic* 95 (May 11, 1938):10-12; ''Federal Writers' Number,'' *New Masses* 27 (May 10, 1938):97-127.

[46] *Poetry* 52 (July, 1938):224-27; *New Masses* 27 (May 10, 1938):127. A proposed anthology of verse by twenty-five project workers, submitted for Maas's editing, was never published. The best selections, from such writers as Clifton Cuthbert, Miriam Allen de Ford, Weldon Kees, William Pillin, Mark Turbyfill, and Charlotte Wilder, were recommended for deposit in the Library of Congress in 1941. Original scripts, D.C. file, Box 14, LC FWP.

[47] *Story* file, Box 34, FWPN.

publication of "Big Boy Leaves Home" in *American Caravan* (1936), and the contribution to *American Stuff* led to his becoming Alsberg's first choice to assume Sterling Brown's editorial position in the central office when Brown received a Guggenheim fellowship. Wright's plan for a portrait of the Negro on the social scene of the preceding twenty years, based on the files of the Associated Negro Press, ran parallel in part to Brown's proposal, and he had a keen interest in the project's work in this unexplored field. However, Alsberg did not have his way and only got Wright on the New York City project after experiencing much difficulty over relief requirements. While rewriting the Negro essay for that guide and the sections relating to Harlem on a $95.44 security monthly wage, Wright worked on four short stories—about the cruel prejudice of whites and the unyielding resentment of blacks—and submitted them under the significant title of *Uncle Tom's Children* for the contest that would bring him a wide audience for the first time.[48] A Negro author, who until a few years previously had had to get books from a Memphis library by writing a note, "Please let this niggar [*sic*] boy have the following books" and then signing the name of a white man who had befriended him, saw his first book published by Harper & Brothers. So was launched a distinguished career.[49]

Native Son, which the $500 prize money permitted Wright to finish, proved the award no mistake. The author, at last having what he called "a riding tag clear across the Jordan," recognized the FWP's importance in his literary career. His publisher emphasized Wright's connection with the project and wrote Alsberg that the author's securing a place in American letters would be "a feather in the cap of WPA." A few months later, the *New Masses* collection of project material included his "Bright and Morning Star." This obvious piece of "revolutionary literature" would not be followed by others, as Wright moved away from the Communist party orbit through the influence of Maas, Roskolenko, and others on the New York City project and some bitter disillusionment with Communist officials soon afterwards. With the help of *Uncle Tom's Children* and Alsberg's recommendation, he

[48] Alsberg to Woodward, Oct. 27, 1937, Box 56, FWPN; Alsberg to Hopkins, Apr. 13, 1938, Box 30, FWPN; *Uncle Tom's Children* (New York, 1938). For additional background on this novel, see Keneth Kinnamon, *The Emergence of Richard Wright*, pp. 72-73.

[49] *American Stuff*, p. 51. For reviews, see *New York Herald Tribune*, Mar. 25, 1938; *New York Post*, Mar. 25, 1938; *New Masses* 27 (Mar. 29, 1938):23-24.

won a Guggenheim in 1939. Wright left the project with the hope that he could justify, by creative work, the "kind faith" placed in him by the national director.[50]

Wright's success alone might justify the existence of the writers' project (were it not for its other numerous and varied achievements), but his story could hardly be considered representative for the other creative writers on its rolls. Indispensable to the progress of the state guides, they could not be spared to produce creative work of their own. Unlike other artists attached to Federal #1, most professionals on the FWP had little opportunity to exhibit their talents. *Material Gathered, The Coast, American Stuff*, and the special issues of *Direction* and *Poetry* were small reward for writers who resented guide work and often had to face incompetent superiors. Of the various attempts to permit greater leeway, only *Cape Cod Pilot* saw print during the project's existence, and that volume had practically been completed as a private venture before the FWP began. For various reasons, the creative project had to be closed, and Alsberg's idea for an anthology of foreign-born writers in the United States also had to be scrapped.[51]

The FWP had limited value for professional writers. The project never became the spearhead for a permanent writers' bureau, and it extended official support for a literary cause only when Harris wrote to the president of Vanguard Press against the anti-vice squad's suppression of James T. Farrell's *A World I Never Made*. However, it did represent what Harry Roskolenko later termed the "spiritual and financial wherewithal" to continue their work for a number of professionals besides Wright. Washington did not give Mark Turbyfill a hard time when he worked on the Illinois Guide and some radio scripts; Ralph Ellison took this rare opportunity to learn his craft. His work with the New York City unit saved Ted Poston from going back to a dining-car waiter's job, instead of forward to a future with the *New York Post*. An unknown just out of college, bored with compiling lists of magazines in Chicago's Newberry Library, found his project work writing biographical sketches of midwestern authors more enjoyable; years later,

[50] "Who's Who in Writers," Box 74, FWPN; Yezierska, *Red Ribbon on a White Horse*, p. 195; Aswell to Shaw, June 1, 1938, Box 30, FWPN; *New Masses* 27 (May 10, 1938); Maas interview; Richard Crossman, ed., *The God That Failed*, p. 115-63; Wright to Alsberg, Mar. 27, 1937, Box 462, WPA.

[51] Adamic to Alsberg, Apr. 10, 1938, Box 26, FWPN.

Saul Bellow would recall this experience, in "the days before gratitude became obsolete," fondly.[52] The writers' project served to tide a number of established writers over the country's worst economic crisis and to give many younger aspirants the chance to develop their talents.[53] In the process, it also supplied them with varied, if few, means of literary achievement which became the harbingers of eventual individual success.

[52] Harris to Henle, Feb. 2, 1937, Box 34, FWPN; Roskolenko interview; Mark Turbyfill telephone conversation with author, Mar. 31, 1968; Poston interview; Mangione, *Dream and Deal*, pp. 123, 95.

[53] A representative example is Stuart Engstrand, who came to the Arizona project "at the end of his stake rope," penniless, with an expectant wife, and "so worried he couldn't write." Santee to Alsberg, July 22, 1936, Box 2, FWPN. Shortly thereafter, Knopf published his first book *(The Invaders)*. He later became editor of the Illinois project, placed a close second to Vardis Fisher for the *Harper's* book prize of 1939, and finally left for Hollywood, where he became a millionaire writing movie scripts.

OF THE VARIOUS CHARGES HURLED against the Federal Writers' Project, none had more force than that accusing it of being a "Red Nest"
and "a festering sore of communism." That a sizeable number of
Communists and fellow travelers worked on the project cannot be
denied, nor should this fact be surprising. Strong emotional factors, as
well as the Communist party's seemingly valid analyses of the Depression, led many creative artists to link their destinies with that of the
party in its attempts to solve the nation's ills.[1]

This allegiance did not, fortunately for them, prevent their getting
jobs on Federal #1. In a decision which reflected idealism and concern
for the needy, FDR and Hopkins emphasized that WPA would neither
discriminate because of political beliefs nor inquire of its employees
the nature of their politics. No "red hunt" would be conducted in the
Federal Arts Projects, resolved Hopkins and Baker in mid-1936, because it could easily disrupt work on other relief agencies and merely
give credit to rumors of all sorts. Performance alone would serve as the
criterion for employment.[2]

Using the WPA standard, the fundamental question in studying this
aspect of the writers' project is not the number of party members or
sympathizers on its rolls, but whether their ideology interfered with
their duties as federal employees. In most states, they constituted only a
small number of the project's workers and had little if any influence on
its activities. Desperately needing their relief checks, they rarely risked
any move which might deprive them of this newly found security.
A former party candidate for attorney general of Milwaukee and a
sociologist kicked out of the University of Kansas because of radical
teaching were among those who worked unstintingly for the project
without resorting to left-wing activity. An investigation of a Writers'

[1] *New York Times*, Nov. 2, 1936; pp. 3-4 and Prologue, note 7, above.
[2] Baker interview.

Union group by a G-man confirmed that the Marxist sympathies of the Oklahoma project's executives and staff did not interfere with responsible FWP duties. Sexual rather than political activity interested Nebraska's "parlor pinks," in the opinion of that project's assistant director. The Illinois unit had a few professed Communists, but the only embarrassment Director John Frederick suffered from their presence was a result of their tendency to quarrel with employees with different views.[3]

Proof of valuable work did not prevent radicals who worked on the project from being dismissed or transferred from their jobs, however. With the approval of the central office, Jay Du Von moved to the Illinois unit from the Iowa directorship partly because the WPA administrator was leery of his leftist inclinations. A "red-baiter" in the Orlando office transferred an avowed Communist to a park project, despite his fine work on Florida Guide copy, on the claim that the worker in question might destroy valuable books and private papers—"as a Communist doesn't believe in private property."[4]

On the California project, as elsewhere, Communist party members who engaged in political activity during FWP hours focused their attention on the maintenance and expansion of jobs. The *Los Angeles Times,* refusing to condone this activity, editorialized, "This government owes no alien a living, whether it owes citizens one or not." Yet militants did not use that project for the furtherance of any subversive philosophy. Like its Chicago counterpart, the California unit had a Trotskyite faction feuding with Stalinists, a staff writer who later made the Hollywood blacklist, and even a right-wing group, but ideological disputes had no influence on the quality or quantity of manuscripts produced.[5]

[3] Cunningham to Alsberg, Dec. 30, 1936, Box 39, FWPN; Rudolph Umland to author, May 28, 1968; John Frederick to author, Apr. 6, 1968. Umland added that an FBI probe, inspired by charges from Nebraska's director that he and Mother Bloor had instigated a farmers' march to gain a state mortgage moratorium in 1933, finally concluded in 1941 that the only thing red about him was his moustache.

[4] Morris to Alsberg, Nov. 5, 1935, Box 59, FWPN; Harris to Rogg, Apr. 18, 1936, Box 55, FWPN. Another prospective candidate for the directorship of the northern California project was turned down because his sentiments about the Spanish Loyalists had aroused the ire of the Catholic church and it was felt that his presence might embarrass the project. Laning to Alsberg, n.d., Box 938, WPA.

[5] *Los Angeles Times,* Jan. 24, 1936; Edward to Hopkins, Mar. 14, 1936, Box 4, FWPN; Leon Dorais to author, Mar. 14, 1968.

Various factors explain the successes which the party did realize. Communist influence could help one to get a job, especially in the larger urban centers of Chicago, Los Angeles, and New York. In Chicago, sympathetic social workers tipped off the party's Unemployment Councils when cuts were pending; as a result, one council did some effective work in getting "403'd" workers back on the project. But here, too, "no one in an administrative post acted like a Communist." Toward the close of the Los Angeles project, left-wing militants made up the bulk of its rolls, much to the consternation of professional, politically independent writers like Kenneth Patchen and Harvey Breit. The fact that WPA approved of unionization and that Washington received the party's labor delegations with the same respect shown all others contributed, in no small measure, to its successes. Because the various City Projects Councils, Writers' Unions, and local Workers' Alliance units proved the most aggressive and unified of all groups in presenting their demands, the party managed to unionize relief workers, hold mass protests, and score its varied triumphs in this regard.[6] Yet it exerted limited influence, since WPA officials were primarily governed by congressional whims and fixed appropriations.

In spite of the generous attitude adopted by WPA administrators regarding employment and political beliefs, the fulminations of "front" unions in various state projects hardly bespoke gratitude. Indeed, these groups often proved annoying as well as embarrassing to FWP officials in sympathy with their objection to slashes in the relief rolls. When the cuts inevitably occurred, the Workers' Alliance of Essex County, New Jersey, was particularly adamant in charging that its project members "got the axe" because of union discrimination. Pennsylvania's director admittedly placed several members of the Writers' Union on the Philadelphia project and permitted them to solicit funds for Spanish Loyalists and seamen's strikes, post notices of their meetings, and picket WPA headquarters without incurring severe penalties.[7]

In the case of the Massachusetts Guide, the tactics of the predom-

---

[6] Jack Conroy to author, Mar. 20, 1968; Anderson to Alsberg, Jan. 14, 1939, Box 4, FWPN. For New York City, see pp. 186-94 below.

[7] J. David file, Box 26, FWPN; French to Brown, Apr. 7, 1938, Box 2446, WPA. For the Writers' Union as a party front, see chap. 1 above.

inantly Communist Boston Writers' Union proved so disruptive that state officials awarded one concession to its members to save the project. Mediocrity became perpetuated not only through relief regulations, but also because of the union's constant strike threats and slowdown methods. Its members finally succeeded in getting a separate essay inserted in the Massachusetts Guide which stressed the commonwealth's literature from the aspect of group movements like Brook Farm. This addition, they reasoned, would counter Conrad Aiken's original piece accenting New England individualism. In effect, the guide had two essays on one topic arguing against each other, but, as director Ray Allen Billington later wrote, "the division was too great to be compromised except in this way."[8]

An even more disturbing case of party influence occurred in the Minnesota project, where the Communist party executive drew bored and grievance-nursing relief workers into the local Workers' Alliance and threatened a strike which finally led to the project director's resignation. When Director Mabel Ulrich ordered the transfer of two incompetent workers, because of relief cuts and with the approval of the state WPA administrator, the president of the alliance called for an immediate investigation and a possible strike. Despite an impartial review by John Frederick that fully supported Ulrich's position, the power of the alliance and the solid backing which it received from the CIO carried such weight in Washington that Alsberg wired that no further transfers were to be made. When the governor and the alliance joined forces with the newly formed Farmer-Labor party to oust WPA's state administrator and gain control of state relief appointments, Hopkins listened. This removal led to the director's "collapse of faith" in WPA's "disinterested leadership" and, concomitantly, the loss of her last hope for a writers' project in Minnesota "that intelligence or even pity could justify."[9]

Other accusations of radical activity on the FWP had little basis in fact. "The presence of Communists was accidental and they were of low virulence," concluded a visiting state director after observing that most so-called radicals on the Oregon project were workers who

[8] Ray A. Billington to author, Apr. 7, 1968. Regional director Frank Manuel later found it necessary to question the bald Marxist dialectic which ruined a potentially valuable study entitled *Living in New England*; its chief editor was dismissed from the state project because of this. McDonald, "Federal Relief," p. 784.

[9] Ulrich, "Salvaging Culture for the WPA"; Ulrich to Alsberg, June 8, 1938, Box 21, FWPN.

squirmed under incompetent supervisors. A "red scare" was thrown at the professionals who went out on strike against the inefficient Missouri director. "A stool pigeon," Jack Conroy later wrote, "tried to get projecteers to make inflammatory statements, pressing radical literature upon them, but with absolutely no success." The fears of Indianapolis's civic leaders to the contrary, one state director informed Alsberg that "if all the Communists in Indiana were laid end-to-end and stretched across the steps of the state house, it would still be possible to leave the building without having to step over anyone." A former state editor reported that no factors other than ability and personality motivated the state of Washington's director to make various selections and removals in her rolls, notwithstanding the accusations of State Senator Mary Farquharson. In some instances, incompetents fired from the project denounced supervisory officials as radicals.[10]

The central office found it difficult to squelch false rumors, especially in the case of its tour editor. The appointment of Katherine Kellock, referred to as the "wife of the publicity director of the Soviet Embassy," convinced the National Republican Builders' Organization that the New Deal was "permeated with Communism." When the Soviet government achieved recognition from the United States, Harold Kellock received an opportunity to serve as the Soviet Embassy's publicity director. Like many other newspapermen, he took the position that provided the best chance to use his talents. Despite replies by Washington officials to senators, civic organizations, and the Democratic National Committee, the lie did not get spiked for a number of years.[11]

Charges of radicalism leveled against the FWP and its employees often came from a conservative perspective. William Randolph Hearst's *New York American* editorialized that the detailed information on state resources and the communication maps given in the Guide Series again proved to be "indisputable evidence of the COMMUNIST CHISELING that is being winked at in high quarters"; project writers might expose America's military installations to the Soviet Union. Frank accounts of labor and the Negro in the state guides also led to

[10] Scammell to Alsberg, Oct. 5, 1937, Box 40, FWPN; Jack Conroy to author, Mar. 20, 1938; Dunton, Aug. 4, 1936, report, Box 59, FWPN; Burns to Alsberg, Feb. 20, 1939, Box 48, FWPN. For use of the project as an issue to discredit the liberal wing of the state Democratic party in Washington, see Taber, "Writers' Project in Pacific Northwest," pp. 66-71.

[11] *New York Times,* Feb. 20, 1936; McClure to Godwin, Feb. 27, 1936, Box 55, FWPN.

such accusations. The American Vigilance Committee, with headquarters in Colonel Robert McCormick's *Chicago Tribune* tower, had no doubts that the local unit was full of boondoggling Communists.[12]

A distinction must be drawn between the ideology and the actual performance of most Communists on the FWP. Except in Massachusetts, Minnesota, and the New York City project, discussed in detail below, membership in the party resulted in little substantial harm to guide manuscripts. A few state units exercised favoritism in employing party card carriers, but throughout the FWP's existence project executives evaluated most workers on the grounds of capability. At the same time, while its liberal analyses of then controversial subjects antagonized a number of self-appointed patriots, the central office never allowed any state guide to become what one Hearst editorial termed a ''red Baedeker.''[13]

II

One exceptional case of Communist activity during project hours led to widespread dissension and the subsequent deterioration of morale. With the formation of the Reporters Project, under the direction of the poet Orrick Johns, the FWP in New York City began in September, 1935, to write about local WPA activities. The central office next appointed Walter Van Olinda, a former editor of encyclopedias, and Samuel McCoy, author and Pulitzer Prize–winning newspaperman, as state and associate director, respectively, of the guidebook project. The Communist party saw the project as the perfect opportunity to recruit members via the Writers' Union, and it began staging mass demonstrations and sending delegations to Washington to ask for additional jobs.[14]

In a bold attempt to gain control of the membership, party councils first succeeded in having the director transferred from the local unit. Van Olinda had not exhibited administrative ability, but he had made it plain to the union that politics would not play any part in work on the guide. In the absence of strong executive leadership, McCoy, the associate director, drew up new employment forms (which established

[12] *New York American*, Feb. 15, 1936; Frederick to Alsberg, n.d., Box 12, FWPN.

[13] *New York American*, Feb. 15, 1936.

[14] *New York Sun*, May 9, 1939; MacLeod, *You Get*, pp. 66, 77-78. (Ivan Terry is substituted for Ivan Black, the representative.)

personal criteria for hiring to avoid political appointments to the project) on his own and against WPA regulations when Washington permitted increases in the rolls during early January, 1936. He persisted in his actions (which he would later repudiate as wrong and insubordinate), thereby contributing to the continuing chaos in editorial procedure and appointments. The situation became aggravated by the increasing hostility and political wrangling between the union and a newly formed group (the Federal Writers' Association) which resisted the party's growing power and had the strong support of McCoy and, to a lesser extent, Van Olinda. As a result, little was accomplished in the way of concrete work. One of the association's members correctly noted the union's support of loafers and incompetents, as well as its threats against supervisors demanding worthwhile copy. The party then mapped out a strategy which called for throwing pickets around project headquarters every day, saying that Van Olinda had displayed incompetence and had aligned himself with Fascists on the local unit. With the factions at daggers' points and with little substantial progress on the guide, Alsberg decided to transfer Van Olinda to the central office, where his editorial experience could be well employed, and have Orrick Johns take over the directorship.[15]

The national director's attempt at an amicable settlement satisfied the union's executive, since the new director had been a party member and a former editor of the *New Masses,* with strong sympathies toward worker unionization, but McCoy refused to cooperate. He telegraphed the Democratic National Committee and summoned police to the project's office at 113 East Thirty-second Street on his own initiative to halt the party's influence on the local unit. They found nothing tangible and left; WPA's Federal #1 representative immediately dismissed McCoy for "obstructive insubordination and incompetence." McCoy insisted that the removal followed his efforts to "prevent Alsberg from loading his organization with Communists" and that all delays and lack of organization resulted from the union's subversive activities. A veteran newspaperman named Travis Hoke was appointed in his place to assist Johns on the guide. The central office transferred the worst troublemakers of both factions to the Reporters Project (now located in offices removed from the local unit), and the assistant WPA adminis-

---

[15] Ralph De Sola to author, Dec. 17 and 26, 1967; Alsberg report and McCoy to Alsberg, Jan. 31, 1936, Box 2114, WPA.

trator in charge of labor relations decreed that factional activities henceforth would be forbidden during office hours.[16]

The union's central committee, which had gained the allegiance of some 75 per cent of the workers by manufacturing fears about a Fascist dictatorship on the project and by its success in having Van Olinda removed, had no intentions of following the ban on political activity. With other front organizations like the Workers' Alliance, the City Projects Council, and local Unemployment Councils, the union maintained boisterous picket lines daily and sent delegations representing the unemployed streaming in and out of the office at all hours. The frequency of demonstrations caused the owners of the building housing the local office to issue a dispossess order to the project as undesirable tenants; the work lost in relocation added to the New York unit's sluggish performance. In response to the WPA administrator's appeal for "loyal" elements in the project's ranks to organize against left-wing agitators, a group of workers formed the American Writers' Association to combat communism, and various accusations about party activity put the project on page one of the *New York Times* with increasing frequency.[17]

Various compromises did not satisfy the Writers' Union, and Johns failed to maintain executive control. The union got Johns's promise, after resorting to a sit-down strike, that its members would receive 40 per cent of an additional fifty openings, but this required the hiring of many writers of dubious qualification. Having succeeded in this attempt, it soon called for another sit-down against a new WPA investigation of the home life of every project worker to determine need for the job; this time police evicted its members. In December, 1936, when Hopkins's office ordered cuts across the board, a third sit-down took place. Despite the police, sympathizers hauled up sandwiches to the strikers from the outside via a ripped-out eighty-foot telephone line, and those inside held a barn dance and community sing. WPA's new administrator, Colonel Brehon Somervell, finally forced the issue by locking the toilets in the building; after an eighteen-hour siege, his action led to the voluntary exit of the strikers. Johns officially resigned in protest against the cuts and reiterated his point in an autobiography

---

[16] *New York Times,* Feb. 14, 1936; Alsberg report, Feb. 11, 1936, and Alsberg to Baker, Feb. 13, 1936, Box 2114, WPA; *New York Sun,* Feb. 25, 1936. In the MacLeod novel, Sam McClellan and Van Loon are McCoy and Van Olinda, respectively; Vincent Jones is Orrick Johns.

[17] *New York Sun,* May 9, 1939; *New York Times,* Mar. 21 and Apr. 14, 1936.

remarkably silent about the party's influence on the project's workers. Actually, Johns's incompetence and heavy drinking, as well as his hospitalization for some six weeks after a severe beating by a disgruntled office seeker, forced Washington to ask for his resignation.[18]

Some welcome changes at the administrative level had limited value. Travis Hoke succeeded Johns but drinking and neuroses forced him to resign after about a half-year, whereupon his assistant, a former newspaper editor named Donald Thompson, became executive director over his "shrill protests." The novelist Vincent McHugh, known for *Caleb Catlum's America* and his subsisting on milk shakes for reasons of health, was put in full charge of guide editorial work. This fragile-looking executive brought new life to the New York unit by first rescuing the guide manuscript from Mayor La Guardia's office with a promise of thorough revision and then convincing the national office to adopt his plan for the volume. To some extent, the quality of the project did improve, but the "backlog of incompetents" who Thompson felt would have better served a bookkeeping project kept the guide merely shuffling along. By continuing to employ its militant tactics, the union gained concessions from the local Federal #1 representative and sought to have all employees in the office rerated to the "Master Writer" category. Deadlines had to be pushed up regularly, an especially sad state of affairs considering that the New York project had no equal in terms of talent.[19]

In some instances, those who denied that a "red nest" had gained control of the New York City project could not claim objectivity. The City Projects Council's executive secretary derided accusations that it dominated the project as "the imaginative phantasies of a diseased mind." Travis Hoke dismissed remarks about Communist activities during project hours as "a lot of baloney."[20]

When the executive secretary of the National Civic Federation declared, in July, 1937, that party members and the Workers' Alliance controlled a vast majority of the project's personnel and contributed to "gross inefficiency and waste," while "a startlingly large proportion of supervisors included convicts, former bootleggers, drunkards . . . professional agitators and moral perverts," he met with a spirited

---

[18] Donald Thompson report (copy in author's possession, gift of Carl Malmberg); *New York Times*, Dec. 4-5, 1936; p. 43 above; Harris interview.

[19] Thompson interview; Thompson report; Mangione, *Dream and Deal*, p. 170.

[20] *New York American*, Apr. 29, 1936; *New York Times*, Apr. 15, 1936.

reaction. Project directors in Michigan and New York State objected to the President that their states were free of such influence, and Alsberg discussed the productivity and literary competence of the FWP in general. As if beside himself, WPA's Colonel Somervell branded the charges "a lot of fatuous twaddle" and "illogical, irrational, unreasonable, imprudent, careless and specious." Robert Morss Lovett of the *New Republic* insisted that the accuser had "exploited the prejudices and fears of his country" for years through such politically animated attacks.[21]

However, although the mixture of Communist charges and counter-charges often resulted from differing ideological motives, and although it is true that "practically every worker dropped accused the project's administration of prejudice because of either union or non-union activity," the influence of the party's fronts could not be doubted. Sit-downs took place in darkened project buildings relit with red candles, and, as party songs were sung, its members "established nocturnal dictatorship over the covered typewriters." Wearers of red armbands labeled all those who attempted to cross picket lines "rats" and "scabs." A number of radical supervisors formed a council in support of Writers' Union and City Projects Council demands against relief cuts; some colleagues joined after receiving threats that their homes would be picketed if they distributed pink slips. Workers who refused to enter the union and then were dismissed often had less chance of getting back on when new openings became available. Party members openly recruited on behalf of the Abraham Lincoln Brigade's forays in the Spanish Civil War. The *Federal Writer* and the more infamous *Red Pen* rolled off project mimeograph machines to expose "stool pigeons" like Trotskyites Harry Roskolenko, Lionel Abel, Philip Rahv, and Ralph Manheim and to uncover their alleged efforts to break up unionization efforts. As late as April, 1938, union representatives planned a *Red Pen* issue, with the project's name on its masthead, to call out workers to march in the May Day parade.[22]

Opposition to the party's influence brought especially harsh retaliation. Henry Lee Moon and Ted Poston refused to join the Supervisors'

[21] *New York Times*, July 18, 1937, VII, p. 11., and July 27, 1937; Lovett to Roosevelt, July 25, 1937, Box 462, WPA.

[22] Thompson report; Roskolenko, *When I Was Last on Cherry Street*, p. 152; Forrest to McAdoo, July 12, 1937, Box 2115, WPA; *Red Pen* (Jan., 1938) enclosed in Shaw to Alsberg, Apr. 12, 1938, Box 33, FWPN.

Council in an extended strike until they were promoted from subsupervisory posts, and both ended up in the lower ranks within a week of their insubordination. Trotskyites found it physically impossible to distribute *The Militant* outside the project office. Their one broadside against the slanderous innuendoes and the "internecine warfare" fomented by the union's *Red Pen*—they called it the "poison pen"—had little effect. When Liston Oak, a former party member, returned from Spain and had the courage to publicize the Stalinist faction's suppression of anarchists, he could not get back on the project until offered a job in the natural history section by its sympathetic supervisor. Edward Dahlberg left the project rather than endure the spleen vented against him by "Marxist mutes" for opposing the party's proclamations on literary matters.[23] Supervisors turned down Donald Thompson's suggestion that John Dos Passos head an advisory committee, to give the local unit prestige, on the ground that the author was a "Fascist" and a "reactionary" because of his disillusionment with the Communists in Spain. The acting director concluded that they "probably only would have wanted Earl Browder and his cousins." When Alsberg appointed Harold Strauss, a book editor who succeeded an NYU English instructor as director toward the end of 1938, to try to pull the guide copy together, Thompson left the project.[24]

A lengthy study by Robert Bruere of the Labor Department for Hopkins's office in 1937 left no doubt as to Alsberg's blame for this deterioration in the New York City project: "Where authority rests, there responsibility rests also." Orrick Johns had been allowed to remain as director for almost a year, and Travis Hoke for half that time, despite the illness and inefficiency of both. Such laxity notwithstanding, a fundamental organization with clearly defined tasks and ample

[23] Poston interview; Max Nomad telephone conversation with author, Feb. 11, 1968. I am grateful to Mr. Nomad for his copy of the reply to *Red Pen*. Frank interview; Dahlberg interview. The opportunism of Communist party project workers regarding Guggenheim winners was also recalled by Dahlberg and Nomad. In one instance, party members refused to publish an introductory volume of Kenneth Fearing's work (compiled and later brought out privately by Dahlberg and Sol Funaroff), but rushed to do so after he had won a Guggenheim. On the other hand, they dropped all plans to boost the local unit by broadcasting Nomad's receipt of that award when they discovered that he was an anti-Stalinist.

[24] Thompson interview. The English instructor, Harry L. Shaw, Jr., had received official WPA approval simply by assuring Hopkins's deputy (worried about the local project's reputation) that he had never set foot in Russia; he resigned after nine months for the tranquil world of academia. Mangione, *Dream and Deal*, p. 189.

authority to perform these duties effectively had not been established by Washington. The report had little effect on the national director, however, and the New York City project continued to be a source of contention and political dissension.[25]

Although Bruere pointed out that Alsberg had allowed the New York project to slide, his report did not refer to the national director's tolerance of the activities of Communist party fronts during working hours. Various accusations to the contrary, Alsberg never was a Communist (at times in the project's history people accused him of being a Fascist and a censor of "social issues"). A philosophical anarchist, he had once looked at the Russian Revolution as a victory over corrupt bourgeois institutions and had excused its initial aberrations as the reaction to "the threat of internal dissolution and of partition by outside forces." But Alsberg soon became disillusioned with Bolshevik corruption, bureaucracy, and treatment of so-called counter-revolutionary anarchists, Menshiviks, and Social Revolutionaries. With the aid of Roger Baldwin's International Committee for Political Prisoners, he edited and published *Letters from Russian Prisons,* a compilation largely based on smuggled material obtained by the foreign correspondent Isaac Don Levine. In later years, he wrote against Communist pogroms which took the lives of at least 250,000 Jews in the Ukraine. Always maintaining independence of judgment, Alsberg objected to his friend Emma Goldman's belief in violent revolution and refused to sign a "blank check" backing the Communist-dominated Amsterdam 1932 World Congress against War.[26]

Alsberg's views of the party and of revolutionary values carried over to his work on the FWP. While differing with the dictatorial methods of various Communists on the New York writers' project, he could still remain very sympathetic to their goal of unionization and additional jobs. Always the armchair philosopher, however, rather than the political realist, Alsberg dismissed Harold Rosenberg's concern with the party's growing control over that project by remarking, "They can't do anything . . . they have not one idea between them."[27]

[25] Bruere to Kellogg, June 17, 1937, Box 2115, WPA.

[26] Henry Alsberg, "The Soviet Domestic Program," *Nation* 111 (Aug. 28, 1920):221; Alsberg, "Tyranny by Prophets," *Nation* 111 (Sept. 4, 1920):268-69; Alsberg, "Russia: Smoked Glass vs. Rose Tint," *Nation* 112 (June 15, 1921):844-46; *Letters from Russian Prisons;* Committee on Un-American Activities, *Hearings on H.R. 282,* IV, pp. 2889, 2893-94.

[27] Rosenberg interview.

Along with political naïveté went the highly personal approach he often took toward workers, an attitude which, in the opinion of his first chief regional supervisor, "often made him secretive." Surrounding himself and sharing his apartment with a circle of male friends (a number of whom were Communists or fellow travelers), Alsberg dealt with a disciplined mechanism like the Writers' Union in an undisciplined manner. Rather than interfere when it became necessary, the national director silenced Reed Harris's complaints with "I like him, he's a good writer" and "they'll be all right." Although WPA's Harold Stein warned Hopkins that union activities such as the June, 1937, sit-down strike would ruin the project's original plans, Alsberg did not back him, and he was moved to Washington.[28]

Eager for power, the young retinue which shared Alsberg's apartment grew resentful of the national director's coterie of loyal, old friends like Philip Coan, Harold Kellock, Lawrence Abbott, and Roderick Seidenberg and slowly ousted these individuals from his confidence. As Seidenberg observed the attempts by the new inner circle to undermine Lawrence Morris, he became "very nauseated" with the situation and left his post. Isaac Don Levine also found that "some of Henry's closest friends were politically noxious" to him after he wrote a best-seller condemning Stalin's tyranny. Levine recognized the group's captivating influence on his old friend as they got on the Washington project, and he and Alsberg slowly drifted apart. One of these editors took an active role in the Communist wing of the Government Employees Union and later defended the Soviet-Nazi pact, and a field representative openly expressed views which could have been considered subversive by the federal government.[29]

Alsberg's personal friendships, in addition to his ineptitude as an administrator, enabled the party to strengthen its control of the New York City project. It is interesting that his reply to charges against the party's control in New York concerned itself with the quality of the FWP's work in general and that he claimed not to know the politics of one supervisor (because "he came from a relief agency"). In fact, the national director shared a Greenwich Village apartment with the individual in question, a former party member who had left the fold because of its behavior during the Spanish Civil War. Holger Cahill was greatly

[28] L. Morris, Harris, and Thompson interviews.

[29] Seidenberg and Levine interviews; Hefferman-Adams file, Box 29, FWPN.

surprised to find that a secret decision, arrived at by the Federal #1 directors in Washington, had reached his New York executive office via that man, the supervisor of the local writers' project. Reed Harris, like Seidenberg, objected to Alsberg's permissiveness toward the New York unit in particular, and this was one reason why he decided to leave the FWP in mid-1938. By his bad administration, Alsberg did more than alienate old companions and let the entire unit deteriorate. He also gave worried congressmen an opportunity to investigate party activity in the FWP as a whole.[30]

III

The question of Communist influence on the FWP finally came to the fore in the latter part of 1938. It did so through the investigations of the House Committee on Un-American Activities, more popularly known as the Dies Committee because of its guiding spirit and "chief publicity getter," Chairman Martin Dies (D., Tex.). This cigar-smoking Orange County populist had long echoed his constituency's suspicion of foreigners, cities, organized labor, and big capital. Under his direction, the committee, initially formed to examine the activities of the German-American Bund, soon transferred its main energies to the hounding of suspected Communists and to thinly veiled attacks against the New Deal. Seizing upon stories about the much-touted "subversion" in New York's theatre and writers' projects, Representative J. Parnell Thomas (R., N.J.) began holding hearings in the Federal Court Building on New York's Foley Square in mid-1938, preliminary to the committee's investigation in Washington.[31]

WPA's New York administrator began an independent investigation and, at the same time, instructed all Federal #1 workers to cooperate fully with the Dies Committee. The revelations Representative Thomas turned up convinced him that the writers' project was "worse than the Federal Theatre Project and a hotbed of Communism." WPA's administrator denied these charges "most emphatically."[32]

The first open session of the subcommittee, held in New York, produced three project workers who told of Communist infiltration and

[30] *New York Times,* Nov. 2, 1936; Thompson, Seidenberg, and Harris interviews; chap. 10 below.

[31] D. A. Saunders, "The Dies Committee: First Phase," *Public Opinion Quarterly* 3 (Apr., 1939):223-28; *New York Times,* July 27, 1938.

[32] *New York Times,* Aug. 5, 19, 25, and 26, 1938.

political activity in the local unit. A former newspaperman testified that the party had gained considerable control of the project through the Workers' Alliance and had used project employees as *agents provocateurs* in Jersey City, Pennsylvania, and Florida. Edwin Banta further revealed that his knowledge came firsthand, as he had joined the party's 36-S Federal Writers' Unit shortly after getting on the project in October, 1935. As a member of the Communist party, he had secured advertising for the *Red Pen* and had collected dues for the alliance during project hours until leaving the party in September, 1938. The witness submitted his dues book and a volume of Earl Browder's *The People's Front*, given him "in recognition of his devotion to and untiring efforts in behalf of our party and Communism," as further proof of his claims. (The names of party members on the project had been inscribed in both.) Banta expounded at length on the extracurricular activities of workers and supervisors belonging to the party and discussed the power of the alliance in getting jobs on the project. He also noted the party's threats of physical violence against him for appearing before the sub-committee and its printing of his picture in the *Daily Worker* under the caption "Workers' Enemy Exposed." Two other witnesses bore out elements of Banta's testimony.[33]

Only with the publicity given this testimony did WPA officials request Dies to grant them and the directors of the projects under attack a hearing. Hallie Flanagan of the theatre project had sought to testify since August, and Alsberg had informed Dies, a few days before the hearings began, that he would be glad to appear at any time and furnish any information at his disposal.[34]

The committee kept project officials waiting until early December, and meanwhile charges against the FWP continued to mount. A magazine which investigated the New York unit concluded that "the Writers' Project is the Communist Party's joy," and one New York newspaper broadcast Dies's warning that the theatre and writers' projects were "doing more to spread Communist propaganda than the Communist Party itself."[35]

Members of the central staff raised other issues relating to subversion when they appeared before the committee in mid-November. Three

[33] Committee on Un-American Activities, *Hearings on H.R. 282,* II, p. 1026; *Daily Worker,* Sept. 2, 1938.

[34] Jane De Hart Mathews, *The Federal Theatre, 1935-1939: Plays, Relief and Politics,* pp. 199-210; Alsberg to Dies, Sept. 13, 1938, Box 1, FWPN.

[35] *The Commentator* (New York), Oct., 1938; *New York Journal and American,* Oct. 19, 1938.

employees testified to insertions of "incendiary propaganda" appealing to class hatred in various state guides and to the unnecessary addition of radicals to the Washington staff. They also noted the publication of *WPA Perspectives* by party members in California's federal projects. To confirm their testimony, they recommended that certain galleys be subpoenaed by the committee.[36]

By the end of November, the Dies Committee had heard additional testimony from two project workers, and it released some of the galleys from the New Jersey and Montana guides as evidence that the impartiality required of official government publications was in serious doubt. As the former secretary of the party faction of the New York unit, Ralph De Sola described its control of the project's Workers' Alliance local. The zoology editor, supplementing testimony he had given earlier, revealed party efforts, through *Red Pen* (which he had once edited) and two leaflets, to counter any opposition to its aims. With C. V. Sutcliffe, who had photographed the sit-down strike of May, 1937, for members of the red-armbanded "defense squad," he identified, in those photos, various party members using federal property to print strike passes and other material, guarding barricaded doors, planning strike strategy, and giving the Communist salute behind a card reading "Striking writers support Spanish democracy." Reviewing the book given Banta in March, 1938, with such inscriptions as "to a real builder of the People's Front," "with comradely love," and "next the Order of Lenin," De Sola concluded that at least 106 of the 300 writers on the New York City project held cards in the Communist party.[37]

Such testimony added strength to the committee's more fundamental attack against "the New Deal masterminds." These administrators, according to Representative Thomas, had "pawned themselves out to the Communist strategists." Dies included Hopkins and Harold Ickes in his committee of "purveyors of class hatred" and called upon them and Frances Perkins to resign. The committee showed its true colors when it noted that De Sola's castigation of party dictatorship was "very finely stated," regularly led witnesses into charging that the central office made appeals for "class hatred" material in the guides, and

[36] Committee on Un-American Activities, *Hearings on H.R. 282,* IV, pp. 3109-39; chap. 5 above.

[37] Committee on Un-American Activities, *Hearings on H.R. 282,* III, pp. 2396-2426; *ibid.,* IV, pp. 2427-35, 2645-55.

thanked one member of that staff for her "patriotism and courage" in submitting "important information."[38]

The presence as a witness, in early December, of Ellen Woodward, Jake Baker's replacement as overseer of Federal #1 and other WPA professional relief projects, afforded Dies an excellent opportunity to continue his crusade against all foreign "isms." Woodward, sympathetic to the arts projects, had earlier told Hopkins that silence on contemporary concerns among project employees could only be imposed by a censorship "as vicious and depraving to the spirit" as that in Hitler's Germany.[39] This proud Southern belle had rehearsed a statement for the occasion to vindicate the work of her subordinate directors. Dies and his associates had no intention of letting her off so lightly, however.

After allowing the witness to note the achievement of both the theatre and writers' projects in brief, Representative Joe Starnes (D., Ala.) accused Richard Wright's autobiographical piece in *American Stuff* of being "the most filthy thing I have ever seen," and Dies judged the other contributors to the volume "somewhat mentally handicapped." When Woodward charged that testimony from Banta, who had recently been a mental patient, should be checked with that of responsible officials, Starnes pointed out that Hopkins had also been in a hospital, and his condition, too, "might be a matter of opinion." In the face of repeated badgering and interruptions, Woodward did manage to express her "deep concern and disappointment over the very un-American way" in which the committee had handled its investigation of the projects under her jurisdiction. It had denied her the opportunity to testify until now, and had not called on the local unit directors or examined their files. Such investigation, she insisted, would reveal whether the signees were still (if they had been then) members of the party. The committee forced the assistant administrator to acknowledge that her lack of close personal contact with the production of projects and their personnel put her reliability as a witness for the defense in doubt. Realizing her weakness on this point and confident in her subordinates, she brought along Hallie Flanagan and Henry Alsberg to testify.[40]

[38] *Chicago Tribune,* Oct. 17, 1938; *Baltimore Sun,* Nov. 14, 1938; Committee on Un-American Activities, *Hearings on H.R. 282,* II, pp. 1024, 3121-22, 3125.

[39] Cited in McKinzie, *New Deal for Artists,* p. 157; Cronin interview.

[40] Committee on Un-American Activities, *Hearings on H.R. 282,* IV, pp. 2729-2838.

The forthright nature of the theatre director distinguished her entire testimony and so ruffled the committee's feelings that her extensive defense brief never found its way into the official transcript. Hallie Flanagan displayed superb irony in informing Representative Starnes that Christopher Marlowe was not a Communist, but it certainly boded ill for her cause, as far as the committee and congressional opponents of Federal #1 were concerned. Flanagan, moreover, had to admit that she could not speak with certainty about the extent of party influence in the local FTP units.[41]

Henry Alsberg's approach, by contrast, proved more deferential, as he primarily sought to preserve the FWP rather than defy conservative politicians. Half of Alsberg's testimony dealt with his past opposition to "the tyrannical Russian situation" under Soviet rule. As for the much-publicized New York City project, he admitted that factional rivalry had created "a ball-up" until the central office recently "cleaned up the mess as best we could." The amiable witness disclosed a "running battle" with the New Jersey project to tone down "offensive and unfair" copy, and he confessed that the central staff's attempt to fix an edited version of Montana's labor essay appeared "hopeless" because "we didn't know enough about it." Alsberg concluded with the assurance that nothing coming out of his office would be "censorable for being unfair." His "frankness" and cooperation led to a personal commendation "in the highest terms" from Dies.[42]

The Dies Committee hearings did not represent the ideal forum for a thorough airing of Communist activity on the Federal Writers' Project. The committee made little attempt at cross-examination (except in the case of Ellen Woodward, a spokesman on behalf of the project), regularly put words into the mouths of witnesses, and allowed persons critical of the project great latitude in expressing opinions based on subjective judgment or hearsay. When De Sola explained his disillusionment with the party line, Dies tried to obtain a link to Bruce Bliven, Lewis Mumford, and Roger Baldwin, and indicated that "front" organizations sought to involve the country in some foreign war to

[41] *Ibid.*, p. 2885. Mathews's study (*Federal Theatre*, pp. 227-32) agrees that the party was strongest in New York City, but gives no details on the other FTP units. Also see John Houseman, *Run-Through: A Memoir*, chaps. 4-6.

[42] Harold Strauss interview, Oct. 4, 1967; Committee on Un-American Activities, *Hearings on H.R. 282*, IV, pp. 2886-2908. This distinction between Alsberg and Hallie Flanagan is overlooked in Mathews's *Federal Theatre* (p. 232).

provide support for Soviet Russia. Though insisting that the committee just wanted "facts, not feelings," its members permitted Washington project workers to speculate on the extent of "class warfare" propaganda in the state guides and on the possibility that Alsberg and Gaer were working toward a country-wide Communist propaganda organization.[43]

The Dies Committee reflected the bias of its members, particularly in their judgment of project publications, and the Washington office's attempt to inject more balance into conservative views of controversial matters received the label of Communist propaganda. Contrary to slanted testimony, the *Poetry* issue of creative writing by project employees did not remain open only to party members (the party had actually denounced that magazine's "reactionary" tendencies). *American Stuff* lacked the mark of blunt class propaganda, and the same was true for the *Direction* issue (which had led to attacks by the Writers' Union against Harold Rosenberg). At one point, De Sola did question the claims of other witnesses that the central office had inserted and instructed state projects to bring in material along "class-angle" lines; the committee did not follow up his demurrer. Alsberg, unlike Flanagan, had skirted this vital point, and his failure to mention it led one citizen to conclude: "His remarks seem to have been a little on the duller, more unintelligent side. His red-baiting is nauseating and ill-befits a New Dealer."[44]

The other test of "subversion"—Communist political operations during project hours—was also inadequately investigated. Far more FWP personnel should have been called in to testify. If they had been, the committee could have learned about the unmistakable influence of party fronts on the Massachusetts and Minnesota projects. Priority in employment that did exist for Communist party members in Chicago and Los Angeles would also have come to light. When the committee received substantial briefings about the one sustained case of party activity, the New York City unit, it failed to call for further clarifica-

[43] Saunders, "Dies Committee"; Committee on Un-American Activities, *Hearings on H.R. 282,* II, pp. 1010, 985, 989, 1007; *ibid.,* III, pp. 2409-10; *ibid.,* IV, pp. 2827, 3122, 3114.

[44] Committee on Un-American Activities, *Hearings on H.R. 282,* IV, pp. 3129-30; *Washington Post,* Jan. 8, 1939; Committee on Un-American Activities, *Hearings on H.R. 282,* IV, p. 3131; *ibid.,* III, p. 2406; Rerenberg to Flanagan, Dec. 7, 1938, Box 16, Federal Theatre Project files, Works Projects Administration records, Record Group 69, National Archives, Washington, D.C.

tion. Alsberg's testimony hardly "proved quite satisfactory," in terms· of either procedure or content.[45] His confession about factional battles on the New York project should have immediately led the committee to ask for additional details, especially on the very basic question of why the central office tolerated this situation for such an extended period of time. A thorough investigation would have revealed his responsibility for the party's divisive strength in that unit and raised serious doubts about his entire administrative function.

Yet, although the Dies hearings did not get to the heart of the question of subversion, they did raise a number of serious matters which would affect the continuation of the FWP. With all its limitations, the Dies Committee directed the public's attention to some of the party's activities on at least one project and got an acknowledgment from the national director himself that factional rivalry had hampered the progress of his most talented unit. Such testimony could easily lead the concerned citizen to wonder about the project's other branches. Even more important, the effect of these introductory investigations on a newly elected Congress in revolt against the President's relief program could not be doubted. Dies had briefly noted, in the course of Hallie Flanagan's testimony, that "lack of funds or some action by Congress" might interrupt the theatre project's work.[46] The same held true for the FWP and, as the year 1939 opened, its independent lifeline became the focus of some legislators who, sharpening their knives, moved in for the kill.

[45] August Ogden, *The Dies Committee*, p. 95, in drawing this conclusion, offers no analysis of Alsberg's testimony.

[46] Committee on Un-American Activities, *Hearings on H.R. 282*, IV, p. 2872.

CHIDED ONE DAY FOR HIS irrepressible optimism, Henry Alsberg declared, "No one who is not an optimist has any business on this project." "Henry," his listener responded, "that's the most pessimistic thing I have ever heard you say." As the year 1939 opened, however, neither Alsberg nor anyone else concerned with the project could have viewed the political climate with much enthusiasm. The President's irresistible popularity and the specter of long breadlines at the beginning of the new administration six years earlier had led Congress to accede without delay to the initiation of New Deal measures and the relief program in particular. However, the start of WPA, with power focused in Washington, moved congressmen to challenge the relief structure's encroachment on the states. Countless editorials thundered against the evils of centralized relief. Extravagant federal spending to subsidize boondoggles had to yield to local jurisdiction. Critics also charged the administration with creating a vast political machine, especially prior to major elections. Influential spokesmen railed against WPA. Talk of retrenchment and balanced budgets increased, and cuts soon befell all WPA projects. The FWP itself became doubly damned as part of WPA and as an assumed sanctuary for lazy louts who should have been pushing wheelbarrows instead of pens.[1]

By the start of the new congressional session in 1939, the President's entire relief program faced serious challenges. The Supreme Court fight, the recession, and the failure of a poorly conducted "purge" of New Deal opponents had all resulted in significant GOP–conservative Democratic victories in the elections of the previous year. Not expected to run in 1940, Roosevelt could no longer command certain legislative

[1] Ruth C. France to author, Nov. 20, 1967; *New York Herald Tribune,* Oct. 20, 1936; chap. 3 above.

support, and the opposition, until then on the defensive, began to seek control of relief expenditures in the session that followed.[2]

The WPA and Federal #1 projects now had more down-to-earth administrators at their helm than Harry Hopkins or Ellen Woodward. Hopkins had taken FDR's advice that he would have a better chance at the presidency if he left WPA to join the cabinet as Secretary of Commerce. His successor in the WPA, Colonel Francis Harrington, carried years of military service and administrative experience in the construction relief projects to his new post, along with a stress on protocol and deference to Capitol Hill. Where Hopkins had been experimental, direct, and compassionate about relief, Harrington concentrated on the proper channels and conventional, useful work. Neither thought highly of the administrative talents of Ellen Woodward, whose strong temper and impulsiveness had enabled her to stand up to Martin Dies, but whose constant worries about Federal #1 forced two assistants to spend hours allaying her fears about its "blowing up." As the volatile, dedicated Woodward accepted a social security commissionership to avoid confrontations with Harrington, the shrewd, efficient Florence Kerr, who had worked under Hopkins in the Gulf Division of the Red Cross and WPA, took her place.[3]

These changes in personnel, however, did not deter the opposition from quickly launching an attack against the relief projects. The House Appropriations Committee immediately lopped $150,000 from Roosevelt's special request for an additional $875 million to WPA. Representative John Taber (R., N.Y.), calling for more cuts, advised his colleagues to read the Dies report. He indicated that he would later move to cut off all funds for the writers' project because its products were "subversive." An amendment calling for $22 million for Federal #1 was defeated in both houses.[4]

With 10 million words out in book form (not counting more than 100 minor publications), more than 5 million words of manuscript ready or on presses, and more than 1 million miles of roads having been covered

---

[2] Leuchtenburg, *Roosevelt and New Deal*, p. 272. Roosevelt had also failed in his attempt to reorganize the administrative structure of government at this time. See Richard Pollenberg, *Reorganizing Roosevelt's Government: The Controversy over Executive Reorganization, 1936-1939*.

[3] Robert E. Sherwood, *Roosevelt and Hopkins, an Intimate History*, pp. 94-98; Asher interview; Kerr interview, July 7, 1968.

[4] *New York Times*, Jan. 13, 26, and 29, 1939.

by its employees, the FWP found itself in grave trouble. Defenders rushed to point out that liquidation would be a calamity for the project's workers and a cultural disaster for the country; one writer considered its rediscovery of America vital "in these days of dictators, wars and intolerance rampant." The chief of the Pan American Union's travel division praised its "unprecedented and monumental work" and hoped that the FWP's example would be copied in Latin America. But congressional circles had no desire for "strange fish" any longer, and the President himself indicated in February that he would refrain from pushing any further legislation. Senator James Byrnes proposed a bill withdrawing all funds from white-collar projects, and Representative Clifton Woodrum of Virginia, another Southern Democrat, suggested direct aid to the states as an alternative to federally controlled relief. At the end of March, the House Subcommittee on Appropriations passed a resolution to investigate all activities on WPA projects.[5]

For congressmen suspicious of the East, culture, and WPA controls, "subversion" represented a convincing as well as convenient word with which to brand Federal #1. Alarmed at certain facts which had emerged from the Dies hearings of the past winter, the now-powerful opposition could read of similar charges raised in the state projects of Washington and California. The Washington director had been cleared of all accusations by the local WPA, and closer study indicated that the other claims had been made by disgruntled employees discharged in January cuts. Yet adverse headlines boded ill for the FWP at a time when a magazine releasing the results of its own investigation of the New York City unit confirmed the infiltration of Communists on the project's supervisory level. Continued publicity of this sort served to mark the entire FWP as a "hotbed" of Communism.[6]

On April 6, Representative Frank Keefe (R., Wisc.) charged the central office with allowing "the influence of communistically inspired agitators" to insert "insidious propaganda" into the D.C. Guide. The congressman focused his attention on a portion which reported that George Washington Parke Custis, foster son of the nation's first President and father-in-law of Robert E. Lee, had left a tract in Arlington to

---

[5] Jan. 23, 1939, report, Box 464, WPA; *New York Times,* Feb. 15, 1939; Tercéro to Alsberg, Feb. 22, 1939, Box 467, WPA; Mathews, *Federal Theatre,* p. 263.

[6] *Seattle Post-Intelligencer,* Feb. 17, 1939; *San Francisco Call-Bulletin,* Feb. 28, 1939; *Headlines* 2 (Mar. 25, 1939), in Box 2116, WPA.

a black daughter named Maria Syphax. This information, in Keefe's opinion—"whether it be right or wrong"—could only lead to "stimulating racial intolerance"; it merited "reproach and condemnation." Keefe informed his appreciative audience that Sterling Brown (who had responsibility for the final writing of the essay, according to Alsberg) had failed to answer his letter or telephone calls about the matter. Keefe's personal study revealed no such information regarding Custis, and he called on his colleagues to consider that the dissemination of the material of which this calumny was a part had cost the taxpayer over $15 million. Senator Robert Reynolds (who would later lead an attack against the theatre project) inserted into the *Congressional Record* an article from the *Baltimore Sun* about the episode, together with a reference to the "rumbling on the Senate side," without comment.[7]

For all readers who held a stereotyped view of blacks, further comment on the essay in question was superfluous. "The Negro in Washington" appeared shocking, beginning as it did with Thomas More's observation on the city in its early years:

> Even here beside the proud Potowmac's [*sic*] streams
> The medley mass of pride and misery
> Of whips and charters, manacles and rights
> Of slaving blacks and democratic whites.

Alongside its description of cultural advances, a gay social life, and the black community's avid interest in education, the essay quoted proud black Reconstruction congressmen, noted the bloody race riot of July, 1919, and the current high rate of tuberculosis among blacks, and warned of their political and civil apathy arising out of disfranchisement. Having no voice in government and facing economic proscription and rigid segregation, Negroes in the capital city might blind themselves with pleasure-seeking, with "a specious self-sufficiency" and a well-earned sense of pride at having achieved much over insuperable odds. Yet, concluded the authors of this pioneering, critical essay, bitterness could not be avoided: ". . . there is a denial of democracy, at times hypocritical and at times flagrant."[8]

Those primarily responsible for the object of the representative's concern reacted far differently from Keefe and Reynolds. Sterling

---

[7] *Congressional Record* 84, (1939), pt. IV, pp. 3930-33 and Appendix, pt. XII, pp. 1359-60.
[8] *Washington, City and Capital* (Washington, D.C., 1937), pp. 68-90.

Brown saw the charges as "badges of honor." The essay in which the Syphax matter appeared, he believed, was the most "hard hitting" in any state guide. (The FBI seemed to agree, for it questioned Brown, as well as his colleagues at Howard University, about his affiliations; the diligent agency informed Brown by formal letter in 1945 that he was not a Communist.) His black research assistant, Ulysses Lee, who had used the Library of Congress, interviews, and the files of the *Washington Evening Star* for much of the original research, was surprised that this particular item had been picked up; no member of the Custis family had made any objection. He also found, to his amazement, that the files could not be relocated on his return to the public library. Lee realized that the assault really focused on the project as a whole; however, it was to prove instrumental in having this reference and quotations from black Reconstruction congressmen deleted from future editions. For the present, the attack added fuel to the fire being stoked by the opposition.[9]

By the time the House subcommmittee investigating WPA (often called the Woodrum Committee because the representative from Virginia spearheaded the attack) declared itself ready to accept testimony, additional criticism had caused the federal relief program to be cast in an even less favorable light. Some newspaper editors, concerned over testimony given by officials of the Workers' Alliance before the Woodrum Committee in April, editorialized against the alliance's alleged plan to use the WPA for political purposes. While searching for alliance and Communist party members on the New York arts projects, a committee investigator informed the press that officials in Washington had refused to prepare and distribute inquiries regarding political or organizational membership on the grounds that to do so would be contrary to WPA laws prohibiting discrimination of any sort. Such disclosures led another paper to call for "a thorough house-cleaning, followed by the return of administrative control to the local governments in direct touch with the problem," as the proper way to handle relief.[10]

Highly receptive to this argument, the Woodrum Committee, with an irony no doubt unconscious, called its first FWP witnesses on May Day, 1939. Ralph Burton, an investigator for the committee, notified

[9] Brown interview; McKinzie, "Writers on Relief," p. 139; Lee interview.

[10] *Augusta Chronicle*, Apr. 20, 1939; *New York Times*, Apr. 27, 1939; *Cincinnati Times Star*, Apr. 29, 1939.

it of his conviction that WPA officials in Washington had supported a protest from the *Daily Worker* and the Workers' Alliance against requiring relief clients to answer his questionnaires. The alliance, in his opinion, had "very definite control" of Federal #1 in New York City through its use of grievance committees and delegations. To prove his charge, he supplied the next witness to indicate the alliance's part in the sit-down strike of May, 1937. The former managing editor of the local project testified that conditions had become "intolerable" after he could not prevent Writers' Union strike meetings, the sit-down strike itself, or the noticeable presence of both "fish peddlers and dishwashers" who had no literary experience and supervisors who read the *Daily Worker* and *Red Pen* before assigning work. He further charged that the guidebook had cost $51.09 per thousand words, and that the supervisors, 60 per cent of whom were Communists, had helped union members with pink slips to get reinstated against his wishes. Colonel Somervell, according to additional testimony from the past business manager of Federal #1 in New York City, had been denied complete authority by superiors in Washington to deal with the alliance-organized demonstrations against cuts in the local area.[11]

Two former witnesses before the Dies Committee also appeared that day. Ralph De Sola repeated the gist of his testimony at the earlier hearings. He then added the accusation that the national director had previously advised him to say as little as possible at the hearings and subsequently had "severely reprimanded" him for giving "voluntary information not called for" and then denied him an expected promotion. Supervisor Joseph Barrett noted that he himself had been demoted as the result of a combination of his previous testimony, his refusal to accept class propaganda in guide copy, and Alsberg's mistaken assumption that he had brought about a recent exposé of the local project. He backed De Sola's observations and accused the national director of telling the supervisors how to initiate a sit-down strike against impending cuts.[12]

[11] U.S. Congress, House, Subcommittee on Appropriations, *Hearings on H.R. 130,* 76th Congress, 1st sess., 1939, I, pp. 209-11, 225, 233-48, 279-82.

[12] *Ibid.,* pp. 249-68. The lengths to which De Sola's former comrades went in trying to discredit him can be seen, De Sola later recalled, in the report of one to a Labor Relations Board investigator that he was harboring an emissary of the Nazis in his home. Actually, De Sola's talk of "Emmy the Emissary," while he showed her picture to fellow project writers, referred to the pet name of his dachshund. De Sola to author, Feb. 8, 1968.

Opponents of the project reacted swiftly. "It is high time that Congress dipped into that mess," editorialized the *Wichita Eagle*. When WPA's deputy administrator challenged the committee's investigator by pointing out that his refusal to permit questionnaires had nothing to do with protests of Communist-influenced groups, Representative John Ditter (R., Pa.) nonetheless objected that the refusal was "entirely out of order" and "far beyond" his authority. The *New York World Telegram*, taking up this point, editorialized that Congress and the country "certainly would not be red-baiting if they objected to Communists muscling in on the management of WPA projects, especially if the result is waste, strife and tax-financed propaganda." About this time, Senator Millard Tydings (who had survived FDR's "purge") received an answer to his request for the project's complete cost to date. The total, Florence Kerr's office informed him, came to $15,420,770.[13]

As the writers' project came under increasing attack, rumors about the close of Federal #1 in general became more frequent. A detailed critique of the testimony given by New York FWP employees, in a report by the local WPA administrator, was buried in the back of the official record without public notice. Instead, unverified reports circulated that the House subcommittee had tentatively decided to draw up a carefully earmarked relief appropriation for 1940 to insure greater congressional control of expenditures. For the first time in WPA's history, the President's request for funds came itemized with great care to the Appropriations Committee; "it was said on good authority" that the committee would recommend abolition of Federal #1.[14]

Defenders of the FWP tried their best to rally support for it. The president of the American Hotel Association praised the project's "excellent progress" in meeting the shortage of adequate guidebooks and hailed its contribution to the current movement to encourage travel in America. A letter from forty-four prominent publishing houses to the chairman of the House subcommittee affirmed that the guides represented no instruments of subversive propaganda but "a genuine,

[13] *Wichita Eagle*, May 5, 1939; House Subcommittee on Appropriations, *Hearings on H.R. 130*, I, pp. 281-91, 851-56; *New York World Telegram*, May 3, 1939; Howe to Tydings, May 19, 1939, Box 465, WPA. "Perhaps some of the Dies revelations were not so fantastically conceived after all," concluded the *New York Herald Tribune* (June 8, 1939).

[14] House Subcommittee on Appropriations, *Hearings on H.R. 130*, I, pp. 1315-20; *New York Times*, May 10, 1939.

valuable and objective contribution to the understanding of American life.'' These volumes offered material which no single publisher could have collected, and their availability gave a "most timely impetus" to the publishing industry and its related trades. That the FWP managed, during its operation, to produce some 300 volumes in three and a half years and maintain throughout "a uniformly high level" seemed "remarkable." The publishers thought that, aside from endangering the livelihood and self-respect of the writers, hampering the project at this time would represent a "severe deprivation to the reading public and to the enrichment of our nation's literature."[15]

The central office felt itself adrift in this period of overlapping crises. Investigators for the Woodrum Committee had raided Alsberg's safe in February, to find only a pair of the director's suspenders and quantities of Bisodol. (Alsberg had transferred personal files to his home after experiencing the smear tactics of Dies and his associates.) The national director desperately wrote to New Dealer Benjamin V. Cohen in an attempt to set up the project as a permanent agency within the well-established Department of the Interior. Amidst the general hubbub, he also came under secret attack by some of his own staff, who felt that he had groveled before Dies and who thought that only by deposing him could their jobs and the project be saved. Older members also resented Alsberg's appointment of young Clair Laning to the assistant directorship. Although broad hints emanated from Colonel Harrington's WPA headquarters that he should resign, Alsberg still had faith that a mid-May invitation to the White House for Jerre Mangione could be used to win Eleanor Roosevelt's support once again and thereby rescue the FWP. The President's focus on the possibility of a second world war and the "obituary style" in which Mrs. Roosevelt reminisced about the project's successes, however, convinced Mangione that his mission was hopeless.[16]

On the first day of June, the *Washington Post* carried a story that the Woodrum Committee had finally decided to eliminate the theatre project and to continue its other creative counterparts on a "strictly local basis." The Federal Arts Sponsoring Committee, led by the novelist Louis Bromfield, was immediately organized to protest any curtailment in Federal #1. Its membership passed a resolution that the

[15] Greene to Alsberg, May 19, 1939, Box 460, WPA; *New York Times*, May 22, 1939.
[16] Mangione, *Dream and Deal*, pp. 6-14.

projects be expanded under federal control and supervised by a federal arts bureau to be established for that purpose. But a Congress which had already defeated various bills for a similar purpose between 1935 and 1938 had no interest.[17]

In mid-June, the House committee "aimed at radicals" in reporting out a relief bill which reflected the strength of the opposition. It transferred $125 million from WPA to PWA construction projects, ordered the dismissal of any worker who had been on WPA more than eighteen months, required a loyalty oath for all future employees, and eliminated the theatre division from the relief program. The other arts projects would be allowed to continue their work after September 1 only by securing local sponsorship. The House overwhelmingly accepted the bill, leading the *Chicago Daily Times* to caution against "profligate economy."[18]

Supporters of the FWP rushed to present their case before the issue was decided for good. Regional Director William Couch urged the Florida and Louisiana directors to write congressmen about the central office's high standards and "absolutely indispensable" service, as well as of the inevitable dangers that would occur if the House relief bill were to pass. While the Senate Subcommittee on Appropriations began debating the bill, Couch wrote Chairman Alva Adams, with reference to the local sponsorship provision, that it would appear "the height of folly" to change from an experienced organization, whose planning, supervision, and direction were "beyond question of the highest quality," to an untried one under which standards would be gradually lowered and remain highly susceptible to local political control. It would be "a national misfortune," Columbia University's Allan Nevins declared, if the greater part of the Federal Arts Projects' work did not continue. WPA's Colonel Harrington asked that the local sponsoring feature, if retained, be postponed until January, 1940, and include the theatre project as well.[19]

Despite some last-minute efforts on behalf of the Federal Arts Projects, the opposition won. The idea of a march on Washington by

[17] *Washington Post*, June 1, 1939; *New York Times*, June 4, 1939.

[18] *New York Times*, June 14 and 17, 1939; Mathews, *Federal Theatre*, pp. 275-95; *Chicago Daily Times*, June 20, 1939.

[19] Couch to Corse and Saxon, June 20-21, 1939, and Couch to Adams, June 21, 1939, Box 2182, WPA; *New York Times*, June 27, 1939; U.S. Congress, Senate, Subcommittee on Appropriations, *Hearings on H.J. Res 326*, 76th Cong., 1st sess., 1939, p. 96.

notable figures in the arts fizzled out when Heywood Broun decided not to lead it because of his past identification with left-wing causes; the non-political Alexander Woolcott, his choice as a substitute, promised to do so only in a few months, when he would have more time. Senators Robert Wagner, Sheridan Downey, and Claude Pepper were successful in getting their colleagues to set aside three-fourths of 1 per cent of the WPA appropriation for all of Federal #1, but the House retained its preference for its original bill. The lower chamber sent the Woodrum resolution back to the Senate, which, under the threat that the entire relief program otherwise would expire in a few hours' time, passed the relief bill. Having lost to a rebellious Congress on neutrality, tax, and farm measures—all in the last weekend of June—FDR also felt obligated to sign this measure, rather than jeopardize the welfare of 2½ million workers. As it saw the curtain come down on "an act of defiance," one editorial raised some fundamental questions: "What is this America of ours, after all? Is it made up only of buildings and roads and sewers? Is there such a thing as the soul of America, and if so, is this American soul capable of appreciating only the things of cement and stone?"[20] To the defeated directors of Federal #1, the answers seemed bleak, indeed.

II

The writers' project, in its new form, survived the fate of Hallie Flanagan's theatre division because of the state and local guidebooks. As a federal agency, it had suffered widespread publicity about the insertion of "class propaganda" and especially about the strong influence of the Workers' Alliance and the Writers' Union in the New York City unit. The disquieting headlines, together with congressional doubts about "boondoggling" writers and the value of centralized relief, persuaded legislators to pare down the project.[21] But its offerings

[20] Mangione, *Dream and Deal*, pp. 18-20; *New York Times*, July 1, 1939; *Jacksonville Journal*, June 28, 1939. For Roosevelt's view of the opposition's victory, see Mathews, *Federal Theatre*, p. 309.

[21] The influence of party fronts in New York was far greater in the FWP than in the FTP, since old-time unions had jurisdiction over 85 per cent of the FTP's performers and technicians. *New York Times*, Aug. 20, 1939, IX, p. 1. For this reason, the claim (*Washington Post*, Dec. 2, 1939) that the issue of Communism closed the FTP must be doubted. Dies's later assertion (*Martin Dies' Story*, p. 158) that his thorough findings convinced "a predominantly liberal Congress to abolish both projects" also overlooks the facts that Congress strongly opposed FDR after the 1938 elections, that his committee's disclosures were limited in the case of the FWP, and that the writers' project was not abolished entirely.

had no influence on these legislators compared with live performances of the *Living Newspaper,* during which actors quoted the words of congressmen and Supreme Court justices opposed to New Deal measures as part of the script. The FWP, in contrast, produced guides which boosted the state pride of most congressmen. For that reason, the writers' project escaped termination.[22]

Despite a partial victory, the FWP had no clear future. It had been permitted by Congress to continue in any state where 25 per cent of the cost could be met by local sponsorship after September 1—a questionable existence in view of state retrenchment. Harassment mounted when, in mid-July, WPA suddenly ordered the national office to move to a temporary building near the mall and to move its files to WPA headquarters downtown. Even the optimistic Alsberg went so far as to suggest in the beginning of August that the central coordinating staff be taken over as supervisory personnel on the Federal Security Agency's Office of Education project, to do research and furnish material for its needs.[23] A week later, he was fired from the project's directorship.

The story behind this sudden event reveals much about the Woodrum Committee, Alsberg, and Colonel Harrington, his WPA superior. While defending the Federal Arts Projects before the committee for a few days in March, Harrington and Florence Kerr were confronted abruptly with new "evidence." Representative Woodrum handed them a letter from Alsberg to the editor of the *Nation* in which he had suggested that the country's prisoners might achieve humane treatment by a display of "class consciousness" through passive resistance and hunger strikes. He had then concluded, "I look forward to the time when every convict inside or outside jail will have his union card." Representative Clarence Cannon (D., Mo.) quickly protested that the letter had been written ten years previously, that the writer's view might subsequently have changed, and that no indication apparently existed that any WPA policy embodied such views. Nevertheless, Representatives R. Wigglesworth (R., Mass.), J. Ditter (R., Pa.), Taber, and Woodrum viewed Alsberg's statement as a typical example of the "very questionable philosophies" which the writers' project had en-

[22] Considering the remarkable range of the FTP's accomplishments, the argument that it (unlike the FWP) did not develop "strong and articulate grass roots support" (Mathews, *Federal Theatre,* pp. 310-11) is questionable.

[23] *New York Times,* Aug. 30, 1939; McKinzie, "Writers on Relief," p. 239; Alsberg to Coy, Aug. 2, 1939, Box 462, WPA.

tertained.[24] Stunned by the committee's tactic, the defense had done its best to reply at the time. Alsberg himself, in a statement he had given Florence Kerr for presentation before the committee, pointed out that he had once been engaged in editing a series of articles concerned with lamentable prison conditions when a series of violent prison revolts occurred in various states. "By advancing a somewhat fantastic scheme in a spirit of paradox," rather than a practical proposal, he had intended, by his letter to the *Nation,* to draw attention to the pressing need of mistreated prisoners. After hearing this explanation and receiving Alsberg's assurance that he had not become involved in the field of prison reform since 1930, the committee left the matter.[25]

Florence Kerr recalled years later, however, that "Alsberg might as well have put a match to a tub of gas." Colonel Harrington became furious about the "damn fool letter" and did not want to be embarrassed by its presence in what he considered a leftist magazine. A proper conservative, WPA's head considered the disclosure too much to bear at a time when rumors were circulating about Alsberg's relationship with his male friends. Harrington called Kerr to his office in the Walker-Johnson building the next morning, and commanded: "This is an order. You fire Henry Alsberg." He would not accept her protests. The swift decision astonished Alsberg, but, although he realized that "some snake in the grass" had uncovered the letter for Representatives Wigglesworth and Taber, he shrugged the news off. However, he prevailed upon Kerr to promise to talk to Harrington again.[26] She never did. Had Hopkins still been in charge of WPA, she reasoned, he would have dismissed the *Nation* letter entirely; the military man who had succeeded him, however, held other views. Kerr stalled as long as possible, hoping to get "a cooling-off" period, until Harrington (who had assumed that she had followed his order in good military fashion) called the assistant administrator on the carpet and warned her "to do it or else." Kerr now obeyed, and from that point on Alsberg "scrubbed her off" his list of friends.

[24] U.S. Congress, House, Subcommittee on Appropriations, *Hearings on H.J. Res 209 and 246,* 76th Cong., 1st sess., 1939, pp. 211-14.

[25] *Ibid.* For contemporary conditions of prisons, see *Nation* 129 (Oct. 16, 1929):398 and (Aug. 14, 1929):158.

[26] Kerr interview, July 7, 1968; Florence Kerr, Oct. 18, 1963, interview, American Archives of Art. The Mangione and Kathleen McKinzie studies do not give the circumstances behind Alsberg's dismissal, while Richard McKinzie errs in stating that Alsberg resigned (*New Deal for Artists,* p. 163).

Unable to get an appointment with Harrington, Alsberg asked Kerr to put him in touch with Hopkins. She was aware that Hopkins had gone to the Mayo Clinic for treatment of his nutritional maladjustments arising from a previous operation for cancer, but she claimed not to know where he was because she realized that Hopkins's failing health and his probable refusal to intercede would have made any efforts by Alsberg to secure his aid pointless.[27]

The dénouement satisfied Harrington completely. While she was putting off his original order to get Alsberg's resignation by the end of March, Kerr had tentatively asked Van Wyck Brooks and Cass Canfield to consider assuming the project's directorship "as a public service." Both men left it hanging for lack of definite commitments from WPA. Alsberg, in the meantime, did not wish to take the responsibility for what would happen to the FWP if he left at the time Harrington requested his resignation, and therefore he refused to resign. A theorist who might have toyed with the ideas expressed in his letter to the *Nation,* he could not fully grasp its political effect. As a last resort, Alsberg offered to retire with the provision that he could help name his successor. Preferring someone closer to his own temperament, Harrington finally selected John Dimmick Newsom for the post. Newsom, who had been recommended by his friends Paul de Kruif and Howard Hunter (Harrington's deputy administrator), had a background with the Foreign Legion and had proved his efficiency as Michigan's project director since June, 1938.[28]

On August 9, the day after Newsom's appointment, Alsberg informed Harrington and the press that he had not resigned, but had been discharged, and he reviewed the FWP's accomplishments. The project's record under his direction—321 publications, including about 100 full-sized books, 128 on the presses, and 68 almost completed —constituted a legacy of which any administrator could have been proud. The magazine in which the damaging letter had appeared ten years earlier called for the facts about a dismissal which "looks too much like a living sacrifice on the altar of Messrs. Dies and Woodrum and the redbaiting forces they represent." For Clair Laning, who had helped his former chief write the final letter to Harrington and therefore

[27] Kerr interview, July 21, 1968.

[28] Kerr interview, July 7, 1968. According to Clair Laning, Hunter had wanted de Kruif to write a book on WPA and hoped that the appointment of his friend Newsom would be persuasion enough. Mangione, *Dream and Deal,* pp. 23, 331.

expressed a bitterness that the fatalistic Alsberg must have secretly felt, other forces were also to blame. Writing to Reed Harris of the shabby treatment accorded Alsberg, he concluded: "It is evident that they intend to kill off the Writers' Project by silent treatment. At the present moment, WPA is probably the most anti–New Deal agency going."[29]

As the *Nation* pointed out in a concluding observation, the Writers' Program—as the FWP was designated following passage of the 1939 relief act—could "coast along for months to come on work already done under Alsberg's direction." Beyond this, its significance would be determined by the new organizational structure and Newsom's initiative. Alsberg could take some comfort in letters of condolence from NAACP's Walter White and Hallie Flanagan, ex-director of the theatre project, who agreed that he had made a "real contribution" to American culture "which petty minds do not have the capacity to understand or appreciate." His doting secretary addressed Alsberg by his first name for the first time in their four-year association, writing: "Of course, the new director may do his best, but how can he compare with you? You were the guiding star of our project. You inspired us to do our best, to do the almost impossible by showing us the way."[30] The dejected proponents of the defunct Federal Writers' Project had cause for despair. At the same time, though, they could reasonably hope that the FWP's four-year experience would help the new program to achieve future success.

[29] *New York Times,* Aug. 10, 1939; *Nation* 149 (Aug. 19, 1939):182; Laning quoted in McKinzie, "Writers on Relief," p. 240.

[30] *Nation* 149 (Aug. 19, 1939):182; all letters to Alsberg quoted in Mangione, *Dream and Deal,* pp. 23-24.

11   Aftermath: The Writers' Program

A FEW DAYS AFTER RECEIVING his sudden appointment to replace Alsberg, Director John Newsom wired a friend: "Not at all sure whether I need congratulations or commiserations. Present period is extremely difficult and my path is strewn with pitfalls." Securing local sponsorship—the major stipulation for the existence of the Writers' Program—was the first difficulty. Only with a guarantee from a tax-supported agency to cover 25 per cent of all project costs could a "DPS-18" be filed for each activity in any given state unit. This requirement led the Guilds' Committee to withdraw its sponsorship of the New York City project, and it deposited $6,382.96 in royalties to the U.S. Treasury. However, within a short time New York, Washington, D.C., and all but two states had contributed the necessary funds, in appreciation of the project's value. Between September and March, 1940, alone, sponsors donated $889,598 in supplies and consultants' services.[1]

A number of problems arose with the scheme of local sponsorship, many reminiscent of the difficulties experienced by the program's predecessor. Because publication agreements lacked binding authority, quite a few completed manuscripts had to be relegated to the files, and workers became demoralized. Since the continuation of the Writers' Program could only be insured by sponsorship, an opportunist policy generally prevailed. Although state units obtained permission to proceed with work, sponsors assumed their responsibility lightly and did little investigation into the probability of eventual fulfillment. Contributions often represented little more than paper transactions, as the WPA's financial officer found while unearthing "a lot of air" and padded accounts to cover unavailable lights and library stack space in Florida. Finally, sponsors readily agreed to support less appealing but

[1] Newsom to Navarre, Aug. 22, 1939, Box 1585, WPA; Triggs to Kerr, Dec. 9, 1939, Box 463, WPA; DPS file, Box 1138, WPA.

more profitable publications, such as *Water for Sioux Falls* instead of *South Dakota Place Names*. As a result, Newsom had to complain that sponsored projects had reached almost 570 titles by October, 1940, and had forced all new activities to be postponed until this backlog could be cleared away.[2]

With "a bunch of vultures dashing in to snatch off a piece of a slowly-expiring and rather weakly-struggling animal," the Writers' Program had to face increasing entanglements of red tape. Every letter from Newsom's office went out over the signature of C. E. Triggs, director of Community Service Projects, and was required to be marked for the attention of various state representatives of the division. Procedural channels also required that correspondence first go to state administrators of the WPA (now the Works Projects Administration). In Connecticut, WPA "major generals" opened Director Riley Hughes's mail and stamped it with "all but latitude and longitude." After sponsors signed "301's," state directors forwarded activity form DPS-18 in sextuplicate to Newsom and the director of the Finance Division in Washington. Applications for permission to publish— DPS-19—and for contracts according to Operating Procedure G-5 followed the same pattern. The slightest hitch, such as a delay in receiving the signatures of sponsors who had municipal authority, created great difficulties. When a Stamford, Connecticut, employee, to avoid filling out forms, bought his own typewriter ribbon, state officials considered charges against him for defacing government property.[3]

An even greater problem, as William Couch had predicted during the congressional appropriation hearings of May, 1939, proved to be the susceptibility of the Writers' Program to local attacks and political influence. District offices of Ohio's WPA tended to conceive of the local units as isolated projects, even requiring them to attain separate 25 per cent sponsored contributions. A state senator who sought the mayoralty of Cleveland charged that almost $3,000 had been wasted on an index to newspaper files which told where stories like "Easy to Love" and "8 Girls in a Boat" might be found. Illinois's director, Curtis MacDougall, experienced great difficulty in convincing state

[2] Davidson interview; Newsom to Tyarks, Oct. 14, 1940, Box 467, WPA.

[3] Smith to Newsom, Aug. 24, 1939, Box 1595, WPA; Riley Hughes interview, July 2, 1968. The WPA Finance Division insisted on this procedure after an audit revealed the inefficient manner in which Alsberg had handled guide contracts. McKinzie, "Writers on Relief," p. 243.

WPA officials that the project could not be run like a construction unit, with writing schedules planned two weeks in advance. Southern states deeply resented the investigations of the federal government, terming them the work of "fault- (rather than "fact-) finding" bureaus. One Washington editor had to convince the Birmingham timekeeper that people needed to talk in order to write. And only Colonel Francis Harrington's overriding authority prevented his WPA subordinate in New York City from closing down that unit entirely.[4]

As if "delegations from the Pope to a bishop," Washington editors had to be invited by state WPA officials in a consultative capacity. With diplomatic skill, Harold Rosenberg used executive jargon to convince Ohio's administrator that two additional professionals would "open up the bottleneck" on the local project. Only the promise that two members of his staff could finish up the Washington state guide got Newsom the chance to send Rosenberg and Mary Barrett there after the State Planning Council had withdrawn its sponsorship.[5]

Greater state control also brought increased dangers of local censorship. Immediately after the new cultural programs were established, WPA's Florence Kerr had pointedly instructed state administrators that Washington wanted the projects to be "safe." A folklore essay dealing with Mormons, previously contributed by Vardis Fisher and written in his typical style, was cut from the Utah Guide at the suggestion of consultants from the Latter-day Saints church. Virginia's director eventually acceded to a sponsor's request to suppress from *Your Vacation in Virginia* information regarding stinging nettles in the state's waters. Washington officials held up *The Pursuit of Freedom*, a history of civil liberties in Illinois: local authorities deemed it perhaps "not expedient for the Administration at this time" to be held responsible for the compilation of material dealing with Mayor Kelly's censorship, the

---

[4] Newsom to Kiplinger, June 14, 1941, Box 464, WPA; Curtis MacDougall interview, Apr. 18, 1968; Stella Hanau interview, Sept. 18, 1967. A controversial history of labor halted sponsorship of Oklahoma's unit for a time. The state university was not able to help because it functioned at the mercy of the legislature and had recently come under attack as a bastion of Communism. Mar. 19, 1941, report, Box 464, WPA.

[5] Rosenberg interview; Rosenberg and Barrett to Newsom, Mar. 19, 1940, Box 2733, WPA. The political feud which first began in Washington in early 1939 between State Senator Mary Farquharson and Director Anne Windhusen had caused the council, acting under the governor's orders, to withdraw its support. The University of Washington logically should have been the next sponsor, but it refused to get involved with the political football. Rosenberg and Barrett to Newsom, Mar. 19, 1940, Box 2733, WPA.

Tobacco Road court case, and the Chicago Memorial Day Massacre.[6]

The central office also exercised editorial control over state copy. Contemporaries had to be left out of state factbooks, as did the throwing of tomatoes at Wendell Willkie, mentioned in copy for the Montana *1940 Almanac*. To avoid the arousal of state jealousies, the Florida Guide was forbidden to claim for its state the longest coastline in the United States or to mention Florida's sale of orange seedlings to California—the facts notwithstanding.[7]

In one instance, censorship and state politics almost prevented the publication of a state guide. West Virginia's director of conservation had agreed, with the governor's consent, to sponsor the state volume, and he appointed a consultant to approve its copy. After Viking Press had withdrawn its offer to publish, a new project director executed a contract with the Oxford University Press. The original sponsor refused to sign it without first seeing the manuscript, however, because his reviewer had raised some objections to the contents. Director Bruce Crawford, believing that this "unreasonable position" was based on politics, quietly made arrangements with the superintendent of public education to sponsor the guide. Upon discovering this transfer, Governor Homer Holt immediately wrote to the President and WPA's Colonel Harrington, asking that the original sponsor be given full authority; some parts of the manuscript, in his opinion, were "distinctly discreditable" to West Virginia and her people. At the President's behest, a reluctant Newsom (suspicious of the governor's "antecedents and affiliations") met with Holt.[8]

The governor's objections bore out Newsom's suspicions about Holt's ulterior motives. Pictures of a miner washing coal dust out of his hair, of children (albeit healthy-looking ones) riding to school in an open truck, and of a Mexican miner were vetoed on the grounds that a number of mines had installed showers, West Virginia used modern school buses, and foreign nationals were few and far between in a state

[6] Cited in McKinzie, *New Deal for Artists*, p. 164; McConkey to Newsom, Mar. 26, 1940, Box 2659, WPA; Richmond to Kerr, Dec. 14, 1940, Box 2595, WPA. When the controversial Illinois manuscript was finally published, its preface referred obliquely to the Writers' Program as "a public agency which has asked that no credit . . . be given either to the two score of research workers or to the agency." MacDougall interview.

[7] Corse interview.

[8] Crawford to Alsberg, July 26, 1939, Box 2767, WPA; Homer Holt, *State Papers and Public Addresses* (Charleston, W. Va., 1942), pp. 614-33.

proud of its Anglo-Saxon origins. A miners' march, the profits made by coal operators, and reports of a congressional committee investigating silicosis all represented the insertion of "propaganda from start to finish," in the governor's opinion.[9]

A few months later, a compromise edition went to the publisher —along with the state seal on every page of the manuscript. Holt, who had warned the Governors' Conference that same year to be on guard against the "present trend toward the centralization of all sovereignty in the federal government," refused to write a foreword to the volume. Oxford's editor noted that Holt really wanted the West Virginia volume to be "nothing more than a guide to historical monuments." The incident finally came to a close when separate essays on industry and labor were written, and a new governor gave the guide his approval.[10]

Policy errors occasionally got by in the rush to publish, but, following the example of its predecessor, the Writers' Program remained steadfast in producing worthy volumes. The final proof for the South Carolina Guide did contain the familiar recriminations over the "War between the States" and Reconstruction, as well as justification of the Klan, a patronizing attitude toward the Negro, and a booster account of contemporary labor conditions. On the other hand, the Washington office forced more attention upon blacks, sharecroppers, and the Commonwealth College in the Arkansas guidebook, while it inserted information on Ohio farm cooperatives and a significant 1932 strike in the Bryan and William County Guide and on a Salisbury lunching in the Maryland volume. Newsom also halted the inclusion of a revised history essay for the Los Angeles Guide. It had glossed over the existence of vast Catholic church estates and their Indian workers, the Pope's transfer of the church's missions from the Jesuits to the Franciscans, the bombing of the *Los Angeles Times* building, and other incidents related to local labor history.[11]

The encroachment of private concerns on the project's domain pre-

[9] Crawford to Anderson, Oct. 26, 1939, Box 2767, WPA.

[10] Newsom to Holt, Feb. 29, 1940, Box 2767, WPA; Holt, *State Papers*, pp. 470-79; Holt to author, Dec. 4, 1967; Vaudrin, Mar. 7, 1940, report, South Carolina, 1941, file, American Guide Series, Oxford University Press files. Wisconsin's guidebook was held up by conservative legislators who objected to a long section praising Senator La Follette's Progressivism until a new sponsor, the Wisconsin Library Association, approved the manuscript as objective. McKinzie, "Writers on Relief," p. 247.

[11] Nicholson to Newsom, Aug. 8, 1940, Box 466, WPA; Los Angeles Guide file, Box 938, WPA.

sented a final problem. In the year 1941 alone, Dodd, Mead and Co. started the Sovereign States series, D. Sloan and Pearce began its sectional portrayals of American folkways under the editorial supervision of Erskine Caldwell, and books like *The Vacation Guide, American Vacations*, and *101 American Vacations from $25 to $250* came out to meet the demands of domestic travelers.[12] These private efforts enjoyed freedom from the threats of bureaucracy, sponsoring difficulties, censorship, and state politics, but none matched the publications of the Writers' Program. A few gifted workers made the project something more than a mere caretaker operation, sliding along on the work of its predecessor, and gave the new undertaking function and value.

II

John Newsom brought a new perspective to the national directorship. Where Alsberg had been relaxed ("I'm doing the best I can"), Newsom proved very precise, disciplined, and efficient in handling executive detail. Newsom's first visit to the state units convinced him that the former practices of the FWP could not be tolerated. The exacting standards of the past, along with an "acidly superior and complacent tone," had resulted in innumerable delays, as well as feelings of neglect and hurt in many states. The first item of Newsom's agenda, therefore, was to finish the state guides quickly and then encourage the development of local activities. Editorial supervision would be held to a minimum, with a great deal more latitude being given state supervisors.[13]

At this time, a letter from Newsom praising his predecessor's "high standards of excellence" and requesting the future collaboration of state directors drew fire from Alsberg. The deposed director believed it should have referred to the facts behind his dismissal rather than give the impression that he agreed with the project's administration. WPA's Florence Kerr was unable to convince Alsberg that Newsom had paid him a gracious and sincere tribute.[14]

Newsom proved to be the exact opposite of Alsberg: he was a good administrator with limited skill at editing or developing new programs.

[12] *Pittsburgh Press*, July 6, 1941, IV, p. 10.

[13] Frese interview; Newsom to Wood, Nov. 27, 1939, and Newsom to Triggs, Dec. 21, 1939, Box 463, WPA.

[14] January, 1939, file, Box 465, WPA.

He called for regular reviews of state progress, and full and prompt replies to correspondence from the field gained the appreciation of his staff. Tennessee's director congratulated the new executive on the "excellent manner" in which he finally obtained a settlement with the University of North Carolina Press and interested its director in pursuing new arrangements with the Writers' Program. A secretary for the central staff later recalled that "he commanded everyone's respect and was well liked." But the creative minds regarded Newsom as "very stiff—maybe like Wellington." He never held the loyalty and devotion of state executives as had his predecessor; Florence Kerr thought that the project never had a director that "amounted to a hill of beans" after Alsberg's forced dismissal. Newsom's stress on immediate results led to a distrust of research projects of an investigative nature and evoked Ben Botkin's later claim that "the heart of the project was gone."[15]

To attain his first objective, that of finishing the state guides, Newsom sent six editors from the central office (now sponsored by the Library of Congress) into the field. With the loan of a worker from the Historical Records Survey and a former project employee, Daryl McConkey ran the Utah Guide "through the condensary," thereby gaining the sponsor's gratitude for the "zealous and unselfish manner" in which he finished the volume in record-breaking time. The rush by Harold Rosenberg and Mary Barrett on the Washington state guide could not prevent a rather drab religion essay, but it enabled them to then help the Missouri and Tennessee projects, respectively. Aided by the assistant HRS supervisor, Rosenberg sat in a hotel for three weeks, for eight to ten hours a day, and "made a book out of marvelous research." George Willison traveled to Colorado, Stella Hanau covered Alabama and Oklahoma, and Katherine Kellock ventured forth to Nevada and New Mexico. Kellock managed to get sufficient background in seven weeks to upgrade the copy for publication. Stella Hanau, finding that Alabama's libraries contained only chamber of commerce material ("there are no discontented laborers in Dothan"), added a balanced viewpoint to that state's guide, "cleared the decks" of masses of rough material, and thereby saved the volume.[16]

The Writers' Program underwent significant changes on the admin-

[15] McDaniel to Newsom, Oct. 12, 1940, Box 2576, WPA; Jean Lee to author, Aug. 26, 1968; Kerr interview, Oct. 18, 1963, American Archives of Art; Botkin interview.

[16] Martin to Newsom, July 18, 1940, Box 2659, WPA; Rosenberg interview; Kellock to Newsom, Mar. 11, 1940, Box 1833, WPA; Hanau to Newsom, Feb. 21, 1940, Box 801, WPA.

istrative level. Regional offices, representative of centralized control in FWP days, were not included within the new organizational framework. This particularly disturbed William Couch, who had previously objected to the delay and confusion resulting from the fact that people unaware of the regional situation dispatched "orders from the Walker-Johnson building" to the state units. He wrote to the Librarian of Congress (Archibald MacLeish), sponsor of the central Technical Project, suggesting that the procedural operation be simplified and that competent people cut from the rolls be reinstated, to continue work of the "life-history" type. Newsom, while informing his WPA superior that this appeared "inexcusable," tactfully reminded the former regional director that reorganization signified "not an arbitrary undertaking dictated for the sole and problematical purpose of increasing our efficiency," but a compliance with the 1939 Relief Act. Nationwide activities might be organized only by approaching the regular administrative channels and requesting cooperation, all with the exercise of "patience and tenacity of purpose." But these qualities could not be appreciated by North Carolina's director or by his Southern California counterpart, soon dismissed because he antagonized WPA state officials with his self-sufficient manner.[17] John Frederick and Vardis Fisher left the Writers' Program a few months after it began; other veterans like Saxon and Santee stayed on for some time.

Even more than its predecessor, the Writers' Program suffered from a dearth of competent writers. Outside of New York City, Chicago, and San Francisco, state units rarely had personnel who could do more than parse a sentence, if that. Stella Hanau located only three employees who could write or edit on Virginia's staff, and a poll indicated that only seven of 104 workers in Texas could produce final copy. Not one professional writer existed among Boston's twenty-five non-security personnel. Montana had more than its quota of alcoholic ex-newsmen, and only three of South Carolina's project could write factual copy.[18]

Faced with such circumstances, state executives expected little from their workers. Illinois's director sometimes felt like "a superintendent

[17] Couch to Kerr, Aug. 17, 1939, Box 81, WPA; Couch to MacLeish, Nov. 3, 1939, Box 2183, WPA; Newsom to Kerr and Newsom to Couch, Nov. 8, 1939, Box 2183, WPA; Newsom to Triggs, Mar. 15, 1940, Box 938, WPA.

[18] Hanau to Newsom, Oct. 14, 1941, Box 2694, WPA; Newsom to Kiplinger, Nov. 19 and Sept. 29, 1941, Box 464, WPA; George Marsh to author, May 24, 1968; Hanau to Newsom, Oct. 21, 1941, Box 2532, WPA.

of a mental institution,'' forced to spend most of his time listening to heartbreaking tragedies, coaxing a paranoiac not to jump from a window, sending housewives and widows to a library just to rid himself of them. The Minnesota office published for its personnel a manual on place-names, Illinois put out a remarkable eighty-one page manual, *Training in Basic Research Methods*, and South Dakota's Lisle Reese planned to offer a course in news feature writing. It soon became obvious, however, that written expression could not be taught. For that reason, one or two people in each state did most of the final writing for project publications.[19]

These conditions could not be altered significantly at a time when WPA relief regulations were changing to meet the increasing needs of a war economy. The number of workers on the writers' project when Congress passed the 1939 relief bill—3,623—increased to 3,654 by January, 1940, and to 3,667 by the end of December, then fell to 3,188 in April, 1941. The last figure represented one-fifth of 1 per cent of all WPA workers, almost exactly the percentage of relief appropriations that was received by the project. In addition to sizable cuts since the days of federal jurisdiction (by November, 1941, the number of employees had fallen to some 2,200), the eighteen-month clause in the Emergency Relief Appropriation Act of 1939 forced many competent people off the rolls. As a result, project directors found operations completely disrupted. More than 50 per cent of northern California's professional employees received pink slips, New York City's rolls sagged from 350 to 150, and the author of *Cape Cod Pilot* could not get back on the project after his Guggenheim expired.[20]

With fewer and less competent personnel, creative opportunities had to be severely limited. The central office ended the practice of permitting the names of editorial staff to be published, which created considerable friction between the University of North Carolina Press and the

[19] MacDougall interview. Stella Hanau received the following as sample copy: "We must follow Florence through the terrible reconstruction, those evil days when in bitter poverty, her best and bravest, many of them asleep on Virginia battlefields, her civilization destroyed, the iron entered her soul. And now, when the darkest hour had struck, came a flash of light, the forerunner of the dawn. It was the Ku Klux Klan." n.d., Hanau papers.

[20] U.S. Congress, House, Subcommittee on Appropriations, *Hearings on Work Relief and Relief for Fiscal Year 1941*, 76th Cong., 3d sess., 1940, pp. 448-49; U.S. Congress, Senate, *Hearings on H.J. Res 193*, 77th Cong., 1st sess., 1941, p. 6; Bernard De Voto, "The Writers' Project," *Harper's* 184 (Jan., 1942):221-24; Newsom to Clayton, Aug. 28, 1939, Box 2116, WPA; A-Z file, Box 1966, WPA.

national WPA office when it came to the publication of *God Bless the Devil*. William Couch, now full-time director of the press, believed that credit should be given the author of this folklore study (as he had credited the authors of *These Are Our Lives*), and he debated the new rules with Colonel Harrington. As he recounted years later, "they sat on their permission and I sat on the book." With the approval of Frank Graham, president of the university, Couch held up publication until federal acceptance could be obtained. Washington finally relented via telegram and the presses were set in operation. A few days later, a second wire noted that the previous one had been sent in error; the press rolled on anyway, and the volume came out without further difficulty. *Liars' Bench Tales, South Carolina Folk Tales,* and *A Bundle of Troubles and Other Tarheel Tales* were also published during this period. The work of Montana's last supervisor largely accounted for its magnum opus, a history and tales of Butte, *The Copper Camp.*[21]

Newsom's lack of interest in seeking creative outlets beyond the project, in sharp contrast to Alsberg's concern, as well as the problems of reorganization and the growing concentration on defense activities, prevented further work which might have satisfied the project's professionals. Ralph Ellison found many evenings free to practice "five-finger exercises of fiction," which, although not published, enabled him to learn a new style. South Carolina's assistant director testified to the "added sense of security" given Chalmers Murray—who first came to the project with "baggy frayed trousers, wool coats that were half cotton, lopsided shoes, and a paper suitcase with a lock broken"—that enabled him to write *Here Comes Joe Muggin* on free weekends.[22] This represented a far cry, however, from the FWP's creative project, *American Stuff,* or its offerings in various magazines.

The precariousness of the project's existence made it susceptible to boondoggling. Tennessee copy had many *c*.s for dates of construction and did not mention the tomb of President James Polk in Nashville. The absence of order in Alabama files and copy stultified that project. Even those units wanting and able to do valuable work had to face the effects of tenuous sponsoring arrangements, timekeeping checks done by mail

[21] Couch interview; Couch memoir, pp. 352-57; George Marsh to author, May 24, 1968.

[22] Ralph Ellison telephone conservation with author, May 30, 1968; DuBose to Newsom, Sept. 27, 1941, Box 464, WPA. A WPA Literary Fellowship, sponsored by Dodd, Mead and Company, was abandoned because of the publisher's fears about the program's reorganization and its concentration on defense activities. Dodd to Newsom, July 31, 1941, Box 466, WPA.

which were delayed because of war preparations, and the competition of defense jobs.

Although the state projects experienced more boondoggling than their predecessor, their employees gave them far less worry about subversive activity. The FBI later arrested a German draftsman from the Florida project on charges of passing maps to submarines off St. Johns Island and signaling the enemy, but this was an isolated case. Although the charge of party control arose in Oklahoma and Ohio, investigators found nothing conclusive to substantiate it, and the West Virginia director who tried to cover up his ineptitude by accusing his predecessor of infesting Bluefield with "Reds" later admitted that he had made a mistake. [23]

Even in New York City, Communist party activity had disappeared. In an effort to clamp down on WPA, the 1940 Relief Act required all its workers to sign affidavits that they were not Communists, Bund members, or aliens. [24] Referring to the names inscribed in the book shown the Dies and Woodrum committees, WPA investigators suspended a number of workers still on the New York unit who had signed such affidavits. On the instructions of WPA's Colonel Brehon Somervell, 404 workers had received dismissal notices by August, 1940, because of alleged subversive party activity. In April of that year the local administrator informed the House subcommittee investigating WPA that many avowed and alleged Communists on that unit until 1939 had been dismissed in accordance with the eighteen-months rule, that production assignment sheets had been instituted by his order, and that copy for a book which had compared New York and Moscow subways would be edited. [25]

Despite red tape, cuts in the relief rolls, and incompetent personnel, the Washington office succeeded in completing the last of the guides by the end of 1941. Louisiana's project edited the Arkansas manuscript and Pennsylvania's workers checked the Alabama Guide maps. Roy

[23] Corse interview; *Huntington Herald Dispatch*, Oct. 8, 1941.

[24] *San Francisco Chronicle*, June 26, 1940. There were obvious difficulties, since few would openly admit this fact. A month after the act took effect only four of 1,600,000 on WPA's rolls had done so (*Baltimore Sun*, July 13, 1940). The law was further complicated by the later ruling of a district judge in Newark that "communism" could not be easily defined (*New York Herald Tribune*, Feb. 21, 1942).

[25] *New York Times*, July 21 and Aug. 1 and 3, 1940; Newsom to Triggs, Aug. 7, 1940, Box 463, WPA. For Somervell's intolerance toward the art project, see McKinzie, *New Deal for Artists*, p. 165.

Basler examined the Alabama history essay, Douglas Freeman and Dixon Ryan Fox contributed the contemporary essays for the Virginia and New York State guidebooks, respectively, and a university professor worked one day a week on the Delaware volume. Newsom formed a National Advisory Committee, including Paul de Kruif, Randolph Adams, and the publishers Walter Frese and Quincy Howe.[26]

Publishers generally received a free hand to finish the guidebooks. Oxford University Press split up the maps in the Maryland volume and decided on the type face for chapter titles in its Florida counterpart, and Hastings House cut the Utah Guide to make it approximately the length of the products of comparable states. Although Oxford's editor could not rid the Virginia book entirely of its heavy concern with Confederate landmarks and Jeffersonian architecture, he did modify assertions couched in such prose as "Social discriminations have not brought about a myopia that impairs a vision of social justice."[27]

Standing on their own feet without a federal crutch, the state guides continued to merit the warm praise given their predecessors. Critics vied with one another in assigning superlatives to the volumes. Even regular opponents of WPA boondoggling like the *Cleveland Plain Dealer* and the *Baltimore Sun* approved of the attention given Ohio's tour descriptions and the genealogy of Maryland's thoroughbreds. The lack of booster spirit was also impressive, leading Louis Bromfield to consider the entire American Guide Series "able and even noble in conception."[28]

Reviewers stressed the guidebooks' fostering of pride in state and nation as war clouds gathered. When the Oklahoma Guide reached completion the series won plaudits as one of the best peacetime efforts to unite the populace. The American Booksellers' Association also sounded the theme in its proclamation of American Guide Week (November 10-16, 1941) and the slogan "take pride in your country." To complement this gesture, the President had a letter drafted (at the request of WPA's Florence Kerr) which commended the guides' portrayal of the nation's unity and diversity. Even the *New York Sun*, a

[26] National Advisory Committee file, Box 463, WPA.

[27] Vaudrin to Nicholson, Oct. 3, 1939; Virginia file, American Guide Series, Oxford University Press files.

[28] *Baltimore Sun*, Aug. 11, 1940, I, p. 8; *Cleveland Plain Dealer*, Nov. 10, 1940, Feature Section, p. 2; *New York Herald Tribune*, Jan. 28, 1940, IX, p. 5.

formidable critic of Roosevelt and the WPA, thought that the presence of the series in every American home might result in a reduction of intolerance. Stephen Vincent Benét said that the books made good reading for "these troubled times," suggesting as they did the nation's motto, *E pluribus unum*.[29]

With 12 million words of Americana, the Guide Series's description of the United States thus came to a close. In their candor, irony, and humor, the larger volumes constituted a unique enterprise, a major triumph in cooperative authorship. Behind their covers lay the story of many dedicated, albeit anonymous, individuals who accomplished a demanding and often boring task. These project employees overcame numerous difficulties to portray collectively the patchwork quilt of the country in informed and interesting prose. Through their resolve, they charted a nation.

III

While the state guidebooks were being completed, the Writers' Program worked on other publications. *The Oregon Trail, The Negro in Virginia*, and *Drums and Shadows*, begun under the FWP, had to be edited and published, as did a few "tall tale" anthologies and a condensed version of the D.C. Guide. Guides to San Francisco, Los Angeles, Mt. Hood, Atlanta, Raleigh, Houston, and Cleveland saw print. In the process of researching old newspapers, South Dakota's director came across an uncopyrighted daily column in the *Aberdeen Saturday Pioneer* by the author of *The Wizard of Oz* and published the articles as *Our Landlady*. The New York City project put out the American Wildlife Series, which sold close to 25,000 copies; the Rhode Island unit produced a summary of labor laws. Arna Bontemps edited *The Cavalcade of the American Negro*, a brief survey distinguished by its prose and balanced views, for the Illinois Diamond Jubilee Exposition of 1940. The Illinois project also contributed a history of baseball in Chicago, the *Annals of Labor and Industry*, and the Art Institute Series. The latter consisted of twenty radio scripts written by Studs Terkel and others for the Art Institute of Chicago: it was broad-

[29] Kerr to E. Roosevelt, Sept. 22, 1941, and F. D. Roosevelt to Kerr, Sept. 30, 1941, Box 16, OF-444C, FDR papers, FDRL; *New York Sun*, Dec. 31, 1941; *New York Herald Tribune*, Dec. 28, 1941.

cast over WGN, which was owned by a leading New Deal opponent, Colonel Robert McCormick.[30]

The Writers' Program also undertook various new series. The American Recreation Series, begun in August, 1940, with a volume on Georgia, sold 18,000 pamphlets by 1942. Picture books on Montana and Virginia started the American Pictorial Guides. The sales of the Elementary Science Series reached 180,000 copies. County histories first appeared in 1940–41 in Minnesota, Wisconsin, Iowa, Kentucky, and New Jersey. The South Dakota, North Carolina, and Massachusetts projects came out with place-name books, and the central office instituted the Factbook Series under the editorship of Katherine Kellock. Social-ethnic studies of Italians in Omaha and Finns in Minnesota, a history of San Francisco theatre, a guide to Las Vegas, Arizona Indian bulletins, and childhood stories by ex-slaves in Arkansas were representative of the over 750 activities listed in the central office's DPS files by mid-1941.[31]

The scope of these efforts gradually narrowed, however, as sponsors demanded trivial material in return for final contributions. Under these circumstances, the project often became a service rather than a production unit. Since sponsors' contributions proved essential to its existence, the Writers' Program would perform editorial services which secured it publicity but also stalled work on worthwhile volumes. A history of Hamtramck High School, a record of "kills" in Michigan before 1925 (for the state game and fur departments), and *Plants Hardy in Butte* had questionable value. Significant efforts did emerge: the indexing of Floridiana for the State Historical Society (including the British Colonial Office's records), a history of Jesuit explorers and Ohio's Maumee missions, a study of nursing in Kansas entitled *Lamps along the Prairie*, and historical articles from unpublished volumes that were serialized for local newspapers. Many of these represented the by-products of previous research, however, not anything beyond work accomplished by the FWP.

Under the central staff's direction, the Writers' Program did work on a number of notable projects besides the factbooks and the recreation and pictorial guide series, but none of these were printed. These

[30] Everett to Kerr, June 19, 1941, Box 2366, WPA; *The Cavalcade of the American Negro* (Chicago, 1940); Terkel interview.

[31] Bacon to Newsom, Jan. 18, 1942, Box 472, WPA; Newsom to Kerr, Apr. 22, 1941, Box 1, LC FWP.

terminated activities included a social-ethnic analysis of Scandinavians and Lithuanians in the Northwest, a U.S. travel atlas, a "Lexicon of Trade Jargon," volumes on Negroes in Florida and Illinois, and books on the ports of New York City and San Francisco. Pearl Harbor ended plans for Latin American Guides and also halted Katherine Kellock's lessons in Portuguese for a trip to Brazil. A national picture book to be entitled *USA: A Democracy*, with its text in various languages, had been suggested by Ruth Crawford and had received the sponsorship of the National Education Association; war preparations shelved this as well.[32]

The country's entry into World War II had the same effect on volumes which provided more opportunity for the exhibition of creative talents. "Men at Work," an anthology covering such professions as cannery workers, sponge divers, cowboys, and Navaho sheepherders, could not be completed. Its editor, Harold Rosenberg, had also begun preparations for a six-volume regional history of the country's handi-crafts entitled "Hands That Built America," with plates from the Federal Art Project's Index of American Design, but war also forced this to a halt. With the thought that literature on the American Indian was either too technical or overpopular, Stella Hanau had convinced the University of Oklahoma to sponsor her prospectus for a regional history; her return to Washington on December 7, 1941, presaged that volume's fate. "Victims of the Depression," "Men against Granite," and "Big Ivy," all based on Couch's "life-history" idea, would have provided additional creative possibilities; so would have "America Eats," Mrs. Kellock's proposal to publish accounts of ethnic dinners and local favorites like Arizona Son-of-a-Bitch Stew and Kansas Corn Fritters. These and numerous suggestions—for an encyclopedia of the Negro (W. E. B. Du Bois's original proposal), a "Flying Guide," a world gazetteer, and an "Angler's Guide"—had to be discontinued and left untried because of the steady decrease in the project's rolls and the reorganization of its activities in the direction of defense mobilization.[33]

With the establishment of the National Defense Program, the project, now under the Community Service Program Division, had to justify itself anew. Only days after the Nazi invasion of Poland,

[32] Kellock interview, June 23, 1968; Ruth C. France to author, Nov. 20, 1968.
[33] Rosenberg and Hanau interviews.

Newsom suggested to his superior that the project's efforts be tied to the "national emergency." Another memo, dated June 1, 1940, argued that the Writers' Program alone could supply "cultural content" to patriotism by providing the realistic awareness of "a unified tradition—the most powerful stimulus to integrated action." Katherine Kellock repeated this theme a few months later, in a defense of the project's work: "Books like these are needed as never before if Americans are to understand their heritage and the culture they are now called on to defend." The guides were soon found on the shelves of military cantonments.[34]

The Writers' Program shifted its work to war themes. A National Defense Series commenced with a guidebook to the U.S. Naval Academy; military area guides, requiring the work of only two or three people, came out regularly. A military history of Kentucky, a history of the American Legion of Delaware, and a biography of aviation pioneer Octave Chanute by the Illinois unit constituted other efforts. At the request of the Jacksonville Naval Air Station, one Florida project employee turned out a series of lectures for the use of instructors on aerial target and gunnery bombing. New York City's *Motion Picture Index* aided Washington agencies on the lookout for war films. Air-raid manuals appeared frequently, while the Florida and Montana units prepared bulletins on home gardening to overcome many existing food shortages.[35]

Such developments drew the fire of some prominent men of letters, summoned by WPA's Howard Hunter at the end of 1941 to evaluate the federal arts program. Bernard DeVoto objected to this "trivial" work which had resulted in the shift of authority to the local offices. John Steinbeck wondered about the more fundamental question: "Are we feeding artists or creating artistic expression?" In response, WPA's Florence Kerr, though prepared to praise the cultural programs, did not commit herself to government support divorced from relief concerns. Finally, when none of the participants could agree, Archibald MacLeish berated the WPA administrators present: "What you people did was completely hypocritical . . . you kept telling yourself [*sic*] you

[34] McDonald, *Federal Relief Administration and the Arts*, pp. 688-89; Greene to Brummet, June 1, 1940, Box 463, WPA; Katherine Kellock, "The WPA Writers: Portraitists of the United States," *American Scholar* 9 (Oct., 1940):473-82.

[35] Corse interview; Box 9, WPA Service Division files, Works Progress Administration records, Record Group 69, National Archives, Washington, D.C.

were actually giving people a job, but you were really more interested in your program." "You must admit," Kerr shot back with accuracy, "it was one of the higher forms of hypocrisy."[36]

Some project officials resisted the new emphasis on minor publications and offered alternatives which would prove of more significant value while still fitting the general national defense pattern. Newsom proposed an "Encyclopedia of the Americas"; Hanau, a volume on a few strategically located port cities and a whole series of regional public health studies. Ruth Crawford thought of a history of women in the United States, to counter "the present ideal of the Nazis—Kinder, Kirche and Küche." Daryl McConkey noted that a history of blimps might prove useful for the Atlantic patrol. These remained only suggestions, however, as priority went to already-begun defense materials requiring far fewer personnel.[37]

Even the proposals that received approval met with difficulties arising out of the defense effort. As the war drew closer, military commanding officers grew more suspicious of the project's servicemen's guides, and soon these could only touch on available recreation in the vicinity of bases. After Congress declared war, the revision of the D.C. Guide omitted the locations of buildings and made descriptions more general. An analysis of community reaction to the December blackout at the Golden Gate, completed in three weeks by Walter McElroy and a few San Francisco project workers, had to be abandoned after the Army raised minor objections. This, notwithstanding the fact that the volume had previously received both the sponsor's approval and an appreciative review from the deputy executive of the Office of Civilian Defense for a "splendid morale-building job." McElroy could not alter the situation, especially since Newsom (sympathetic to such efforts) left in February, 1942, for a post with the U.S. Navy.[38]

Faced with the reorganization of WPA for war service, project officials in Washington focused their attention on the permanent safeguarding of all manuscripts. Sensing in July, 1939, that the writers'

[36] "Conference on the Arts Program of the WPA, October 8, 1941," cited in McKinzie, "Writers on Relief," pp. 267-70.

[37] Newsom to Coons, Jan. 4, 1941, Box 2116, WPA; *passim*, Box 209, WPA; McConkey to Newsom, Nov. 3, 1941, Box 208, WPA.

[38] Newsom to Drought, Jan. 17, 1942, Box 2633, WPA; "Blackout at the Golden Gate" file, folder 2, KK papers, LC.

project would lose its federal character, Archibald MacLeish (newly appointed Librarian of Congress) had suggested that he sponsor the Washington staff as a future unit under the District of Columbia WPA. In this way, he reasoned, its members could index and arrange the project's "gold-bearing ore." On October 21, 1939, the Library of Congress Writers' Project began work under the supervision of Gorham Munson, former editor of *Secession* (1922–24), writer, and teacher at the New School, who had also served on the central staff for one month before it closed. Of the twenty-seven workers on the editorial and production staff, thirteen were transferred four months later to concentrate on project publications, and Ben Botkin became chief editor of the section.[39]

The Library of Congress project lasted for only a brief time. Under Botkin's direction, employees filled out evaluation sheets to cover all surplus records of the state writers' projects. Despite its record of progress, however, Munson became disappointed with the way the vast filing process seem to inch along without any tangible result. He resigned after a subtle power struggle involving Luther Evans, Holger Cahill, and the Government Employees' Union. Botkin, who could not gain approval for an Index of American Folklore, got tired of this "salvage operation"; he later received an appointment to head the library's folklore section. MacLeish, who had tried unsuccessfully to keep Harold Rosenberg off the unit, thinking him "a rigid doctrinaire Marxist," was never completely satisfied with the project. Consequently, it suspended operation on July 3, 1941, after having accessioned 79,483 items and approved for deposit 28,322 items, a total of 114,408 pages.[40]

While the cataloging continued, Washington officials arrived at a decision regarding the final deposit of project material. MacLeish and Philip Hamer (the head of the National Archives' reference department) had debated whether or not the project's unpublished material would

[39] MacLeish to Kerr, July 21, 1939, Box 463, WPA; Munson interview; Newsom to Triggs, Feb. 9, 1941, Box 212, WPA. Roosevelt had approved this set-up on the advice of the Bureau of the Budget that "supervision . . . will undoubtedly eliminate any radical tendency, and . . . provide probably the best technical supervision available." Cited in McKinzie, "Writers on Relief," pp. 243-44.

[40] Munson and Botkin interviews; Botkin to Bianco, July 7, 1941, Box 213, WPA. MacLeish's attitude stemmed from Rosenberg's attack on his article in the FWP *Poetry* number. See *Poetry* 52 (July, 1938):212-19 and (Sept., 1938):332-43.

be considered records of the project or archives, and the Librarian of Congress won the argument in 1939. However, the sheer bulk of the project's files made it impractical for either government agency to serve as a permanent central depository. The records would also be more accessible and of more use in state institutions. In the Federal Writers' Project's first year, requests were made by such agencies as Baltimore's Enoch Pratt Library, Louisville's Filson Club, the University of Maine, and the Tennessee Planning Commission to serve as future depositories. Newsom, primarily interested that large numbers of researchers and readers be given the opportunity to use the project's data, asked state units in June, 1940, to send all publications to ten centrally located institutions. Two months later the Washington office sent a circular to advise projects how to set up efficient filing procedures. Soon after Pearl Harbor, a memorandum ordered state directors to evaluate all manuscripts and to select, with the sponsor's advice, an appropriate state agency which could house project material if the need arose.[41]

Despite a few difficulties, the complex undertaking proceeded smoothly. By the end of April, 1942, forty state depositories, usually universities and libraries, had been approved. In each case, the grant was conditioned on the new acquisitions' being subject to recall for the project's use and on the possibility that procedures eventually would be worked out for evaluating the material and making it available to the public if not recalled.[42]

Having taken steps to insure the safety of the project's records, the Washington staff made one last attempt to substitute an important project for the secondary pamphlets which "salved local egos and created the impression of usefulness." Newsom's plan for "sampling information of the United States at war," on which his staff would exercise its proven talents as an independent unit under the Office of Civilian Defense or the Office of Government Reports, received the strong approval of his advisory committee. A telegram signed by Fannie Hurst, Elmer Rice, Cass Canfield, Louis Untermeyer, John Dos Passos, and Freda Kirchwey was sent to Florence Kerr in January, 1942, in support of the plan, and the historian Randolph Adams, in an

[41] Davidson interview; Newsom to Stolte, June 14, 1940, Box 1632, WPA; Circular, Aug. 8, 1940, and Memorandum, Dec. 19, 1941, Hanau papers.

[42] Kerr to Eaton, Apr. 27, 1942, Box 384, WPA.

allusion to certain congressional investigation committees, discounted the danger of this unit's becoming a propaganda bureau. However, the activity did not receive approval, and, after Newsom's resignation a month later, the Writers' Program became the Writers' Unit of the War Services Subdivision (formerly the Community Service Division) of WPA.[43]

The new Writers' Unit, in issuing a practical statement to Congress which stressed a Military and Civilian Defense Series, seemed far from the project's original dream of an American Renaissance in culture. Only those state programs which "directly build morale or promote the public welfare" would be allowed to continue operations, noted the central office. This "post-mortem life" saw a publication exclusively devoted to Illinois's Scott Field and Mississippi's *Our Army* first-level readers (for illiterate rejectees); also issued was Ohio's *Bomb Squad Training Manual*. By the end of April, 211 activities of the Writers' Unit had been reported in the states, including seventy servicemen's recreational guides. At the same time, Merle Colby, its principal editor, expressed his desire for future collaboration with the art section on regional studies of popular art and also tried to get publishers to undertake the one-volume American Guide and "Hands That Built America." Waiting for the final word on the project's future, members of the Washington office could only hope that WPA's "first frenzy" to prove that it was doing "war stuff" would be replaced by a new appreciation of the project's primary efforts. Only in this way, they reasoned, could it "limber up again."[44]

"Writers' Project—Morituri," wrote Katherine Kellock in her diary for March 25, 1942, as the "wild racket of moving desks, falling file cases, ripping papers" gave way to a scene suggestive of the prophetic Valley of Dry Bones. The next day, while she was rephrasing letters and noting policy slips in the *USA* pictorial guide, a memo arrived which informed the central staff that henceforth the technical aspects of project operation would be delegated to state administrators of the War Services Division. Realizing that the District of Columbia unit would soon be disbanded, its members spoke of keeping in touch with one

[43] Graff, Jan., 1942, report, and Adams to Kerr, Jan. 14, 1942, Box 208, WPA.

[44] McDonald, *Federal Relief Administration and the Arts*, pp. 690-91; "Writers' Project: 1942," *New Republic* 106 (Apr. 13, 1942):480; Merle Colby memo, May 1, 1942, Box 384, WPA; Colby to Huxley, Feb. 11, 1942, Box 1844, WPA; Hanau papers.

another by meeting once a month for lunch at some quiet restaurant in Washington "in a sort of unofficial way."[45]

The signs of decay and depression increased daily. The once-crowded central headquarters, moved from the Ouray Building back to the project's first location in the old Washington Auditorium, now had vacant spaces and sounded harsh echoes. Katherine Kellock answered mail and held down the office, Stella Hanau helped her reduce the project's files to seven cases and went on the "job hunt," and McConkey and Colby sought contracts for odd volumes in Florida and New York City. Rumors rose and fell about the date on which the remaining staff would be moved.[46]

At 3:30 P.M. on May 14, 1942, Walter Kiplinger (director of War Services) called Katherine Kellock, Stella Hanau, Ruth Crawford, and Daryl McConkey into his office and, "without even an expression of regret or perfunctory courtesy," handed them formal two-weeks notices. Having no other recourse to action, the three women decided to go straight to the Powhattan Hotel for a drink. Although Kellock claimed considerable seniority and administrative experience over Colby, Kiplinger's choice for consultant to the new program, she resigned herself to "the survival of the fittest." In her last contribution to the project, she rushed the remaining master set (276 volumes, 701 pamphlets, and 340 "numbers," subject to recall until 1945) over to the Library of Congress before those "jockeying for final place in the musical chairs game" could get to it for private copies. As the project drew to a close, her forlorn note of adieu captured its sorry dénouement: "The last day we dribbled out, without anyone's even saying good-bye."[47]

As the project, now geared solely to the defense effort, declined inexorably, the country shifted to a war economy. By the early autumn of 1940, the Federal Reserve Board's index of industrial production had risen nearly seven points, and almost 2 million persons found private jobs during that year. "Our day was done," recalled WPA's Florence Kerr, and the labor surplus of the Depression years quickly gave way to the labor scarcity of the post–Pearl Harbor months. Washington

[45] Mar. 25, 1942, report, KK papers, LC; Hanau to Clair, Apr. 20, 1942, Hanau papers.

[46] Mar. 25, 1942, report, KK papers, LC.

[47] Kellock to Coy, May 14, 1942, KK papers, LC; Kellock interview, Aug. 18, 1968.

officials sold the projects under her supervision "on the hoof," for instance the Los Angeles sewing unit that "went lock, stock and barrel" to a parachute company with a government contract. The House Appropriations Committee proposed giving WPA (which had always been considered a stop-gap measure) close to half a million less for 1942 than for the year preceding.[48]

The country's entry into World War II and its subsequent rise in economic fortunes adversely affected the Writers' Unit. What the *New Republic* termed the "martial ghost" of the project, with about 2,000 on state relief rolls, had to restrict its activities to such publications as health almanacs, a pamphlet for the Los Angeles Defense Council entitled *General Rumor Says "If You Stop Talking I Stop Living,"* and servicemen's guides. New York State's unit of four folded in July, leaving manuscripts on Yonkers, Ft. Slocum, Albany, and the Buffalo-Niagara frontier close to final presentation. The California project's doors closed in December, with the Long Beach and San Bernadino County guides and a study of "California and the Confederacy" almost finished. Curtis MacDougall, eager not to be in at "the absolute kill," left the Illinois directorship to join the editorial staff of the *Chicago Sun*.[49]

Merle Colby, presiding over the shadow of a once vibrant, creative organization, unsuccessfully tried to revive it somehow. He kept talking "idea file" and "feature publications," and thought that regular meetings should be held to which distinguished visitors could be invited to discuss past and future activities. In January, 1943, he also called on all remaining projects to forward an evaluation of their past work to the Federal Workers Agency Library for possible future use. Massachusetts began work on an anthology of quotations showing the development of the "Four Freedoms" in the state from 1620. Delaware continued its government book and New York City its multivolume film index, and Virginia finished a study of Roanoke. However, work could not proceed with the steady transfer of workers to defense training courses, and OPA's Leon Henderson opposed continuing WPA beyond the fiscal year. He did not want to touch the program,

[48] Wecter, *Great Depression*, p. 311; Kerr interview, July 21, 1968.
[49] "Writers' Project: 1942," *New Republic* 106 (Apr. 13, 1942):480; Malone to DuVon, July 9, 1942, Box 1957, WPA; California report, Box 9, WPA Service Division files; MacDougall interview.

with its grim reminders of relief, unemployment, breadlines, and high labor costs.[50]

Under these circumstances, the passing of what Florence Kerr had called the "Elysian Fields" proved inevitable. Lyle Saxon, who had finally left the project on July 15, 1942, ended up in charge, as national consultant for WPA, when the Writers' Unit finally closed its doors exactly seven months later. "The biggest literary project in history," having spent a total of $27,189,370 in a little over seven years, ended with enough material to fill seven twelve-foot shelves in the library of the Department of the Interior. In April, Colby submitted a final report to the Library of Congress, "Disposition of Unpublished Writers' Project Materials," with the concluding hope that "here and there in America some talented boy or girl will stumble on some of this material, take fire from it, and turn it to creative use."[51] Washington liquidated the entire WPA on June 30, 1943. The epic of federal support of the arts was over.

[50] Kellock to Coy, May 14, 1942, KK papers, LC. These final reports (Box 9, WPA Service Division files) discuss the failings of the projects along with proposals for a future program. Merle Colby file, Box 384, WPA; Kerr interview, Oct. 24, 1963, American Archives of Art.

[51] Kerr interview, Oct. 24, 1963, American Archives of Art; 211.7 N-Z folder, Box 384, WPA; "WPA Accounting," *Time* 41 (Feb. 15, 1943):95-96; LC Feb. 14, 1942, folder, Box 384, WPA.

Conclusion

NEVER INTENDED AS A SUBSIDIZED cultural enterprise, the Federal Writers' Project was established to provide work relief for writers and other white-collar personnel caught in the toils of the Depression. Under the circumstances, the project could not be divorced from relief regulations. The clear majority of its personnel, as a result, were not writers, but simply willing workers in need whose sincerest literary efforts only affirmed Pope's observation that "true ease in writing comes from art, not chance, /As those move easiest who have learn'd to dance." Yet, without the contribution of the lawyers, ministers, news-papermen, librarians, and teachers who made up the bulk of its rolls, the FWP would never have been able to arrive at its outstanding record of success.[1]

The writers' project admirably achieved its primary objective—to serve as an agency of conservation and rehabilitation of threatened personalities. Its researchers in dusty archives, interviewers, and editors gained the right to walk on the same side of the street as other citizens. Many took pride in their work, and this fact reflected itself in the relative absence of boondoggling. Universities which at first were "very, very leery about associating with anything as disreputable and with such an 'x' quality" as a government project and libraries which hesitated to let reliefers handle rare books soon changed their initial assumptions. White-collar workers underwent significant transformations almost overnight. With their awakened enthusiasm, they proceeded to display a diligence worthy of Scotland Yard in ferreting out information for the American Guide Series and other volumes. Often with their offices in their hats, the federal writers poked their noses everywhere and set out in battered Fords to log back roads and chart a nation. Observing the "generosity, dignity and integrity" with which

[1] Alexander Pope, *An Essay on Criticism* (1709).

project employees responded to the opportunity to do constructive work, Director John Frederick claimed to have regained from them his faith in human nature and American democracy. Even the highly critical investigation of the embroiled New York City project spoke of its members' "new sense of social purpose [and] their relation as writers to the mainstream of American culture." This conservation of skills and professional pride, rather than the production of books, marks the true significance and revolutionary nature of the federal program for writers.[2]

This "daring experiment in social psychology" was necessitated by the economic crisis of the thirties, but it is questionable whether the FWP would have emerged under an administration other than Roosevelt's. The project represented one of FDR's many experiments to alleviate the needs of his constituency. Roosevelt's personal approach to relief strengthened his close ties with the individual he chose to run WPA, a devoted public servant who measured efficiency primarily by "whether the food got into people's stomachs." As a former social worker, Harry Hopkins could understand the immediate needs of destitute white-collar people, and he had no reservations about bringing creative minds to Washington to help solve the crisis. Only in this way did Jake Baker come to spearhead the planning for Federal #1 and, subsequently, call Henry Alsberg to head the FWP.

Because of Hopkins, the project was also freed of much red tape by the WPA Finance Division and other agencies. Thus, too, it received the services of Ellen Woodward, Florence Kerr, and various other state directors who represented the new presence of women in government circles. At a time when other Washington officials were expressing concern over soil erosion, Arthur Goldschmidt and his subordinates in the inner circle of professional project organizers spoke of avoiding "skill erosion" and made every effort to come up with exciting, worthwhile proposals.[3]

The FWP also justified itself artistically. Despite the dearth of qualified writers, the absence of worthy guidebook examples, and the persistent attempts to reduce the project to a political football and an

[2] Cahill Memoir, p. 434; Corse interview; Frederick to Kerr, n.d., Box 1225, WPA; Bruere to Kellogg, June 17, 1937, Box 2115, WPA.

[3] Bruere to Kellogg, June 17, 1937, Box 2115, WPA; Cahill Memoir, p. 415; Goldschmidt interview.

auxiliary of local chambers of commerce, the FWP succeeded in fulfilling its *raison d'être*—the American Guide Series. Marked by neither drumbeating nor ponderous criticism, these books were relieved of the dullness of most of their predecessors by good writing, intelligent editing, and a wealth of interesting information. Unlike the traditional "intimate" guidebooks—"usually so damnable intimate as to drive tourists into bars for information if not for drink"—the project's state and local offerings substantially filled the gap between armchair knowledge and practical application. To emphasize that the guides lacked sufficient interpretive depth or historical perspective is to minimize the difficulties constantly entountered by the project and to misconceive the fundamental purpose of a guidebook. It is also to disagree with the judgment, for example, of Bernard DeVoto, who noted the "astonishingly high" average level of literary and historical competence of these volumes. Escaping both the internal danger of purple prose and the external one of censorship, the American Guide Series gained the warm praise of such additional observers as Harry Hansen, Lewis Gannett, Louis Bromfield, and Van Wyck Brooks for containing some of the best reading of the day and for providing the country with "its first candid self-portrait."[4]

At a time when WPA sought to prime the pump to national recovery, the guides' contemporary import and that of the project's numerous other publications lay in their priming the pump to national self-awareness. With considerable scholarship, the federal writers uncovered a land which lay hidden behind billboards and boosterism. Their painstaking research reached far beyond the countless movie houses, highway restaurants, and chain stores to discover the nation's rich diversity. Cities and towns were found to have an individuality of their own. State pride quickened. The North Carolina Guide convinced one reviewer that "Tar Heelia" would no longer be called "the Rip Van Winkle of the Union." A local resident hoped his New York friends would read the Arkansas volume so that it might "drive from their nostrils the stench of the subway" and "make them even forget the

[4] *New York Times*, July 5, 1939; Daniel Fox, "The Achievement of the Federal Writers' Project," *American Quarterly* 13 (Spring, 1961):3-19; DeVoto, "The Writers' Project"; *The Pathfinder* (Washington, D.C.), Dec. 17, 1938. Thus the fears of Vermont's director that in the "auto-conscious guidebook deference is paid to pedestrianism only in the matter of prose style" could be forgotten (Doten to Morris, Apr. 15, 1938, Box 25, FWPN).

cockroaches of Greenwich Village." "Florida" and "florid" would no longer be considered synonymous, nor would Iowa be confused with Ohio or Idaho.[5]

In increasing understanding, according to many reviewers, the state and local guidebooks also strengthened national unity by placing the particular within the framework of the whole. As domestic and international unrest tested the Republic's very foundations, and as it turned to take stock of itself, the critical guides did their part in making this inspection fruitful. While conserving skills and human dignity, the project also conserved history and folklore which otherwise might have remained unexplored or fallen victim to mildew. Digging deep to recover roots and a sense of community with the country's past, FWP writers put out publications which, in Director Harlan Hatcher's words, would ultimately "stand as a heartening monument to the stability of America, long after the bitter years of the 1930s have been forgotten."[6]

Even aside from the seminal guidebooks, the FWP made significant contributions in a number of areas. Its black studies were pioneering ones. Its social-ethnic and folklore research represented novel approaches, as did the "life-history" technique of *These Are Our Lives*. Booklets on place-names, local legends, and many other subjects appeared regularly. Pamphlets for school use, publicity for newspapers, indexing of library files, and the verification of data for various federal and private concerns exemplified the project's diverse efforts. These auxiliary projects resulted in a total achievement which thirty years later seems almost incredible.[7]

One aspect of the project's publications is, in some respects, reminiscent of the note sounded by literary America at the close of the thirties.[8] An insular "literature of nationhood" swept the land, as writers, seeking new certainties, stumbled upon and then deeply reexamined America's life and landscape for a "usable past." Doubters became devotees, and the restoration of America to herself was ex-

[5] *New York Herald Tribune,* Jan. 28, 1940; J. Selvy, Sept. 21, 1941, review, cited in Box 83, WPA Division of Information files.

[6] Harlan Hatcher book column, *Columbus Citizen,* Nov. 16, 1941.

[7] *London Times* (July, 1939) clipping in Box 1, LC FWP.

[8] I have already made the distinction between the FWP's final product and the indiscriminate self-celebration which marked American writing at this time. See, especially, the conclusion to chap. 5 and chaps. 4 and 7 above.

pressed in titles like *The American Cause, The Flowering of New England*, and *The Ground We Stand On*. The debunkers of the 1920s were often criticized for abandoning the country's needs to focus on art and Europe. A popular interest in history, aroused by a spate of scholarly biographies in quest of heroes (especially Lincoln, ultimate symbol of unity) and the two most successful novels of the decade, *Gone with the Wind* and *Anthony Adverse,* came into full bloom. Constance Rourke and John Lomax revived frontier legends and ballads, and James Truslow Adams's widely read *Epic of America* beckoned its readers to recapture the American dream. WPA furthered the cause not only with the writers' project but with the Historical American Buildings Survey, the Historical Records Survey , and the Index of American Design.[9]

The way the project's discoveries came to light and finally reached expression also reflected trends of the 1930s. Its very collective effort, which "helped explode the romantic notion of the genius as someone solitary, irresponsible and unique," suggested the shift from the individualistic ethic of the twenties to a community spirit. The FWP's stress on the pooling of various contributions typified the greater contemporary dependence on such approaches as cooperatives and county planning boards, as well as emphases in the field of education which played down the child's individual role in favor of social concerns.[10]

On a broader scale, the project's development along regional lines mirrored certain other tendencies of this period. The project's regional efforts were paralleled by a quickening interest in TVA and the National Resources Board. Howard Odum, examining such developments, praised the FWP's exploratory ventures in this regard. The findings of the FWP also had an affinity with the resurgence of regional social consciousness expressed in the novels of Faulkner, Steinbeck,

[9] Kazin, *On Native Grounds*, chap. 1; Alfred H. Jones, "The Search for a Usable American Past in the New Deal Era," *American Quarterly* 23 (Dec., 1971):710-24; James Truslow Adams, *Epic of America* (Boston, 1934), pp. 412-28. For one such discovery, see Thomas Wolfe, "The Story of a Novel," *Saturday Review of Literature* 13 (Dec. 21 and 28, 1935):14f. The dramatic shift from the 1920s is well seen in a comparison of Harold Stearns's anthology *Civilization in the United States* (New York, 1922) and *America Now* (New York, 1938). For the use of history in various civilizations for sanctification, rather than as a quest for truth, see the provocative essay in J. H. Plumb, *The Death of the Past* (Boston, 1971), chap. 1.

[10] Charles I. Glicksberg, "The Federal Writers' Project," *South Atlantic Quarterly*, 37 (Apr., 1938):157-69; Wecter, *Great Depression*, pp. 154-55. For the unfortunate consequences of this change, see Pells, *Radical Visions and American Dreams*, pp. 310-29.

Farrell, and Wright and in the paintings of Grant Wood, Charles Burchfield, and Thomas Hart Benton.[11]

The various publications of the FWP, analogous to contemporary trends in another respect, viewed the nation in human (if somewhat romanticized) terms. *These Are Our Lives, The Negro in Virginia, American Stuff,* and the state guides, with their focus on the common-man hero, the forgotten American (of any color), were in the warp and woof of a literary tapestry interwoven with *Let Us Now Praise Famous Men, You Have Seen Their Faces, An American Exodus,* and the "proletarian literature" of the decade. "The key to the '30's," as Muriel Rukeyser later expressed it, "was the joy to awake and see life entire, and tell the stories of real people." This search for the "acknowledged life in all its forms" helps explain the interchangeability of word and camera in these troubled times, as revealed in the previously mentioned books or in the lean, documentary "newsreels" of Dos Passos's *U.S.A.* And, in this quest, a modern-day Whitman could assess his neighbors—their successes, failures, and hopes—and conclude: "The People, Yes."[12]

In this fashion, the FWP made a unique contribution to the New Deal quest for a "cultural democracy." Because the FWP's program was not specifically geared to professional talent, it never could hope to bring the art of writing to the nation's millions through creative workshops, readings, lectures on literature, or the encouragement of gifted unknowns through contests and other means. In contrast to the other WPA arts projects, the FWP was thus of necessity not so concerned with the integration of artist and public and the creation of a new, public intelligentsia.[13] However, its final works, as some project administrators had hoped, also pointed to the promise of a new national art. More than any other project on Federal #1, the FWP brought its

---

[11] Howard Odum, *American Regionalism,* pp. 428-29, 615.

[12] Rukeyser interview; Carl Sandburg, *The People, Yes.* The most comprehensive study of the use of documentary forms in the decade, including the WPA arts projects, refers to the FWP guides as the "WPA's finest monument." Stott, *Documentary Expression and Thirties America,* p. 111.

[13] For the best analysis of the hopes of New Deal cultural enthusiasts, see Jane De Hart Mathews, "Arts and the People: The New Deal Quest for a Cultural Democracy," *Journal of American History* 62 (Sept., 1975):316-39. The limitations regarding personnel and purpose under which the FWP operated, in contrast to its counterparts on Federal #1, lead Mathews to pass lightly over the FWP's achievement in this connection. The same is true for Harold Rosenberg, "Anyone Who Could Write English."

audience face to face with the factual, rich diversity called America and her people. The guides, in particular, were distinctly an *American* product, transcending Baedeker to become the ultimate road map for the indigenous cultural discovery of the United States. Together with the FWP's auxiliary publications, the guide essays and tours possessed a "phenomenal democracy of retrospection" which included in their purview fact and folktale, rich and poor, realization and failure of the national dream. All Americans could therefore relate in some fashion to the FWP's multifaceted portrait. This extensive documentation was also especially, albeit unintentionally, helpful in forming what Holger Cahill of the Federal Art Project called a "great reservoir" from which "a genuine art movement" might yet flow.[14]

The contribution of the writers' project to the cultural revolution of these years won plaudits both at home and abroad. Harold Ickes ordered twelve sets of the guides for the U.S. Tourist Bureau, and the Pan American Union used the volumes for its first Inter-American Travel Congress. Jake Baker believed that the FWP did more for American culture than any of its Federal #1 colleagues, while some historians argued that the project represented the "most striking" and the boldest of WPA experiments. Its accomplishments, together with those of the other arts projects, led to Fannie Hurst's observation that "this era of ours may chiefly be remembered because of the fact that it assisted at the cultural birth of a nation." Reviewing the guides for the *London Spectator,* D. W. Brogan was astonished at the richness of American life revealed therein. A left-wing magazine paid tribute to the project's "suprising truth and vigor," as well as Roosevelt's endeavor to halt "the wastage of creative energy normally inherent even in an alert and advanced capitalist society." H. G. Nicholas, concluding a strong tribute to the project's work, observed that "social awareness is the only agency of preservation."[15]

Project files and books later turned up in a number of volumes.

---

[14] Henry Alsberg's views on this subject have been given in chaps. 1, 2, 4, 5, 7, and 8 above. I have followed the perceptive observations of Stott, *Documentary Expression and Thirties America,* pp. 114-18. Some of Cahill's opinions are succinctly given in his address "American Resources in the Arts," in Francis V. O'Connor, ed., *Art for the Millions, Essays from the 1930's by Artists and Administrators of the WPA Federal Art Project,* pp. 33-44.

[15] Baker interview; Wecter, *Great Depression,* p. 260; Hopkins radio script, n.d., p. 19, Authors' League papers; D. W. Brogan, "Inside America"; Cedric Dover, "Literary Opportunity in America," *Left Review* 3 (May, 1938):932; H. G. Nicholas, "The Writer and the State."

Material from the FWP's black studies appeared in *Black Metropolis, New World A-Comin'*, and *Any Place but Here*. Vardis Fisher used Mormon diaries discovered by project workers for *Children of God*, and Edna Ferber relied on the New Orleans and Louisiana guides in creating the setting of *Saratoga Trunk*. Henry Seidel Canby, who had formerly opposed writers going on salary, consulted the Delaware Guide for his book on the Brandywine River. Having discovered, while doing research for the Massachusetts Guide, that he did not know "a damned thing" about the Pilgrims, George Willison later continued his studies and found the guidebooks "invaluable," especially for his Pulitzer Prize–winning *Saints and Sinners*.[16]

After the closing of the Federal Writers' Project and its successors, some of those most responsible for its various successes entered new fields of endeavor. Alsberg and Cronyn edited manuscripts for the Office of War Information, Katherine Kellock worked for the State Department, and Seidenberg wrote a widely respected book about the effects of technology on human relations. Morris became the country's cultural attaché in Paris, Harris entered government service (where he fell prey to McCarthyism), and Rosenberg served as the chief art critic for the *New Yorker*. John Frederick resumed university teaching; Harlan Hatcher became president of the University of Michigan. Newsom worked as an editor at Harcourt, Brace and Colby wrote a Literary Club selection *(The Big Secret)*. MacDougall ran on the Progressive ticket for the Illinois senatorship and wrote *Gideon's Army* about that party's 1948 Presidential campaign. Josef Berger employed his talents as a speech writer for the Democratic National Committee, while Ralph Ellison, Saul Bellow, John Cheever, Richard Wright, and Nelson Algren went on to gain literary recognition.[17]

The project's crowning achievement, the guides, having "set a new cultural mode," gained increasing prestige in a monetary respect. A complete set of the state guides, presented by Florence Kerr to Grinnell College in 1961 as a memorial to Hopkins, was appraised at $700. After John Steinbeck expressed his wish that all the guides could have fit into

---

[16] Cahill Memoir, pp. 432-33; p. 7 above; George Willison telephone conversation with author, Mar. 6, 1968. The Spanish edition of the Writers' Program volume *USA* was later published by the State Department for its South American embassies — without mention of its original authors (Ruth C. France to author, Nov. 20, 1968).

[17] Harris, Berger, and MacDougall interviews.

the trailer used during his "travels with Charley," prices of the volumes rose sharply. One Tampa resident had her collection of 300 items insured for $3,500.[18]

The Guide Series also achieved ever-widening use when Hastings House published *The American Guide*, a one-volume condensation of the entire series with a few brief essays by Arthur Cole, Harold Rosenberg, Weldon Kees, and other authorities. A staff of thirty-two under Alsberg's direction, including former project editors Mary Barrett and Edward Dreyer, directors William McDaniel, Walter McElroy, and Lisle Reese, and Alsberg's loyal secretary, Dora Thea Hettwer, took four and a half years to complete the undertaking. The 1,348-page digest was chosen as a Book-of-the-Month Club alternate selection and gave that agency its largest dividend return ever when most subscribers elected to keep it.[19]

Revised editions of most of the state guides appeared regularly (no copyright fee had to be paid beyond the original five-year contractual stipulation). The Alaska Guide took the record with thirteen printings by 1959. While keeping abreast of changing road conditions, some publishers chose either to omit the essays section and pocket maps or change the format: for instance, the Vermont revision included a new alphabetical town arrangement. Reviews of these volumes have been as enthusiastic as those of their predecessors, and suggestions in the press for updating the Guide Series include reissuing them in paperback.[20]

Nevertheless, the FWP's history provides limited value for advocates of permanent federal support of literary talent. An enterprise which made publishing and cultural history, the project did prove that subsidized art could be generally free of censorship. It also indicated that worthwhile productions could be produced at "ridiculously little" cost, as a former project writer later noted, "if we consider what is

[18] George Cronyn to author, July 6, 1967; Kerr interview, July 7, 1968; John Steinbeck, *Travels with Charley* (New York, 1962), p. 121; Powell interview. An interested resident of Pittsburgh, Arthur Scharf, began *WPA Writers' Notes* about the project in 1967 and is currently working on the authoritative bibliography of the project's publications (Scharf to author, Nov. 4, 1968). Scharf recently prepared a selected list for Jerre Mangione's informal memoir, *The Dream and the Deal*.

[19] Henry Alsberg, ed., *The American Guide;* Frese interview.

[20] *Chicago Sun,* May 11, 1947; *New York Times,* Dec. 10, 1967, travel section (letter to editor). For difficulties with royalty payments (originally made out to the state governor) in the case of the Alaska Guide, see Roll 6553A, correspondence folder, Central Office files, Works Projects Administration records, Record Group 69, National Archives, Washington, D.C.

being spent to prevent the Viet Cong from invading San Francisco in sampans.'' Still, the FWP was hampered by relief regulations, as well as by state and congressional politics.[21]

While amply refuting Dorothy Thompson's contemporary reaction—''Project? For Writers? Absurd!''—the project never represented a satisfactory program for creative writers. Richard Wright, especially, benefited from his stay on the FWP, and a number of workers received the opportunity to display their talents in a few literary outlets, but this exposure was limited. The editor of the *Saturday Review of Literature* could no longer contend that ''a writer can never be out of work because there's no work for writers to do.'' Yet some professionals on the project never forgot they were on relief and, like Algren and Cheever, chose to block a disagreeable experience from memory. A sense of futility lingered for many others, knowing they were not performing ''at any maximum or optimum'' and were denied the opportunity for regular individual production. In retrospect, the project did not represent what one professional—not on its rolls— later called a ''temporary but fruitful symbiosis of bureaucratic and creative spirit.''[22]

The FWP of the thirties is far removed from present-day university writerships-in-residence, literary fellowships, and a National Academy of Arts and Sciences, and any future proposals for increased federal aid to writers would perforce call for a different format. The project's experiences are a convincing argument that such a program should be kept under both federal control and the supervision of competent editorial personnel and that the prevailing wage should be paid for each skill employed. Avoiding the necessity of carrying recognized incompetents, such a project would also be free of political cadres and the requirement of private sponsorship. Employees would have to know they were writing for actual publication, and diversified creative outlets would have to be provided for gifted professionals. In the event that white-collar persons such as those who made up most of the FWP's rolls might need employment, they could be put to large-scale research

[21] Jack Conroy to author, Mar. 30, 1968.

[22] Bill Dorais to author, Mar. 14, 1968; *Saturday Review of Literature* 15 (Oct. 31, 1936):8; Maas interview; Harold Rosenberg, ''Anyone Who Could Write English.'' The last assertion can be found in Harvey Swados, ed., *The American Writer and the Great Depression*, p. xvi. Vardis Fisher to author, May 19, 1968: ''Did the project have any literary or historical value? Of course, but not much in proportion to the money spent.''

tasks of a cooperative nature, as indeed the Society for Social Research urged after the project became subject to state control by congressional fiat. Such works could be invaluable and far-reaching.[23]

Until such time as federal support is again granted cultural enterprises on a broad scale, the potentials of the FWP and the other projects which comprised Federal #1 for a fully realized "democratization" and "salvation" of the arts remain unfulfilled. That the creative arts were supported by the American government only in time of dire need represents a paradox which deserves the attention of students of politics and culture. Meanwhile, the national government can look back with satisfaction upon the FWP's diverse accomplishments. In contemplating aid for the development of the arts as a whole, it might also recall and appreciate the advice of a former President: "Any good thing we can do, let us do now. We'll not come back this way, you know."[24]

[23] *Bulletin* of the Society for Social Research, Feb. 21, 1940, report, in Nathan Morris papers, private collection, Chicago, Illinois.

[24] Lewis Mumford, "A Letter to the President," *New Republic* 89 (Dec. 30, 1936):263-65; Abraham Lincoln, cited in Cronyn to Dyess, Oct. 14, 1935, Box 3, FWPN.

Bibliography

MANUSCRIPT COLLECTIONS AND MISCELLANEA

Authors' League of America papers. Authors' League of America, New York, N.Y.

Holger Cahill Memoir. Columbia University Oral History Collection, New York, N.Y.

Clayton, Ronnie W. "A History of the Federal Writers' Project in Louisiana." Ph.D. dissertation, Louisiana State University, 1974.

William T. Couch Memoir. Columbia University Oral History Collection, New York, N.Y.

Anne Cronin interview, March 30, 1965. Archives of American Art, Detroit, Michigan.

Luther Evans Memoir. Columbia University Oral History Collection, New York, N.Y.

Federal Writers' Project file. Schomburg Collection, New York Public Library.

Stella Hanau papers. Private collection, New York, N.Y.

Hirsch, Jerold M. "Culture on Relief: The Federal Writers' Project in North Carolina, 1935-1942." M.A. thesis, University of North Carolina, 1973.

Harry Hopkins papers. Franklin D. Roosevelt Library, Hyde Park, N.Y.

International Committee for Political Prisoners papers. New York Public Library.

Katherine Kellock papers. Federal Writers' Project file. Library of Congress, Washington, D.C.

Florence Kerr interviews, October 18 and 24, 1963. Archives of American Art, Detroit, Michigan.

McDonald, William. "Federal Relief Administration and the Arts." Library of Congress, Washington, D.C., Music Division, Reel MUS 64, 1949.

McKinzie, Kathleen O'Connor. "Writers on Relief: 1935-1942." Ph.D. dissertation, Indiana University, 1970.

Carl Malmberg papers. Private collection, New York, N.Y.

Nathan Morris papers. Private collection, Chicago, Illinois.

Oxford University Press files. American Guide series. Oxford University Press, New York, N.Y.

Eleanor Roosevelt papers. Series 70 and 100. Woodward, Bruce, Flanagan, Kerr, Dewson, and Lazell files. Franklin D. Roosevelt Library, Hyde Park, N.Y.

Franklin D. Roosevelt papers. OF-444C. Works Projects Administration and Works Projects Administration miscellaneous files. Franklin D. Roosevelt Library, Hyde Park, N.Y.

Taber, Ronald W. "The Federal Writers' Project in the Pacific Northwest: A Case Study." Ph.D. dissertation, Washington State University, 1969.

U.S. Congress, House, Special Committee on Un-American Activities. *Hearings on H.R. 282*, 75th Cong., 3d sess., 1938, I-IV.

U.S. Congress, House, Subcommittee of the Committee on Appropriations. *Hearings on H.R. 130*, 76th Cong., 1st sess., 1939-40, I.

————. *Hearings on H.J.Res. 209 and 246*, 76th Cong., 1st sess., 1939.

————. *Hearings on Work Relief and Relief for Fiscal Year 1941*, 76th Cong., 3d sess., 1941.

U.S. Congress, Senate, Subcommittee of the Committee on Appropriations. *Hearings on H.J. Res. 326*, 76th Cong., 1st sess., 1939.

————. *Hearings on H.J.Res. 193*, 77th Cong., 1st sess., 1941.

Wahl, Jo Ann. "Art under the New Deal." M.A. thesis, Columbia University, 1966.

Works Projects Administration records. Record Group 69. National Archives. Washington, D.C.

    Central Office files, Rolls 6353A and 6207

    Civil Works Administration, general subject files

    Dies Committee files

    Federal Emergency Relief Administration files

    Federal Emergency Relief Administration Procedural Publications

    Federal Theatre Project files

    Federal Writers' Project files

    Library of Congress Federal Writers' Project files

    Newspaper Writers' Project files

    Works Projects Administration Division of Information files

    Works Projects Administration general file series

    Works Projects Administration Service Division files, Box 9

    Works Projects Administration state file series

Works Projects Administration Florida Writers' Project file. Jacksonville University collection, Jacksonville, Fla.

Newspapers, private correspondence, and FWP publications that have been used can be found in the footnotes.

INTERVIEWS
Alsberg, Julius. August 5, 1968.
Asher, Robert. August 26, 1968.
Baker, Jacob. June 27, 1967.
Balch, Jack. January 19, 1968.
Baldwin, Roger. November 20, 1967.
Berger, Josef. November 13, 1967.
Black, Ivan. February 15, 1968.
Boni, Albert. February 11, 1968.
Bontemps, Arna. March 31, 1968.
Botkin, Ben. March 28, 1968.
Breit, Harvey. November 16, 1967.
Brown, Sterling. June 11, 1968.
Corse, Carita. October 15, 1967.
Couch, William. January 21, 1968.
Cronin, Anne. September 18, 1967.
Cronyn, George. Telephone conversation, June 30, 1968.
Dahlberg, Edward. April 11, 1968.
Davidson, Julius. June 30, 1968.
Ellison, Ralph. Telephone conversation, May 30, 1968.
Evans, Luther. June 19, 1967.
Frank, Nelson. February 20, 1968.
Frese, Walter. September 13, 1967.
Goldschmidt, Arthur. January 31, 1968.
Guinzberg, Benjamin. August 26, 1968.
Hanau, Stella. September 18, 1967.
Harris, Reed. July 17, 1968.
Hettwer, Dora Thea. July 11, 1967.
Hughes, Riley. July 2, 1968.
Kellock, Katherine. June 23 and August 18, 1968; telephone conversation,
    August 25, 1968.
Kerr, Florence. July 7 and 21, 1968.
Kline, Donald. August 25, 1968.
Lee, Ulysses. August 12, 1968.
Levine, Isaac Don. July 31, 1968, and telephone conversation, August 25,
    1968.
Loewenberg, Bert. April 30, 1968.
Maas, Willard. December 11, 1967.
MacDougall, Curtis. April 18, 1968.
Malmberg, Carl. November 22, 1967.
Moon, Henry Lee. December 7, 1967.

Morris, Lawrence. September 14, 1967.
Morris, Nathan. March 30, 1968.
Morse, Jarvis. July 24, 1968.
Munson, Gorham. February 11, 1968.
Noel, Gerry S. February 27, 1968.
Nomad, Max. Telephone conversation, February 11, 1968.
Ozer, Sol. August 13, 1968.
Peneff, James. Telephone conversation, March 31, 1968.
Portner, Mildred. August 21, 1968.
Poston, Ted. December 4, 1967.
Powell, Eleanor. November 14, 1968.
Rosenberg, Harold. January 31, 1968.
Roskolenko, Harry. November 21, 1967.
Rukeyser, Muriel. March 12, 1968.
Schneider, Isidor. May 30, 1968.
Seaver, Edwin. March 26, 1968.
Seidenberg, Roderick. April 18, 1969.
Strauss, Harold. October 4, 1967.
Terkel, Studs. March 29, 1968.
Thompson, Donald. November 28, 1967.
Turbyfill, Mark. Telephone conversation, March 31, 1968.
Tyler, Parker. February 27, 1968.
Weinberg, Arthur. March 31, 1968.
Willison, George. Telephone conversation, March 6, 1968.

BOOKS

Aaron, Daniel. *Writers on the Left*. New York: Harcourt, Brace & World, 1961.
Alsberg, Henry, ed. *America Fights the Depression: A Photographic Record of the Civil Works Administration*. New York: Coward-McCann, 1934.
———, ed. *The American Guide*. New York: Hastings House, 1949.
American Stuff. New York: Viking Press, 1937.
Anderson, Sherwood. *Memoirs*. New York: Harcourt, Brace, 1942.
Baedeker, Karl. *The United States*. New York: Charles Scribner's Sons, 1909.
Balch, Jack. *Lamps at High Noon*. New York: Modern Age, 1941.
Bendiner, Robert. *Just Around the Corner*. New York: Harper & Row, 1967.
Berger, Josef [Digges, Jeremiah]. *Cape Cod Pilot*. Provincetown, R.I.: Viking Press, 1938.
Bontemps, Arna, and Conroy, Jack. *Anyplace but Here*. New York: Hill & Wang, 1966.

Boorstin, Daniel. *The Americans: The National Experience*. New York: Random House, 1965.

Bulletin of the Writers' Union. New York: Parnassus Press, 1935.

The Connecticut Guide: What to See and Where to Find It. Hartford, Conn.: Emergency Relief Commission, 1935.

Cowley, Malcolm. *Exile's Return: A Literary Odyssey of the 1920's*. New York: Viking Press, 1934.

————. *Think Back on Us: A Contemporary Chronicle of the 1930's*, edited by Henry D. Piper. Carbondale: Southern Illinois University Press, 1967.

Crossman, Richard, ed. *The God That Failed*. New York: Harper & Brothers, 1949.

Curti, Merle. *The Growth of American Thought*. 3d edition. New York: Harper & Row, 1964.

Dies, Martin. *Martin Dies' Story*. New York: Bookmailer, 1963.

Dreiser, Theodore. *Tragic America*. New York: H. Liveright, 1931.

Filler, Louis, ed. *The Anxious Years: America in the 1930's*. New York: G. P. Putnam, 1963.

Fisher, Vardis. *Orphans in Gethsemane: A Novel of the Past in the Present*. Denver, Colo.: Swallow Press, 1960.

Flanagan, Hallie. *Arena*. New York: Duell, Sloan & Pearce, 1940.

French, Warren, ed. *The Thirties: Fiction, Poetry, Drama*. Deland, Fla.: Everett-Edwards, 1967.

Gaer, Joseph, ed. *Gold Rush Period*. Bibliography of California Literature, no. 8. San Francisco: California Relief Administration, 1935.

Goldman, Emma. *Living My Life*. New York: Alfred A. Knopf, 1931.

Harris, Bernice K. *Southern Savory*. Chapel Hill: University of North Carolina Press, 1964.

Hicks, Granville. *Part of the Truth*. New York: Harcourt, Brace & World, 1965.

Hopkins, Harry. *Spending to Save*. New York: W. W. Norton, 1936.

Houseman, John. *Run Through: A Memoir*. New York: Simon & Schuster, 1972.

Howard, Donald. *The WPA and Federal Relief Policy*. New York: Russell Sage Foundation, 1943.

International Committee for Political Prisoners. *Letters from Russian Prisoners*. Edited by Henry Alsberg and Isaac Don Levine. New York: Albert & Charles Boni, 1925.

Johns, Orrick. *Time of Our Lives*. New York: Stackpole, 1937.

Josephson, Matthew. *Infidel in the Temple*. New York: Alfred A. Knopf, 1967.

Kazin, Alfred. *On Native Grounds*. New York: Doubleday, 1952.
————. *Starting Out in the Thirties*. Boston: Little, Brown, 1956.
Kempton, Murray. *Part of Our Time*. New York: Simon & Schuster, 1955.
Kinnamon, Keneth. *The Emergence of Richard Wright: A Study in Literature and Society*. Urbana: University of Illinois Press, 1972.
Leuchtenburg, William E. *Franklin D. Roosevelt and the New Deal, 1932-1940*. New York: Harper & Row, 1963.
McDonald, William F. *Federal Relief Administration and the Arts: The Origins and Administrative History of the Arts Projects of the Works Progress Administration*. Columbus: Ohio State University Press, 1969.
McKinzie, Richard D. *The New Deal for Artists*. Princeton, N.J.: Princeton University Press, 1973.
MacLeod, Norman. *You Get What You Ask For*. New York: Harrison-Hilton, 1939.
Macmahon, Arthur, and Millett, John. *The Administration of Federal Work Relief*. Chicago: Public Administration Service, 1941.
Madden, David, ed. *Proletarian Writers of the Thirties*. Carbondale: Southern Illinois University Press, 1968.
Mangione, Jerre. *The Dream and the Deal: The Federal Writers' Project, 1935-1943*. Boston: Little, Brown, 1972.
Mathews, Jane De Hart. *The Federal Theatre, 1935-1939: Plays, Relief, and Politics*. Princeton, N.J.: Princeton University Press, 1967.
O'Connor, Francis V., ed. *Art for the Millions: Essays from the 1930's by Artists and Administrators of the WPA Federal Art Project*. Greenwich, Conn.: New York Graphic Society, 1973.
————, ed. *The New Deal Art Project: An Anthology of Memoirs*. Washington, D.C.: Smithsonian Institution Press, 1972.
Odum, Howard. *American Regionalism*. New York: Henry Holt, 1938.
Ogden, August. *The Dies Committee: A Study of the Special House Committee for the Investigation of Un-American Activities, 1938-1943*. Washington, D.C.: Catholic University of America Press, 1943.
Ottley, Roi, and Weatherby, William, eds. *The Negro in New York*. Dobbs Ferry, N.Y.: Oceana Publications, 1967.
Overmyer, Grace. *Government and the Arts*. New York: W. W. Norton, 1939.
Pells, Richard H. *Radical Visions and American Dreams: Culture and Social Thought in the Depression Years*. New York: Harper & Row, 1973.
Perkins, Frances. *The Roosevelt I Knew*. New York: Viking Press, 1946.
Pollenberg, Richard. *Reorganizing Roosevelt's Government: The Con-

troversy over Executive Reorganization, 1936-1939. Cambridge: Harvard University Press, 1966.

Rideout, Walter B. *The Radical Novel in the United States, 1900-1954: Some Inter-Relations of Literature and Society.* Cambridge: Harvard University Press, 1956.

Roskolenko, Harry. *When I Was Last on Cherry Street.* New York: Stein & Day, 1965.

Sandburg, Carl. *The People, Yes.* New York: Harcourt, Brace, 1936.

Schlesinger, Arthur M., Jr. *The Age of Roosevelt,* vol. 1: *The Crisis of the Old Order.* Boston: Houghton Mifflin, 1957.

————. *The Age of Roosevelt,* vol. 2: *The Coming of the New Deal.* Boston: Houghton Mifflin, 1959.

Sherwood, Robert E. *Roosevelt and Hopkins: An Intimate History.* New York: Harper & Brothers, 1948.

Simon, Rita. ed. *As We Saw the Thirties: Essays on Social and Political Movements of a Decade.* Urbana: University of Illinois Press, 1967.

Stearns, Harold, ed. *Civilization in the United States: An Inquiry by Thirty Americans.* New York: Harcourt, Brace, 1922.

————, ed. *America Now: An Inquiry Into Civilization in the United States by Thirty-Six Americans.* New York: Charles Scribner's Sons, 1938.

Stott, William. *Documentary Expression and Thirties America.* New York: Oxford University Press, 1973.

Susman, Warren. "The Thirties." In Stanley Coben and Lorman Ratner, eds., *The Development of an American Culture*, pp. 179-218. Englewood Cliffs, N.J.: Prentice-Hall, 1970.

Swados, Harvey, ed. *The American Writer and the Great Depression.* Indianapolis: Bobbs-Merrill, 1966.

Warren, Frank. *Liberals and Communism.* Bloomington: Indiana University Press, 1966.

Warwick, George P., ed. *The American Slave: A Composite Autobiography,* II-XVII. Westport, Conn.: Greenwood Press, 1972–.

Wecter, Dixon. *The Age of the Great Depression.* New York: Macmillan, 1948.

Wilson, Edmund. *The American Earthquake: A Documentary of the Jazz Age, the Great Depression, and the New Deal.* New York: Doubleday, 1964 ed.

————. *The Shores of Light.* New York: Farrar, Straus & Giroux, 1952.

Wright, Richard. *Uncle Tom's Children.* New York: Harper & Brothers, 1938.

Yezierska, Anzia. *Red Ribbon on a White Horse.* New York: Charles Scribner's Sons, 1950.

PERIODICALS

Aaron, Daniel. "The Treachery of Recollection." *Carleton Miscellany* 6 (Summer, 1965).

Alsberg, Henry. "Russia: Smoked Glass vs. Rose Tint." *Nation* 112 (June 15, 1921):844-46.

―――. "The Soviet Domestic Program." *Nation* 111 (Aug. 28, 1920):221.

―――. "Tyranny by Prophets." *Nation* 111 (Sept. 4, 1920):268-69.

―――. "Will Russia Drive the British from Asia?" *Nation* 111 (Aug. 14, 1920):179-81.

―――. "Writers and the Government: Federal Writers' Projects." *Saturday Review of Literature* 13 (Jan. 4, 1936):9.

"American Stuff by Workers of Federal Writers' Project." *Direction* 1, no. 3 (Feb., 1938).

Author and Journalist, 1930-35.

Bell, Clive. "Art in the Planned State." *Forum* 97 (May, 1937):306-9.

Biddle, George, *et al.* "The Government and the Arts." *Harper's* 187 (Oct., 1943):427-34.

Billington, Ray A. "Government and the Arts: The WPA Experience." *American Quarterly* 13 (Winter, 1961):466-71.

Bolles, Blair. "The Federal Writers' Project." *Saturday Review of Literature* 18 (July 9, 1938):3-4.

Brogan, Dennis. "Inside America." *London Spectator* 167 (Nov. 28, 1941):507-8.

―――. "Uncle Sam's Guides." *London Spectator* 161 (Aug. 5, 1938):226-27.

Canby, Henry Seidel. "Should Writers Go on a Salary?" *Saturday Review of Literature* 9 (Nov. 26, 1932):270.

Cantwell, Robert. "America and the Writers' Project." *New Republic* 98 (Apr. 26, 1939):323-25.

Chapman, Maristan. "The Trouble with Authors." *Bookman* 74 (Dec., 1931):368-70.

The Coast (Spring, 1937).

Colby, Merle. "Presenting America to All Americans." *Publishers Weekly* 139 (May 3, 1941):1828-31.

Cowley, Malcolm, *et al.* "Memories of the First American Writers' Congress." *American Scholar* 35 (Summer, 1966): 495-516.

Current-Garcia, E. "Writers in the Sticks." *Prairie Schooner* 12 (1938):294-309.

————. "American Panorama." *Prairie Schooner* 12 (1938):79-90.

DeVoto, Bernard. "The Writers' Project." *Harper's* 184 (Jan., 1942): 221-24.

"Distributing the WPA Guides." *Publishers Weekly* 137 (May 11, 1940):1836-39.

Dover, Cedric. "Literary Opportunity in America." *Left Review* 3 (May, 1938):932.

Editor and Publisher, 1930-35.

Farran, Don. "The Federals in Iowa: A Hawkeye Guidebook in the Making." *Annals of Iowa*, Winter, 1973, pp. 1190-96.

"Federal Poets." *New Republic* 95 (May 11, 1938):10-12.

"Federal Writers' Number." *New Masses* 27 (May 10, 1938):97-127.

"First WPA Guide." *Saturday Review of Literature* 14 (Feb. 27, 1937):8.

Fox, Daniel. "The Achievement of the Federal Writers' Project." *American Quarterly* 13 (Spring, 1961):3-19.

Glicksberg, Charles I. "The Federal Writers' Project." *South Atlantic Quarterly* 37 (Apr., 1938):157-69.

Jones, Alfred H. "The Search for a Usable American Past in the New Deal Era." *American Quarterly* 23 (Dec., 1971):710-24.

Kellock, Katherine. "The WPA Writers: Portraitists of the United States." *American Scholar* 9 (Oct., 1940):473-82.

Larson, Cedric. "Uncle Sam, Printer, Publisher and Literary Sponsor." *Colophon* 1 (1939):83-90.

Littell, Robert. "Putting America on Paper." *Today* 5 (Nov. 30, 1935):6-9.

Mangione, Jerre. "Federal Writers' Project." *New York Times*, May 18, 1969, VII, p. 2.

Material Gathered (1936).

Mathews, Jane De Hart. "Arts and the People: The New Deal Quest for a Cultural Democracy." *Journal of American History* 62 (Sept., 1975):316-39.

"Mirror to America." *Time* 31 (Jan. 3, 1938):55-56.

Morrison, Perry. "Everyman's Archive." *The Call* 18, no. 2 (Spring, 1957):4-9.

Mumford, Lewis. "A Letter to the President." *New Republic* 89 (Dec. 30, 1936):263-65.

————. "Writers' Project." *New Republic* 92 (Oct. 20, 1937):306-7.

Nicholas, H. G. "The Writer and the State." *Contemporary Review* 155 (Jan. 1939):89-94.

Patterson, James T. "The New Deal and the States." *American Historical Review* 73 (Oct., 1967):70-84.

Poetry 52 (July-Sept., 1938).

"Publishers' Letter on Federal Writers' Project." *Publishers Weekly* 135 (May 20 and 27, 1939):1817, 1919.

Rosenberg, Harold. "Anyone Who Could Write English." *New Yorker* 49 (Jan. 20, 1973):99-102.

"Salaries and Working Conditions of Newspaper Editorial Employees." *Monthly Labor Review* 40 (May, 1935).

Saunders, D. A. "The Dies Committee, First Phase." *Public Opinion Quarterly* 3 (Apr., 1939):223-28.

"Their Own Baedeker." *New Yorker* 25 (Apr. 20, 1949):17-18.

Touhey, Eleanor. "American Baedekers." *Library Journal* 66 (Apr. 15, 1941):339-41.

Ulrich, Mabel. "Salvaging Culture for the WPA." *Harper's* 177 (May, 1939):653-64.

"Unemployed Arts." *Fortune* 15 (May, 1937):108-17.

"Unemployed Writers." *Saturday Review of Literature* 15 (Oct. 31, 1936):8.

Weeks, Edward. "Hard Times and the Author." *Atlantic Monthly* 155 (May, 1935):551-62.

"What the Writers Wrote." *New Republic* 92 (Sept. 1, 1937):89-90.

"Work of the FWP of WPA." *Publishers Weekly* 135 (Mar. 18, 1939):1130-35.

"WPA Accounting." *Time* 41 (Feb. 15, 1943):95-96.

"WPA Writers Produce." *Publishers Weekly* 132 (Aug. 21, 1937): 569-70.

Writers' Digest, 1930-35.

"Writers' Project: 1942." *New Republic* 106 (Apr. 13, 1942):480.

Yetman, Norman. "The Background of the Slave Collection." *American Quarterly* 19 (Fall, 1967):535-53.

Index